Micro Level Planning for Regional Development
Indian Experience

Micro Level Planning for Regional Development

Indian Experience

K. Sivachithappa

ADHYAYAN

ADHYAYAN PUBLISHERS & DISTRIBUTORS
New Delhi-110002

Published by
ADHYAYAN PUBLISHERS & DISTRIBUTORS
4378/4B, 105, J.M.D. House, Murari Lal Street
Ansari Road Darya Ganj, New Delhi - 110002
Ph.: 011-23263018, 011-23277156, Fax: 23280028
Email: adhyayanpublishers@yahoo.com

Micro Level Planning for Regional Development
Indian Experience

Edition 2011
ISBN 978-81-8435-276-4

Printed in India

Published by Harish Chandra Yadav for Adhyayan Publishers & Distributors, Delhi. Laser Typesetting at Jain Computers and Printed at Tarun Offset Printers, Delhi

Preface

The planning process in the developing countries is fast changing in keeping with the emerging new needs, issues, goals and realities of development. Till the mid-1960s, countries were more pre-occupied with macro-economic growth opportunities and laid great emphasis on large scale projects and infrastructural developments. Planning was concentrated at the top and tended to be focussed more on strategies of development than on actual spatial potentialities and means of implementation. This inevitably left a wide gap between the plan and ground realities. As inroads into development were made, issues relating to the distribution of investments and the choice of production alternatives in relation to regional and local potentials have assumed great significance. In this context, it has become clear that planning to be more effective has to share appropriately decision-making functions with sub-national levels through a system, that is properly adopted to the needs and characteristics of the country involved, and covering the range of regional and local conditions. With this background, myself and our collegues interested in micro level planning for spatial development has been kindled since last 10 years through many events and circumstances in our life. Hence this book.

The present book entitled "Micro Level Planning for Regional Development - Indian Experience" is purely research oriented book contains 22 research papers written by different scholars in Economics and Rural Development on regional issues. Economic Empowerment of Rural Community Through Panchayath Raj System - A Study, a paper by **Narasimhan M.S.,** is an assessment of the role of PRIs in economic empowerment of the community. He observed that the decentralized planning is the process undertaken at the grassroot level by the people for their development. The growing interest in decentralized planning and administration is due to the development thrust built upon to emphasize the growth-with-equity policies in our country. **T.D.Thimmaiya's** paper "Impact of Women Empowerment Programmes on Rural Women in Hassan District" makes an attempt to evaluate the impact of women empowerment programmes on rural women in Hassan district. He opines that there have been perceptible changes in the living conditions of the rural poor mainly on economic side and relatively on social side.

K. Sivachithappa's paper "Economic Empowerment of Kadu Golla Women Through Stree Shakti Programme—A Case Study in Pavagada Taluk" provides an analysis of the role of Stree Shakti Programme in economic empowerment of tribal women i.e., Kadu Golla Women in Pavagada Taluk. A paper "Role of Micro-Finance and Its Impact on Socio-Economic Development of Women in Karnataka" by **Shivanand Nari,** analyses the role of micro-finance in socio-economic empowerment of women in the state of Karnataka. He opines that Micro-finance implies providing the poor with savings, credit and insurance facilities to set up or expand income generating activities relating to agriculture, allied activities and non-farm Sector, and thereby, increases household income security.

Mahadevaswamy, M.S. in his paper on "Impact of Primary Agricultural Cooperative Societies on Rural Community—A Case Study of Mysore District" observed that, today the India's cooperative scene presents a mixed picture. On the one hand, the cooperative movement has grown, membership has increased, it has become more diversified, there has been great deal of regional dispersal and there are numerous examples of cooperatives in India's landscape where it has made spectacular achievements. **Ziaulla's** paper on "Dimensions of Female Agricultural Wage Rates in India" examines the issues incorporated in wage differentials among female agricultural labourers in India. A paper on "Problems and Prospects of Co-operative Sector underglobalization Regime – A Study in Karnataka" by **Sreenivasaiah K.N.** made an attempt to evaluate the problems of cooperative sector. Umesha C. has made an attempt in his paper on "Social Security Schemes and Socio-Economic Development of Depressed Classes—A Study in Karnataka" to evaluate the dimensions of social security schemes in the state of Karnataka.

Venkatesha, J.N. in his paper on "Commercial Banking in the Development of Mysore District Economy - With Special Reference to Small Scale Industries" observed that the success of economic development depends mainly on the extent of mobilization of the resources and their investment with operational efficiency. Indian banking system, after nationalization, has brought about a speedy transformation of the entire economic structure. Another paper by **Raghava D.H.** on "Socio-Economic Empowerment of Women through NGO Based Micro-Finance—A Case Study in Mandya District" throws more light on NGOs role in order to empower the women. **Prasad** in his paper on "Progress of Self-Help Groups in Karnataka—An Analysis" observed that the rural bankers, NGOs and some government functionaries have done splendid work in the development of self-help groups in the state of Karnataka.

Narayanamma P.N. in her paper on "Performance of Agarbathi Industries in the State of Karnataka – A Study" examined the role of agarbathi industries in the development of women. **Suresha.A.L** in his paper on "Livelihood Security of Women Through SHGs—With Special Reference to Mandya District" observed that the achievement of SHGs and Government programmes are having a positive impact on the economic empowerment and it increases the role of women in decision-making as well as income generating activities. **Divyathejomurthy, V.** in the paper entitled "Issues Before Trade Unions in India" examined that Unions have come to occupy a strategic place in the modern industrial organizations and he observed that industrial production, among other things depends upon cordial industrial relations and committed and contended industrial work force.

Lepakshaiah, S.V. in the study on "Dairy Industry in Poverty Alleviation of Rural Areas – A Case Study" has conducted the micro-investigation in Tumkur district has been made to review the existing structure, growth trend in milk production competitiveness of dairy industry, cost of production and level of efficiency in dairying. Study shall also cover income generation capacity of dairying in rural areas and marketing problems of dairying in the district.

Chandrakala, K.S. in her study on "People Participation in Community Development Programmes–A Study in Mandya District" opined that rural development in India is recognized as a sine qua non for faster economic development and welfare of common masses. Rural development is not merely development of rural areas but also the development of the rural people into self-reliant and self-sustaining modern little communities. **Bhuvanendra, S.K.** in his study on " Economic Empowerment of Weaker Sections Through Bank Credit–With Special Reference to Mysore District" analysed the impact of bank credit on weaker sections in Mysore district. He opined that Massive changes have been witnessed in the entire spectrum of Indian banking in general and in the area of their lending activities in particular.

Gule Ariffa in her study entitled "A Study on the Problem of Non-Performing Assets With Reference to Canara Bank in Mandya" observed that over the past two decades, banking policies and programmes have sought to achieve certain national objectives by reorienting the banking system towards a larger social purpose. As a result, the system has under-gone a structural transformation in both quantitative and qualitative terms.

Krishnappa Madivala in his paper on "Empowering women through expansion of school education in Karnataka" made an attempt to examine *(a)* the poverty reduction efforts leading to enhanced school enrollment of children (male & female) during 1981-2001; *(b)* the efforts to improve the educational infrastructure and the quality of imparting school education has whether led to improvement in girl child school enrollment, attendance and retention positions; and *(c)* the problems of development of school education system in Karnataka.

Narayana, N. in the study of "Visveswaraya Grameena Bank and Rural Development—A Study in Mandya District" opined that Institutional credit system has been playing a vital role in the economic development of rural India particularly at this important juncture when we are entering 21st century. Rural sector plays a significant role in Indian economy. It affects directly or indirectly almost all the economic activities in the country. It employs the maximum number of people. It is also the most important source of national income in India.

Nagesha in his study on "Role of Information Technology in Economic Growth in India" rightly observed that the overall analysis of IT industries of India in this study revealed that the performance of the IT industries in domestic sale of IT software and products as well as in international market accelerating the growth rate of the economy.

Chandra Naik, M. in his study on "Growth in Livestock Population and Its Role in the Development of Karnataka Economy" observed that the most important feature of the cattle and buffaloes population of Karnataka State has been that nearly 90 per cent of it has been the native breed livestock. Therefore, the milk yield from the native breed cattle and buffaloes population is low. This situation has to be changed by increasing the total size of cross breed cows and buffaloes to increase the supply of milk and make dairying a productive employment and economically viable rural enterprise.

Micro level planning for regional developmnt, which may be a narrow specialisation, is yet a vast field. We have not covered all its aspects in this book. With every attempt at factual precision and clarity of presentation, still some errors of commission and omission are bound to be there for which I take the sole responsibility. I hope the book will be useful to students, professionals and practitioners and those who are interested in this field. My greatest debt of gratituted is to the many exceptionally busy academicions who accepted the invitation to write papers on a wide range of topics pertaining to regional planning. Needles to say that the editor is in any way responsible for personal views of the authors. I would like to thank all the researchers who have provided research oriented articles to this book. Finally I am greatful to Sh. Harish Chandra Yadav, Adhyayan Publishers and Distributors, publishing of this book for showing interest to publish this book in a short time.

K. SIVACHITHAPPA

List of Contributors

Bhuvanendra, S.K., Assistant Professor of Economics, Government First Grade College, Holenarasipura, Hassan district.

Chandrakala K.S., Assistant Professor of Economics, Government Arts College, Hassan.

Divyathejomurthy, V., Associate Professor, Department of Rural Development, Acharya Nagarjuna University, Guntur, AP.

Gule Ariffa, Assistant Professor of Economics, Government First Grade College, K.R. Pet, Mandya district.

Krishnappa Madivala, Associate Professor of Economics, Government First Grade College, Bantwal, D.K., district.

Lepakshaiah, S.V., Assistant Professor of Economics, Government First Grade College, Ramdurga, Belgaum district.

M.Chandra Naik, Associate Professor of Economics, Government First Grade College, Harohalli.

Mahadevaswamy, M.S., Asst.Professor of Economics, Government First Grade College, Hanagudu, Mysore district.

Nagesha, Lecturer in Economics, JSS College, Saraswathipuram, Mysore.

Narasimhan, M.S., Associate Professor of Economics, Government First Grade College, Sira, Tumkur district.

Narayana, N., Research Scholar, Department of Economics, University of Mysore, Post-graduate Centre, Mandya.

Narayanamma, P.N., Assistant Professor of Economics, Government First Grade College, Malur.

Prasad, Assistant Professor of Economics, Government First Grade College, Hullahalli, Mysore district.

Raghava, D.H., Assistant Professor of Economics, Jnanadhare First Grade College, Hassan.

Shivanand Nari, Assistant Professor of Economics, Maharaja's College, University of Mysore, Mysore.

Sivachithappa, K., Assistant Professor of Economics, University of Mysore, Post-graduate Centre, Mandya.

Sreenivasaiah, K.N., Assistant Professor of Economics, Government First Grade College, Mulabagal.

Suresha, A.L., Assistant Professor of Economics, Government College Autonomus, Mandya district.

Thimmaiya, T.D., Associate Professor of Economics, FMKMC College, Mangalore University Constitutent College, Madikeri.

Umesha, C., Assistant Professor of Economics, Government First Grade College, Mulabagal.

Venkatesha, J.N., Assistant Professor of Economics, SAC College, H.D. Kote.

Ziaulla, Assistant Professor of Economics, Government First Grade College, Mulabagal.

Contents

1

Economic Empowerment of Rural Community through Panchayath Raj System – A Study

Narasimhan M.S.

Introduction

The main objective of this paper is to analyze the role of PRIs in socio-economic development of weaker sections of the society through the major programmes like swarna jayathi gram swarojgar yojana, and on the basis of the study the major findings have been drawn and finally suggestions have also been offered. The decentralized planning is the process undertaken at the grass-root level by the people for their development. The growing interest in decentralized planning and administration is due to the development thrust built upon to emphasize the growth-with-equity policies in our country. The decentralized development planning process being undertaken at the gross-root level is well suited planning process for development (Abdul Aziz and Shenoy, 1997). So, it is not just changing the level of administration for development by the process of decentralization, but it is for enhancing the capabilities at the local level to ensure people's participation in the decision-making process, (Meenakshisundaram, 1997) for the development with "Social Justice". The social justice may be referred as equal opportunities for all section of people to participate in the process of making development decisions. It is believed that decentralized decision making meant for enhanced participation of people to identify and solve the local problems and also to attend the local needs.

Gandhiji imagine a world within machines should function solely for villagers benefits, turning out those goods which are necessary for his well being, relieving him of the necessity for heavy physical labour and dull routine and meaningfuless activity well-clothed and well-housed. Rural people in this worked lives in balance with his environment, nourished by nature, in harmany with the myriods of other life forms that are beneficial to them. The villagers trust their land wisely, halts erosion and over-cropping and returns all organic matter from the soil from which it has sprung, villagers live efficiently and yet minimises artificiality, Gandhi's world is not over crowded world, people can, if they wish, isolate themselves in the silence of a mountain top or they can walk through primeval forests or across wooded plains.

In the village of Gandhiji's imagination, there is organisation but it is as decentralised as possible compatible with the requirements for survival. In Gandhiji's economy Government exists for men rather than man for the Government. In the Economy of Gandhi's imagination, the various regions are self-sufficient and the people are free to govern themselves as they choose to establish their own cultural patterns.

Results and Discussion

Under educational programmes, various educational schemes have been introduced for the benefit for SC/ST students in Delhi. During 11th FYP, department has fixed the target of 598640 Students of SC/ST/OBC/Min. for scholarships at school/ college level & for vocational & technical courses under various schemes. Under educational programmes for all educational development schemes, the income limit for eligibility has been increased from Rs.48,000/- to Rs.1,00,000/-p.a.

In the current financial year 2007-08, one time grant of Rs.30.00 lakh has been given to DSCFDC for procurement of sophisticated machinery and equipments for setting up an Apparel Training and Design Center (ATDC) by the Apparel Export Promotion Council (AEPC) in the premises of DSCFDC. The objective of this training center is to organize skill up gradation training cum capacity building. The Apparel Training & Design Center will run courses on different subjects for benefit of candidates from all over India including slum dwellers for which it was originally planned.

Under the scheme "Merit Scholarship to SC/ST/OBC/ Min. (Class VI to XII)" Government of India is providing scholarship to meritorious students belonging to SC/ST/ OBC/Min. communities studying in VI to XII from Rs.500/ - to Rs.1700/-p.a. Family income is not applicable to the students belonging to SC/ST communities. However, family income of Rs.1.00lakh is applicable to the students belonging to OBC and Minorities communities. Under the scheme "Merit Scholarship for college & Professional institution students belonging SC/ST/OBC/Min." Scholarship is provided form Rs.350 p.m. to Rs.800 p.m., Family income is not applicable to the students belonging to SC/ST communities. However, family income of Rs.1.00lakh is applicable to the students belonging to OBC and Minorities communities.

Under the scheme "Reimbursement of tuition fee for SC/ST/OBC/Min. students in public school", tuition & other compulsory fee for SC/ST/OBC/Min. students in reimbursement. In case of family income up to Rs.48000/ - p.a., the reimbursement is 100%, whereas for students having family income up to Rs.1.00 per annum the reimbursement is 75%.

Under "Free supply of stationery to SC/ST/OBC/Min. students in school", Financial assistance of Rs.450 to Rs.750/- is being provided to the students belonging to SC/ST/OBC/Min. communities studying in class VI to XII and having family income of Rs.1,00,000/- p.a. for purchase of stationary.

The scheme of "Improvement of SC" was revised during the year 2005-06 and is being implemented w.e.f. September 2005. As per revised scheme a basti which has a population of 33% or more of SCs as per the census report 2001 is considered as a SC basti. The scheme provides that area/ Basti where such improvement work is proposed to be undertaken may be either on private land, Lal Dora/ extended Lal Dora or Govt. land allotted under 20 point programme with at least 60-70% built up area. Under the scheme there is a condition that no improvement shall be recommended/ extended in any unauthorized SC Basti on public or Govt. land. During 11th Five Year Plan, Department has proposed improvement work for 250 basties/ chaupal, out of which during the Annual Plan 2007-08 an expenditure of Rs.2376.85 lakh has incurred for carrying out improvement work in 48 basties & 2 choupals.

In the current financial year 2007-08, one time grant of Rs.30.00lakh has been given to DSCFDC for procurement of sophisticated machinery and equipments for setting up an Apparel Training and Design Center (ATDC) by the Apparel Export Promotion Council (AEPC) in the premises of DSCFDC. The objective of this training center is to provide skill up gradation training cum capacity building. The Apparel Training & Design Center will run courses on different subject for benefit of candidates from all over India including slum dwellers for which it was originally planned.

DSCFDC implements schemes towards promoting self employment ventures or providing Vocational Training. There are composite Loan Scheme & Financial Assistance schemes for purchase of LCV, Tata - 407 & TSR, Providing

Big Loan, Industrial Loan costing upto 5 lakh and Vocational Training.

Swarnajayanti Gram Swarozgar Yojana

The focus of development planning in India has been rightly on the alleviation of rural poverty since Independence. Rural India, however, continues to suffer from high incidence of poverty programmes in successive years. In percentage terms, poverty level has reduced from 56.44 percent of the population in 1973-74 to 37.27 percent in 1993-94. In absolute terms, however, the number of rural poor has remained more or less static. It is estimated to be about 25.40 crore persons. The adverse effect of such a large size of the poor on the country's development is not difficult to appreciate. Quite obviously the situation needs to be redressed quickly. It is in this context that the self-employment programmes assume significance. These alone can provide income to the rural poor on a sustainable basis.

A New self-employment programme namely Swaranjayanti Gram Swarozgar Yojana (SGSY) has been launched w.e.f. April 1999. As a result, the erstwhile programmes viz. Integrated Rural Development Programme (IRDP), Development of Women and Children in Rural Areas (DWCRA), Training of Rural Youth for Self-Employment (TRYSEM), Supply of Improved Tool kits to Rural Artisans (SITRA), Ganga Kalyan Yojana (GKY) and Million Wells Scheme (MWS) ceased to be in operation. It may be pointed out that SGSY has been devised keeping in view the positive aspects and deficiencies of the earlier programmes. The earlier programmes were originally viewed as complimentary to each other to achieve the larger goal of poverty alleviation. But over the years, each one of these started operating almost as a separate and independent programme. Obviously, the concern was more for achieving individual programme targets. The desired linkages among the programmes and the much needed focus on the substantive issue of sustainable income generation were missing. SGSY accordingly came into being after restructuring of all these programmes.

SGSY has a definite objective of improving the family incomes of the rural poor and, at the same time, providing for a flexibility of design at the same time, providing for a flexibility of design at the grassroots level to suit the local needs and resources. The objective of the restructuring was to make the programme more effective in providing a substructure was to make the programme more effective in providing a sustainable income through micro-enterprise development, both land based and otherwise. In doing so, effective linkages have been established between various components such as capacity building of the poor credit, technology, marketing and infrastructure.

The allocation under SGSY during 1999-2000 is Rs. 950 crore (RE). SGSY has also a component for special projects for self employment of the rural poor. Some project proposals submitted by the State Governments are under active consideration of the Ministry. The financial performance of SGSY during 2008-09 is depicted in table-1.

Table - 1
Financial Performance (2008-09)

(Rs. in crores)

Year	*Opening balance as on 1-4-99*	*Total allocation (Centre+ state*	*Total release*	*Total avail- ability (2+4)*	*Utili= sation*	*Percent ages*
1	2	3	4	5	6	7
2008-2009	520.27	1231.36	3999.19	4519.46	209.24	16.99

The Physical performance of SGSY during 2008-09 is as depicted in Table-2.

Table-2
Physical Performance (2008-09)

(Number of Works)

Year	*Total Swarozgaris assisted*	*SCs*	*STs*	*Women*	*Handicapped*
1	2	3	4	5	6
2008-2009	176044 (28.93)	50924 (28.93)	19865 (11.28)	58019 (32.96)	874 (0.50)

Source: Economic Survey,GOI.

The State wise allocation under SGSY is made as per the distribution ratio indicated by the Planning Commission after keeping aside a part of the fund for the special projects. The details of the State wise allocation and releases made have been given in following Table-3.

Table-3
Financial & Physical Performance Under SGSY during 2008-09

State/ UTs	*Financial Performance (Rs. in laks)*				*Physical Performance*
	Opinion Balance	*Total allocation*	*Utilisation*	*% utilisation*	*Total Swarozgaris Assisted*
1	2.	3.	4.	5.	6.
Andhra Pradesh	423	6935	869	12.54	1125
Assam	1691	3962	886	22.37	4512
Bihar	17222	22720	4590	20.20	28522
Gujarat	3.52	2611	134	5.15	566
Haryana	394	1536	202	13.17	27.84

1	2.	3.	4.	5.	6.
Himachal Pradesh	358	647	197	39.43	4591
J & Kashmir	129	800	182	22.78	1746
Karnataka	4040	5237	858	16.37	1419
Kerala	1093	2350	225	9.60	51.66
Madhya Pradesh	2734	11516	1887	16.38	7036
Maharahtra	3929	10353	2570	24.82	30889
Orissa	541	7933	901	11.36	5944
Punjab	312	746	87	11.66	741
Rajasthans	NR	3977	NR	NR	NR
Tamil Nadu	1083	6133	3209	53.34	12558
Uttar Pradesh	11668	25003	1174	4.70	3482
West Bengal	6645	8816	2822	32.01	53767
Total	32028	123136	29924	16.99	176044

Source: Economic Survey, GOI

Total funds made available for JGSY during 2008-09 was Rs.1,50,862 lakh out of which Rs.69.556 lakh was utilised hence the percentage utilisation of total fund available was only 46.11 per cent. In case of utilisation of funds available performance of Rajasthan, Bihar, Assam, Karnataka, Madhya Pradesh, Maharashtra was quite satisfactory.

The seventh plan strategy, in this context, however, emphasized two aspects: (i) consolidation of the progress made during the sixth plan, and provision of supplementary assistance to those who have failed to cross the poverty line: and (ii) selection of new beneficiaries who should be lifted above the poverty line with a single dose of assistance. The progress of banks in providing assistance under the IRDP SGSY is presented in a nutshell in Table- 4.

Table - 4
Advances Under Swarnajayanti Gram Swarojgar Yojana - All India

Years	*No. Of Beneficiaries (No. Lakhs)*	*Total Credit (Rs. Crores)*
1999-00	37.47	1014.88
2000-01	42.47	1175.35
2001-02	37.72	1231.62
2002-03	33.51	1220.53
2003-04	28.98	1190.03
2004-05	25.37	1147.34
2005-06	20.69	1036.80
2006-07	25.39	1408.44
2007-08	22.15	1450.58
2008-09	**20.89**	**1701.33**

Source : Report on Currency and Finance, Various Issues.

The States would be requested to similarly set up their own brand name and logo for the products of the rural poor in their States, which can be solid in the urban markets. Likewise, the District Rural Development Agencies can have their own distinct identity in so far as products sold in the rural areas are concerned. The access to international and metropolitan markets should be through one national agency, at least in so far as brand image development is concerned. Otherwise, there is a risk of products not having sufficient identity and in the process losing out. The Ministry would support all such efforts to promote the brand image.

Table - 5

Performance of the programme in Karnataka Expenditure of SGSY

(Amount Rs in Lakhs)

Year	*balance Opening*	*Allocation*			*Release*			*Total fund*	*Expenditure*	*% of exp.*
		Centre	*State*	*Total*	*Centre*	*State*	*Total*			
2006-07	113.15	1996.54	1288	3284.54	1994.78	664.93	2659.71	2773.22	2717.76	98
2007-08 (Nov. 07)	53.29	3042.75	1288	4330.75	1521.38	507.12	2028.50	2081.79	1546.89	74
TOTAL	166.44	5039.29	2576	7615.29	3516.16	1172.05	4688.21	4855.01	4264.65	88

Source: Economic Survey, GoK.

Total amount of subsidy and credit disbursed to SHGs and individual swarozgaris during 2006-07 and up to the month of November 2007-08 are as follows:

Table- 6
Credit and Subsidy Disbursed

Year	*Credit disbursed to (Rs.in Lakhs)*			*Subsidy disbursed to (Rs.in Lakhs)*		
	SHGs	*Ind. Swaroz-garis*	*Total*	*SHGs*	*Ind. Swaroz-garis*	*Total*
2006-07	2793.03	1136.89	3929.92	1500.43	485.36	1985.79
2007-08 (Nov. 07)	1922.75	694.44	2617.19	863.68	271.05	1134.73
Total4	715.78	1831.33	6547.11	2364.11	756.41	3120.52

Source: Economic Survey, GoK.

A total numbers of 1395 SHGs, started economic activities, covering 18089 members during 2006-07 and in the case of individual swarozgaries, the coverage is 5022. During the current financial year up to the month of November 2007, 757 enterprises covering 9522 members and 2815 swarozgaris were benefited by the programmes as shown in the Table - 7.

Decentralisation and Rural Development in Karnataka

Prior to decentralisation of power in the year 1987 the state itself undertook the responsibility of planning and implementation of programmes including mitigation of poverty, unemployment and rural developemnt ones. The state apart from the Centre's special programmes for poverty aleviaiton, unemployment and other rural development schemes (CSSs and CPSs) adopted its own schemes from time to time for the above problems. A

Table - 7
Achievement of SGSY during 2006-07 & 2007-2008

Year	*Self Help Group (No of members covered)*					*No.of Individual Swarozgaris*				
	Total	*SC*	*ST*	*Women*	*Disabled*	*Total*	*SC*	*ST*	*Women*	*Disabled*
2006-07	18089	5898	700	15650	127	5022	4181	268	2322	557
2007-08	9522	3267	452	7681	156	2815	2183	203	1184	332
TOTAL	27611	9165	1152	23331	283	7837	6364	471	3506	889

Source: RDPR, Bangalore.

sample of such schemes adopted and implemented in recent years are dryland development, ganga-kalyana, vishwa, stree shakthi, swavalambana, namma bhoomi namma thota, kugrama suvarna grama, ashraya, etc.

The CSSs and CPSs relating to the above problems are being implemented simultaneously in the state. In fact, they are the major schemes involving large budgetary support from the Centre. With regard to poverty reducation, Karnataka State seems to be not doing well. To overcome some of the inherent problems particularly the poverty, unemployment, basic services and the overall development of rural areas, the state took a bold policy decision to decentralise power both political and administrative down to the village level in the ear 1987. When democratic decentralsied bodies were established at the sub-state level in the year 1987 a large number of programmes/schemes under development sectors were transferred to them. It amy be noted that the then government enacted a new legislation namely "The Karnataka Zilla Parishad, Taluk Panchayat Samithi, Mandal Panchayat and Nyaya Panchayat Act, 1983" in the year 1985 for creation of rural local governments in the state. Based on this new legislation a two-tier elected panchayats were established throughout the state in the year 1987 and they have been entrusted with a large number of functions and financial resources.

The state governement transferred around 350 plan schemes in about 30 development sectors to panchayaths for implementation. The guiding principle in the devolution of schemes was that all schemes with a Mandal orientation had been transferred to the Mandal Panchayat (MP) and all schemes with an inter-Mandal Panchayat, inter-taluk or district orientation were transferred to Zilla Parishad. The entire special component plan (SCP) and the tribal sub-pla (TSP) were made over to the ZPs for implementation. Further, the District Rural Developemnt Agenc (DRDA) at the district level which was largely implementing anti-poverty and rural development programmes was merged with ZP along with funds and functionaries. The PR Act (1983) had two Schedules specifying the sector-wise programmes of MPs and ZPs. The functions under Scheduel-I pertained to MP and had two categories. One, obligatory functions and two, planning, identification of beneficiaries, supervision and monitoring of the schemes/projects. There were altogether 89 schemes under Schedule - I, Schedule- II had 267 schemes which were brought under the purview of ZPs.

In the post 73rd amendment period a three tier PRIs system was established in the year 1994. During this period also the PRIs were entrusted with large number of functions and resources. Now, the functions/responsibilities are distributed across the three-tier panchayats in contrast to two-tiers earlier. Around 665 schemes under plan and non-plan categories in about 27 sectors have been brought under the purview of PRIs. The sector-wise and tier-wise schemes transferred to PRIs are presented in table - 8. some problems were encountered in the allocation of functions between the tiers. These are : a) overlapping of functions, and b) lopsided distribution across the tiers. The Grama Panchayats till 2004-05 were not assigned any development sector except JRY/SGRY. However, an activity mapping initiated during 2003-04 resolved the above problems to some extent. Grama Panchayat is the lowest tier in the PRI structure has been assigned with 33 schemes during 2004-05 and 2005-06.

In the meantime to give some flexibility to PRIs in their planning, the state RDPR department undertook rationalizing the existing schemes. As a result of mergers and abolition of uneconomical and un-viable schemes the number of schemes has come down to 435 from 665.

Besides functions, the state also undertook redesigning the resource transfers between the three-tier panchayats. The share of GPs in the PRIs total plan grants has increased to around 22 percent in 2004-05 and further to about 34 percent in the year 2005-06. This enhancement in the resources of GPs was made at the cost of TPs and ZPs.

Table - 8
Sector and Tier-wise Schemes transferred to PRIs in Karnataka (in Nos)

Sector	*Plan Schemes*				*Non-plan Schemes*				*Total Plan and Non-Plan Schemes*			
	ZP	*TP*	*GP*	*Total*	*ZP*	*TP*	*GP*	*Total*	*ZP*	*TP*	*GP*	*Total*
General Education	14	11	-	25	17	8	0	25	31	19	0	50
Adult education	3	-	-	3	-	-	0	-	33	0	0	3
Sports and Youth Services	16	-	-	16	9	1	0	10	25	1	0	26
Medical and Public Health	30	6	-	36	43	4	0	47	73	10	0	83
Indian System of Medicine	7	1	-	8	-	-	0	-	7	1	0	8
Family Welfare	15	-	-	15	1	-	0	1	16	0	0	16
Water Supply and Sanitation	23	1	2	26	3	2	0	5	26	3	2	31
Social Welfare	27	26	-	53	34	15	0	49	61	41	0	102
Special Component Plan	-	18	-	18	-	-	0	-	0	18	0	18
Welfare of Backward Classes	12	10	-	22	-	-	0	-	12	10	0	22

Sector	Plan Schemes				Non-plan Schemes				Total Plan and Non-Plan Schemes			
	ZP	TP	GP	Total	ZP	TP	GP	Total	ZP	TP	GP	Total
Welfare of Womenand Children	4	5	-	9	3	1	0	4	7	6	0	13
Nutrition	-	1	-	1	-	1	0	1	0	2	0	2
Agriculture	13	3	-	16	8	4	0	12	21	7	0	28
Social Conservation	-	-	-	-	1	1	0	2	1	1	0	2
Horticulture	9	7	-	16	-	-	0	-	9	7	0	16
Animal Husbandry	9	6	-	15	15	3	0	18	24	9	0	33
Fisheries	22	-	-	22	9	-	0	9	31	0	0	31
Forest	9	-	-	9	-	-	0	-	9	0	0	9
Cooperation	14	6	-	20	-	-	0	-	14	6	0	20
Rural development Programmes	5	3	-	8	-	-	0	-	5	3	0	8
Rural Employment	1	1	1	3	-	-	0	-	1	1	1	3
Other RD Programmes	5	2	1	8	1	2	0	3	6	4	1	11
Minor Irrigation	6	3	-	9	7	-	0	7	13	3	0	16
Cottage and Small Scale Industires	15	-	-	15	19	-	0	19	34	0	0	34
Sericulture	7	2	-	9	-	-	-	-	7	2	0	9
Roads and Bridges	17	1	-	18	8	-	-	8	25	1	0	26

Sector	*Plan Schemes*				*Non-plan Schemes*				*Total Plan and Non-Plan Schemes*			
	ZP	*TP*	*GP*	*Total*	*ZP*	*TP*	*GP*	*Total*	*ZP*	*TP*	*GP*	*Total*
Tribal Sub Plan	-	18	-	18	-	-	-	-	0	18	0	18
Handloom and Textiles	16	-	-	16	-	-	-	-	16	0	0	16
Science and Technology	1	-	-	1	-	-	-	-	1	0	0	1
Secretariat Economic Services	-	-	-	-	3	-	-	3	3	0	0	3
Public Works	-	-	-	-	7	-	-	7	7	0	0	7
Total	**300**	**131**	**4**	**435**	**188**	**42**	-	**230**	**488**	**173**	**4**	**665**

Source: Rural Development and Panchayat Raj Department, Government of Karnataka.

The shares of TPs and ZPs during 2003-04 was 28 and 54 percent respectively and during 2005-06 they stood at 27 and 40 percent. The statutory grant to each GP has been increased to Rs.5 lakhs per annum from the Rs.2 lakhs that was allocated till 1999-2000. The total plan grants (state, Central and UFC) transferred to GPs in the year 2005-06 amounts to Rs.965 crores. This works out to Rs.17 lakhs per GP per annum. The own revenues (tax and non-tax) account for Rs.3 lakhs per year per GP. Thus, the average revenue per GP during 2008-09 works out to Rs.20 lakhs. The average revenue during 2008-09 was around Rs.7 lakhs. It is interesting to observe the allocation of grants across the sectoral programmes at the state level by the GPs.

The major responsibility for programme implementation has been given to the Panchayat Raj institutions

The NREG Act, 2005 gives priority for water harvesting and water conservation, drought proofing including afforestation and plantation, construction of irrigation canals, micro and minor irrigation works and provision of irrigation facilities to land owned by Scheduled Castes and Scheduled Tribes. Renovation of traditional water bodies, land development and rural connectivity has also to be given priority in the Annual Works Programme that is to be prepared by the implementing agencies. Government of India issued the notification on 2.2.2006 to launch National Rural Employment Guarantee Act for 200 selected districts in the country. The act will be extended to the whole Karnataka by April 2008.

Urban Self Employment Programame: Urban Self Employment Programame (USEP) assists individual urban poor for setting up gainful self employment ventures. The project cost is Rs. 50,000 per individual but if two or more eligible persons join together in a partnership, higher project cost is allowed, provided individual share does not exceed Rs. 50,000. Subsidy is provided at the rate of 15 % of the project cost subject to a maximum of Rs. 7500 per beneficiary. Beneficiary share is 5% of the project cost either in cash or in kind or both. Out of the total project cost, 80% is sanctioned as loan by financial institutions including Banks and Thrift and Credit Societies. A house to house survey for identification of genuine beneficiaries is being done. Now economic Para methods are to be applied to identify the urban poor. Women beneficiaries belonging to widows, divorcees, single women, where women are the sole earners is to be ranked higher in priority. Not less than 30% of the beneficiaries should be women, 3% to be reserved for disabled and Scheduled Caste / Scheduled Tribe beneficiaries are given special attention in proportion of their strength in the local population.

Development of Women and Children in Urban Areas: Development of women and children in urban Areas (DWCUA) assist the urban poor women for starting gainful employment through group activity. The scheme is extended to the poor women of urban areas who decide to set up self employment enterprise as a group. Minimum number of a group is fixed as 10. The project cost is Rs. 25 lakhs or less. The DWCUA group is given a subsidy of Rs. 1.25 lakh o r 50% of the project cost whichever is less. To ensure the contribution of members, 5% of the project cost is brought as their share, either in cash or in kind or as both and 45% of the project cost is as bank loan.

From the various aspects that has been touched upon in the preceding pages, I sincerely suggest the following corrective mechanisms.

1. Allow free and frank debates and discussions in the Gram Sabhas.
2. Avoid wastage of funds by keeping a tight check on the money earned and money spent and avoid pilferage of funds through various devious means.
3. Avoid wastage of funds by keeping a tight check on the money earned and money spent and avoid

pilferage of funds through various devious means.

4. Imbibe the canons of good administrative procedures by avoiding duplicity.
5. Use always quality products to avoid depreciation costs (in popular terms-wear and tear).
6. Make it obligatory upon the members of the three-tier Panchayati Raj Institution to understand the basis of the Indian Constitution and intern the73rd and 74th constitution Amendment Acts.
7. Reduce the number of the standing committees at various levels.
8. In order to streamline the fund flow to the gram Panchayats, a mechanism of direct release of Government devolution's through banks has been involves six nationalized banks and 12 Grameen banks. Further greater emphasis has been given for improvement of own finances of Grama Panchayats by way of scientific levy and collection of taxes.

Guidelines standardizing the rules for collection of property taxes have been issued. Further, a process of evaluation of taxes that was transparent and allowed people to participate in the tax determination process has been put into place. Property lists have been publicized and made available on the notice board of the Grama Panchayats for inspection. However the biggest gain according to the deputy chief minister and finance minister was 80 percent increase in the number of properties enumerated to tax. The properties have increased from 74.16 lakh to 104.47 after revision. The property tax and centers have increased from Rs.80.crore to Rs. 200crore.

To sum up, we may say that the SGSY and other programmes implemented through PRIs are an excellent rural development programmes meant for creation of employment and building up economic infrastructure in rural areas. However, it is fraught with some working deficiencies which can certainly be got over with the help of suggestions made here. This study reinforces our hope that a reformed scheme of poverty alleviation and generation of employment in the rural areas.

References

Panda Snehalata, 1999, "Political Empowerment of Women: Case of Orissa Panchayati Raj Institution, Indian Journal of Public Administration, Vol.45.

Pandey, Saroj, 1992, Women's Education and Development in Orissa, Social Change, Vol.22.

Patel, A. R., "Financing of Integrated Rural Development Programme", The Journal of Indian Institute of Bankers, Vol. 54, No.3, (Jul- Sept. 1983), PP.147-55.

Patel, A.R. and Patel,M. R., "Role of Banks in the Implementation of 20-point Economic Programme", The Journal of Indian Institute of Bankers, Vol. 54, No.1, (Jan- Mar 1983), PP. 28-38.

Manikymba, P , P,1989, Women in Panchayati Raj-Promises and Performances, Teaching Politics,Vol.14(3-4)

Manikymba, P ,1990, Women presiding officer at the tertiary political Structure, Journal of Rural development, vol. 9(6)

Manipal, 1994, "Empowering Women through Panchyatati Raj Institution, Kurukshetra.

Bagchee, Sañdeep (1987), "Poverty Alleviation Programmes in seventh Plan", EPW, vol. XXII, No. 4 January 24.

Bajpai, S.I. (1982), "Rural Development: Some Constraints", Kurukshetra, Vol. XXX, No. 23.

2

Impact of Women Empowerment Programmes on Rural Women in Hassan District

Thimmaiya T.D.

Introduction

Enhancing Women's participation in development is essential not only for achieving social justice, but also for reducing poverty. World wide experience shows clearly that supporting a stronger role for women contributes to economic growth, it improves child survival and overall family health and it reduces fertility, thus helping to slow population growth rates. In short, investing in women is central to sustainable development.

In spite of the massive scale of Government intervention towards rural development in India, rural India continues to be reeling under poverty and related problems. Not withstanding the phenomenal progress seen in the rural credit structure in terms of volume of credit extended, concessionality, coverage of weaker sections including Scheduled Caste and Scheduled Tribes, almost all institutions constituting the formal part of the rural credit system suffer from several shortcomings like: (a) Gap between the concern of the policy makers and the quality of the effort. (b) Defects in policy design. (c) Infirmities in implementation. (d) Loans to the poor were considered as a part of social sector lending and not commercial (e) It was felt that poor were not borrowers but beneficiaries (f) An attitude of 'carefully disguised cynicism towards the poor' and (g) An attitude of 'poor are not bankable'.

The above short comings have been due to the absence of the people's participation in the development programmes and also due to the gap in mutual understandings about the perspectives of the programmes between the supply side (the Government, planners and the bureaucracy) and the demand side (the rural poor). This gap is felt to be filled by the micro finance activity through the Self - Help Groups approach for sustainable rural development.

The significant feature of the Self – Help Groups(SHGs) is that they provide credit to the poor at unsubsidized interest rates besides they having relatively low default rates on these loans. SHGs reduce transaction costs of financial institutions that do business with the poor and that of the SHGs themselves. They reduce the cost of financial institutions by acting as intermediary organizations or by providing social collateral that substitute for costly loan appraisals and supervisions. SHG approach has made considerable impact on the development of rural economy in terms of increasing savings of the poor, providing access to credit for the poor at reasonable rates of interest by establishing linkages with the formal financial institutions, improving the production levels and income levels, increasing food security and standard of living improving asset creation and enhancing income generation activities, augmenting environment sustainability and contributing for the much needed women empowerment with the enthusiastic roles played by the NGOs, the banks, the public and the Governments, over a period of one and half decades, the SHGs approach has been transformed into a movement in the rural areas.

Self -Help Groups have been receiving greater attention by all the concerned like the Government, NABARD, RBI, Commercial Banks and RRBs. This innovative form of credit delivery system is catching up the rural areas in a big way. SHGs movement is leveraging the strength of the formal banking system and flexibility of informal SHGs are providing adequate financial-services to the rural poor. This programme has been further in to a social movement with a high rate of expansion in recent years. Fuelled by competence and enthusiasm at all stakeholder levels, it is expanding rapidly throughout India, including tribal areas. It is probably the world's largest and most successful micro finance programme for the rural poor outstanding in its emphasis on self-reliance and local autonomy of the very poor. It is widely felt that there have been perceptible changes in the living conditions of the rural poor mainly on economic side and relatively on social side. It is with this perceptional background that a detailed study has been undertaken to find out the economic impact of the Self -Help Groups on the development of rural economy.

In this context, it is desirable to generate information and analyse to what extent these Self Help Groups have been able to reduce poverty and vulnerability by increasing capital/asset formation at the household level, improving the incomes of household and enterprise, enhancing the capacity of individuals and households to manage risk, increasing enterprise activity within households, expanding employment opportunities for the poor in non-farm enterprises, empowering women and improving the accessibility of other financial services at the community level.

Objectives of the Study

The following objectives are formulated for the study.

1. To evaluate the Impact of Women Empowerment

Programmes on Rural Women in Karnataka in general and Hassan District in particular.

2. To study the changes in the quality of the beneficiary women through women Empowerment Programmes like SHGs.
3. To review the economic benefits of SHGs Bank Linkage Programme and Empowerment of Women in Hassan District.
4. To suggest the suitable measures for further effective improvement of the programmes on the Empowerment of Rural Women.

Results and Discussion

It is truly a innovative scheme sanctioned by the Government of Karnataka in the 1997-98. Udyogini assists women in gaining self - reliance through self employment, especially in the trade and service sector. Udyogini empowers women by providing loans through Banks and subsidy through the Corporation for undertaking business activities/ micro enterprises. Loans are arranged through financial institutions like Commercial banks, District Co - operative Banks and RRBs. The scheme has gone a long way in preventing women entrepreneurs from private borrowing at higher rates of interest.

K.S.W.D.C provides a subsidy about 40% of the loan sanctioned or Rs.10,000/- whichever is less for special category viz., widows, destitute, disable women and women belonging to SC/STs. In case of the general category women, the subsidy is 25% of the loan sanctioned or 7,500/ - whichever is less. Loans are provided through the Banks and the subsidy part is provided through the corporation. Annual target and achievements of Udyogini Scheme in Karnataka State is depicted in the following table - 1.

Table - 1
Annual Target & Achievements under Udyogini Scheme in Karnataka State 2002-03 to 2006-07

Sl. No.	*Year*	*Annual Target*		*Achievement*	
		Physical	*Financial*	*Physical*	*Financial*
1.	2002-03	1726	80.00	1827	95.68
2.	2003-04	2027	75.00	2215	126.95
3.	2004-05	1524	125.00	1635	128.95
4.	2005-06	-	-	-	-
5.	2006-07	882	85-00	980	72.91

Source: Karnataka State Women Development Corporation, Bangalore.

Mahila Arthika Swavalambana Yojane

Karnataka State Women Development Corporation has introduced this project with total amount of 12 crores during 1997-98 for the Economic Empowerment of 12000 Women in Raichur, Bijapur, Gulbarga and Bidar District of North Karnataka in 5 years. This will be achieved through the Self - Help Groups' approach in which women that from SHGs are encouraged to take up thrift and credit activities. The programme includes training the women in various market - oriented skills and thereafter linking up with financial institutions for funding of income generating programmes. For the year 2006-07 a target of 400 groups and financial target of Rs.30.00 lakhs was fixed. An amount of Rs.20.55 lakhs has been spent covering 400 old groups. Annual wise target and achievements of Mahila Arthika Swavalambana Yojane in Karnataka are illustrated in the table - 2.

Table - 2
Annual - wise Target & Achievements under Mahila Arthika Swavalambana Yojane From 2002-03 to 2006-07

Sl. No.	*Year*	*Annual Target*		*Achievement*	
		Physical (Groups)	*Financial (in lakhs)*	*Physical (Groups)*	*Financial (in lakhs)*
1.	2002-03	400	30.00	400	30.00
2.	2003-04	2250	55.00	765	18.90
3.	2004-05	4200	33.00	3585	51.23
4.	2005-06	400	50.00	400	9.28
5.	2006-07	400	30.00	400	20.55

Source: Karnataka State Women Development Corporation Bangalore.

Devadasi Rehabilitation Programme (DRP)

Karnataka State Women Development Corporation (KSWDC) has taken the responsibility for implementation of this programme in Belgaum and Bijapur Districts of Karnataka. The corporation has implemented many programmes for the economic and social development of Devadasis. The main programmes of the Corporation are:

- To set up of training and production centres.
- To undertake housing workshop for handloom weaving trained Devadasis.
- To provide loans through financial institutions with 60% subsidy of the loan sanctioned for Devadasis to undertake income generate activities.
- To implement social programmes like public awareness, formation of SHGs, Vigilance camp, health camp etc.,

The following table - 3 illustrates the target and achievements under Devadasi Rehabilitation Programme in Karnataka State.

Table - 3
Target & Achievements under Devadasi Rehabilitation Programme in Karnataka State (Health camps also included)
2002-03 to 2006-07

Sl. No.	Year	Annual Target		Achievement	
		Physical (Groups)	Financial (in lakhs)	Physical (Groups)	Financial (in lakhs)
1.	2002-03	306	40.00	399	53.79
2.	2003-04	389	30.00	1330	50.99
3.	2004-05	23057	55.00	23057	57.09
4.	2005-06	10352	81.00	10352	129.76
5.	2006-07	14254	92.00	11255	131.15

Source: Karnataka State Women Development Corporation, Bangalore.

CASE STUDY AREA: HASSAN DISTRICT

Some of the important programmes implemented in Hassan District to empower women are analysed here below.

Udyogini Scheme

The target and achievements of Udyogini Scheme in Hassan District are depicted in the following table - 4. The data shows the mixed trend in physical and financial annual target of the scheme in Hassan District. Even in achievement also there are variations.

Table - 4

Annual Target & Achievements under Udyogini Scheme in Hassan 2002-03 To 2006-07

Sl. No.	*Year*	*Annual Target*		*Achievement*	
		Physical (Nos)	*Financial (Rs.)*	*Physical (Nos)*	*Financial (Rs.)*
1.	2002-03	65	335079	65	335079
2.	2003-04	85	459500	85	459500
3.	2004-05	48	329100	48	329100
4.	2005-06	39	330000	39	284900
5.	2006-07	400	1997500	62	1174900

Source: Women and Child Development Department, Hassan.

Marketing Assistance Scheme

The benefited sangas/ societies under Marketing Assistance Scheme in Hassan District are described in the Table - 6.

The data in the table clearly show that there is no drastic change in physical annual target under the scheme in the District. During 2002-03 there were 30 sangas, and even after 2002-03 also this number has not been changed. In financial target also we may found declining trend. Hence, we can say that Government should take care about effective implementation of the scheme for the benefit of the women.

Stree Shakthi Scheme

Details of Self Help Groups under Stree Shakthi Scheme in Hassan District are depicted in the Table - 7.

Table – 5
Category wise Achievements under Udyogini Scheme in Hassan District 2002-03 to 2006-07

Sl. No.	Year	Category wise Achievements											
		Physical	Financial	Physical	Financial	Physical	Financial	Physical	Financial	Physical	Financial	Physical	Financial
1.	2002-03	13	75279	-	-	1	7500	-	-	7	3400	44	218300
2.	2003-04	30	200500	1	7500	3	16500	-	-	3	12500	35	217100
3.	2004-05	6	53000	1	9000	2	20000	2	17500	2	12500	21	141000
4.	2005-06	11	92900	1	7500	2	14500	2	16500	2	12500	21	141000
5.	2006-07	28	233500	3	26000	8	68000	4	39000	8	54000	104	693900

Source: Women and Child Development Department, Hassan.

Table - 6

Annual Target & Achievements under Marketing Assistance Scheme in Hassan District 2002-03 to 2006-07

Sl. No.	Year	Annual Target		Achievement	
		Physical (No. of Sangas/ Societies)	Financial (in Rs.)	Physical (No. of Sangas/ Societies)	Financial (in Rs.)
1.	2002-03	30	30566	30	27286
2.	2003-04	-	-	-	-
3.	2004-05	30	30000	30	30000
4.	2005-06	30	30000	30	30000
5.	2006-07	30	30000	30	30450

Source: Women and Child Development Department, Hassan.

Table - 7

Annual wise details of SHGs under Stree Shakthi Scheme in Hassan District 2002-03 to 2006-07

Sl. No.	Year	No. of Women of SHGs					
		No. of Self Help group (SHG)	Total No. of SC women in SHG	Total No. of ST Women in SHG	Minorities	Others	Total No. of Women of all Categories
1.	2002-03	3003	8599	732	844	37902	48107
2.	2003-04	4493	12528	1264	1188	60287	75267
3.	2004-05	4493	12528	1264	1188	60287	75267
4.	2005-06	4493	12528	1264	1188	60287	75267
5.	2006-07	5392	14702	1571	1365	72096	89734

Source : Women & Child Development Department, Hassan.

The data regarding the performance of the scheme in Hassan District indicates that there is a progressive trend in formation of SHGs. Even in SC/ST women also we can notice the higher trend in the formation of groups. This show that awareness among women is gradually increasing. During 2002-03 there were 3003 SHGs, then it has been gradually increased to 5392 SHGs.

Table - 8

Annual wise Financial Details of SHGs under Stree Shakthi Scheme in Hassan District 2002-03 to 2006-07

Sl. No.	*Year*	*No of Groups who have started saving*	*Savings accumu-lated (Rs. In lakhs)*	*No. of Groups taken loan from the bank*	*Total loan Amount taken from bank (Rs. In lakh)*	*Revolving Fund Released by Govt. (in lakhs)*
1.	2002-03	3003	522.52	1367	250.41	44.25
2	2003-04	4493	891.68	2150	511.07	161.91
3.	2004-05	4493	1560	3281	669	225
4.	2005-06	3281	1676	3281	846.42	7714
5.	2006-07	5392	2251.25	4359	895.35	34.00

Source : Women & Child Development Department, Hassan.

Among the above women empowerment programmes, the data clearly indicates that Stree Shakthi Programme in the major Women Empowerment Programme in Karnataka and especially in Hassan District. Hence much concentration has been made on the analysis of Self Help Groups under Stree Shakthi Programme in Hassan District. The following table - 9 shows the category wise formation of Self-Help Groups under Stree Shakthi Programmes in Hassan District up to 2006-07.

Table - 9
Categorywise formation of SHGs in Hassan District upto 2006-07

Category	*No. of SHGs*	*Percentage of Total SHGs*
SC	865	16.04
ST	89	1.65
General (Including SC & ST)	4438	82.30
Total	**5392**	**100**

Source : Women & Child Development Department, Hassan.

The above table clearly shows that there have been 5392 Self-help Groups in Hassan District upto 2006-07. Among those 865 SHGs have been formed by SC Women only, 89 SHGs have been formed by ST Women only and remaining 4438 SHGs have been formed by the general women i.e., women of all categories including SC & ST women also. Talukwise details of Self-Help Groups under Stree Shakthi Scheme in Hassan District upto 2006-07 and indicated in the following table-10.

The table 10 clearly shows that there is diversification in the number of women engaged in Self-Help Groups in Hassan District. During the year 2006-07, Arasikere taluk has the highest number of women Self Help Groups i.e., 20150, it is followed by Channarayapatna taluk which has 16731 women, Hassan taluk has 13018 women, Belur has 10124 women, Holenarasipur taluk has 9536 women, Arkalagud has 8917 women, Sakaleshpur has 6183 women. The lowest number of women engaged in SHGs' is at Alur taluk i.e., 5075. It is heartening to mention here is that, in Aarasikere taluk highest women are engaged in SHGs' activities and they are matured in respect in SHGs' activities and conducting meeting, book keeping, proper utilization of the fund, repayment and about saving motivation.

Table - 10

Talukwise SHGs under Stree Shakthi Scheme in Hassan District upto 2006-07.

Sl. No.	*Taluk*	*No. of Self Help group (SHG)*	*Total No. of SC women in SHG*	*Total No. of ST Women in SHG*	*Minorities*	*Others*	*Total No. of Women of all Categories*
1.	Alur	329	1408	98	81	3488	5075
2.	Arkalgud	575	1131	133	115	7538	8917
3.	Arsikere	1140	2710	705	254	16481	20150
4.	Belur	625	2557	108	48	7068	10124
5.	Channarayapatna	992	2282	108	48	14293	16731
6.	Hassan	734	1768	30	118	11002	13018
7.	Holenarasipur	595	1825	105	150	7447	9536
8.	Sakaleshpur	402	1021	97	282	4779	6183
	Total	**5392**	**14702**	**1571**	**1365**	**72096**	**89734**

Source: Women & Child Development Department, Hassan.

The savings are actually carried out by the Self-Help Groups. The animator of the group collects the money and deposit in the banks in the name of the group. The savings also can be given weekly and fort nightly to enable them to save the nearer amount then and there itself. Here most of the respondents are in the Rs. 30-50 savings group. It is heartening to note that all the borrowers save some amount of money.

The Government will give a revolving fund of Rs.5000/- to each group which has maintained savings at least for six months. The numbers will start loan activities by using the savings of the numbers and the revolving fund. The Supervisors and Assistant child development project officer will regularly examine and get ensured that the numbers are repaying the loans in time and money is not misused in any manner. The taluk wise financial details about Self Help Groups up to 2006-07 are presented in the following table - 11.

Table - 11
Taluk wise financial details of SHGs under Stree Shakthi Scheme up to 2006-07.

Sl. No.	*Taluk*	*No of Groups who have started saving*	*Savings accumulated (Rs. In lakhs)*	*No. of Groups taken loan from the bank*	*Total loan Amount taken from bank (Rs. In lakh)*	*Revolving Fund Released by Govt. (in lakhs)*
1.	Alur	329	131.58	227	53.66	1.75
2.	Arakalagud	575	256.77	475	80.67	4.75
3.	Arsikere	1140	471.06	980	291.68	5.75
4.	Belur	625	262.91	525	62.19	5.25
5.	Channara-yapatna	992	364.31	775	172.64	5.00
6.	Hassan	734	416.83	669	89.66	3.25
7.	Holenarasi-pur	595	185.69	395	78.43	5.25
8.	Sakaleshpur	402	162.1	313	66.42	3.00
	Total	5392	2251.25	4359	895.35	34.00

Source: Women & Child Development Department, Hassan.

The above table clearly shows that Self-Help Groups have started savings and have benefited from the Stree Shakthi Programme in the District.

FINDINGS OF THE STUDY

Based on the analysis and discussion in the evaluation of the performance of Women Empowerment Programmes in Karnataka State in general and Hassan District in particular, the following findings have been drawn:

1. More importantly, the decentralization of the Bank linkage programme for women was for more pronounced in most of the districts. The members and their federation were playing an active role in the formation of groups, selection of beneficiaries, monitoring the loan utilization and

repayment. Further, the federation was in the forefront in improving the access of members to resources and infrastructure of the Government.

2. In terms of Self Help Groups under Stree Shakthi Scheme, Karnataka State has 130000 total No. of SHGs, 20.00 lakhs total No. of women in SHGs, No. of Groups taken loan from the different banks are 98,133 and total loan amount taken from bank is 5962.60 lakhs among the districts in the State (at the end of December - 2007).
3. Self - Help Groups approach under Stree Shakthi Scheme is enabling empowerment of rural women and this bottom-up approach for rural women empowerment has provided considerable economic and non-economic externalities to low income households.
4. It is evident that the income of the households increased rapidly and resulted in an acquisition of household assets and thereby leading relatively a better life. After joining the Self Help Groups, women purchased T.V, tape recorder, bicycle, fan, tailoring machine, etc. Whereas before joining the SHG, women had only radio and a buffalo. The expenditure towards education, health, nutrition's food items and housing has increased after joining the group. All of them feel that their knowledge in relation to the importance of children's education, health, banks, and their role in the society has been improved. They also feel that their confidence in leading a better life has been improved due to association with the group.
5. SHGs have potentiality to tackle the poverty and they can be an important weapon for poverty alleviation in Hassan District.

SUGGESTIONS

The following suggestions have been offered for the

better implementation and effectiveness of the women development programmes.

1. The study shows that there is an increase in the level of income and assets of the rural women of SHGs and reduction in the level of poverty as a result of intervention of micro finance by SHGs. It is important to note that most of the women beneficiaries are illiterate. Hence, the beneficiaries need to be educated about the formalities to be fulfilled in obtaining the necessary finance. The bank staff should help the uneducated women in getting their credit sanctioned from the banks. If the beneficiaries are educated they can get loans easily from the banks.
2. While loaning to Self - Help Groups right time, right person and right purpose should be kept in mind and the process of loaning should be more easy and convenient for the women beneficiary.
3. For greater acceleration of rate of economic empowerment, further strategy must focus more and more on training and capacity building of members besides ensuring adequate linkage supports.

References

Chandrasekhar R.(ed)., "Women's Resource and National Development: A Perspective", New Delhi, Gaurav Publishing House.

Ankar R.E.Khan M.E., Gupta R.B,(1988) "Women's Participation in Labour Force. A Method of test in India for Improving Measurement", International Labour Office, Geneva.

Ashine Roy, (2003): "Women Empowerment and Gender Planning", Rajat Publications, New Delhi,

Badal Chandra Das (2002): "Rural Women in Micro-

Enterprises: Concern and Challenges", Social Welfare Department , Delhi.

Banarjee, & Nirmala (1989): "Trends in Women Employment 1971-81", Economic and Political Weekly, April 29, P 20-21.

Ackerly & Brooke A.(1995): "Testing the tools of Development: Credit Programmes, Loan Involvement and Women's Empowerment". IDS Bulletin 26(3): 56 - 68.

Bhatt N. and S.V.Tang (1998):" Group Based Microfinance and Economic Development", New York, Handbook of Economic Development.

Chan & Marm (1992)", Conceptual Model for women's Empowerment" unpublished.

Coleman B.E. (2001) "Measuring the impact of micro finance programmes, Finance for the poor", Asian Development Bank, 2(4): 5-7.

Gurumoorthy T.R.(2002): "Economic Empowerment Through Self-Reliance", Social Welfare Department, Delhi.

3

Economic Empowerment of Kadu Golla Women Through Stree Shakti Programme - A Case Study in Pavagada Taluk

K. Sivachithappa

Introduction

In rural India, there is a substantial degree of feminization of poverty on account of an increase in the net population growth rate among the landless agricultural labour households (including SC, STs Other Backward Classes women), low level of human skills, lack of availability of wage employment opportunities and inadequacy of institutional support of create wage as well as self employment opportunities. This list includes economic factors responsible for feminization of poverty, which are much stronger in operation and which function along with socio-cultural barriers and discrimination against women in economic participation.

SHGs have helped micro-enterprises set by Kadu Golla women as individually and groups. The examples are raising vegetables in the land, ready made garments making, developing horticulture and animal husbandry, cultivation of medical herbs, mushroom cultivation, pot making, stone quarrying, sheep breeding and marketing wool, preparation of pickles, canteens in Government office premises, and so on. Therefore it is the right time to make an empirical evaluation of the impact of women participation in literacy, decision making etc., especially weakest section of the society women i.e., Kadu golla women. Hence, the statement of the problem is suitably entitled as "Economic Empowerment of Kadu Golla Women through Stree Shakthi Programme ". This study is intends (a) to examine the initiatives for Empowerment of Women in Karnataka (b) to evaluate the Impact of Women Empowerment Programmes on Rural Women in Karnataka in general and Pavagada taluk in particular (c) to study the changes in the quality of the beneficiary Kadu Golla women through women empowerment programmes like Stree Shakthi Programme and; (d) to suggest the suitable measures for further effective improvement of the Stree Shakthi programmes on the empowerment of weaker section women.

In recent years, the individual approach to poverty alleviation programmes has been increasingly replaced by group made. Studies revealed that the delivery of micro finance to the poor is smooth, effective and less costly if they are organized in to self-help groups (SHGs). The major approach to deliver micro finance from financial institutions for under taking self-employment activities particularly among the rural poor is two types viz. individual and group oriented. The individual approach to micro finance self-employment activities could not yield the expected results due to the relatively high transaction costs and procedural delay involved in it. The launching of National Bank for Agriculture and Rural Development (NABARD) pilot scheme in 1992 on micro finance by linking SHGs with banks, gave further boost in reaching the formal credit to the poor.

In 1980s, there was a considerable rethinking among

the policy makers in India about the existing approaches and strategies towards women welfare. This rethinking among the policy makers resulted in the formulation of a novel programme in the name of Development of Women and Children in Rural Areas (DWCRA), which is essentially an employment programme. The launching of the DWCRA during the period of 1982 under the self-help group strategy with the UNICEF assistance as a pilot project in 50 selected districts in few states, it has been extended in the country by 1995.

The SHG is considered as viable organization of the rural poor particularly women for delivering micro-credit in order to under take entrepreneurial activities. They have to mobilize and manage thrift activities appraise credit needs enforce financial disciplines; maintain credit linkages with banks and effectively under take income generating activities. The joint liability of the group enables the poor to overcome the problem of collateral security and also has an in-built mechanism of peer monitoring leading to better loan recoveries and productive credit utilization.

The Bangladesh Grameen Bank (BGB) is responsible for popularizing the concept of micro finance. The Bank was founded by Prof. Muhammad Yunus, the economist. It was started as a project in Chittagong District in August 1976. It became an independent bank dedicated to poor women of Bangladesh on October 2nd, 1993. The experience of the Bank made one thing clear: the poor are credit worthy.

The Bangladesh Grameen Bank (BGB) has some unique features. A unique feature of the Bank is ownership by borrowers. The target group is the landless poor, particularly the women. Also, all the members have to agree on certain obligations like family planning, growing vegetable, avoidance of dowry and child marriage etc., The group formation is on gender basis, that is, a group is either for women or men. The Bangladesh Grameen Bank (BGB) has now almost more than 7 lakhs groups and 2.2 crore members throughout Bangladesh. At present

Stree Shakthi Programme playing an important role in economic empowerment of women. Under this programme many SHGs have been formulated. Hence to evaluate the role of Stree Shakthi Programme the present study is undertaken.

RESEARCH METHODOLOGY

A planned approach has been employed for data collection so that the facts that are near to reality and free from aberrations are elicited for impact evaluation. This study is based on both primary and secondary source of data. The primary data has been collected from field survey. Primary data has been collected from 80 members of SHGs Stree Shakthi Programme in Pavagada taluk through random sampling basis.

ANALYSIS AND DISCUSSION

The implementation of Stree Shakthi scheme covers the villages spreading in 175 taluks of the state. About 20 lakhs women has been organised through one lakh Self - Help Groups. The data regarding the performance of the scheme in Pavagada taluk indicates that there is a progressive trend in formation of SHGs. Even in SC/ ST women also we can notice the higher trend in the formation of groups. This show that awareness among women is gradually increasing. During 2008-09 there were 3003 SHGs, then it has been gradually increased to 5392 SHGs.

STREE SHAKTHI SCHEME IN KARNATAKA

Honorable Chief Minister of Karnataka Sri S.M. Krishna has introduced the "Stree Shakti Scheme" for the empowerment of rural women. The main aim of this project is to make the rural women self - dependent through organizing 20 lakhs women into one lakh Self - Help Groups. This project has been implemented during 2000-01 leading to all - round development of the women. The state Government has taken a revolutionary step by setting up of this project by investing 72 crore rupees at a time in this project for the empowerment of women and organizing women in such huge number.

Table- 1

Details about the progress of SHGs under Rural Stree Shakthi Scheme in Karnataka State (At the end of December - 2008)

1.	Total No. of Self - Help Groups	1,19,246
2.	Total No. of SC women in SHGs	3,56,362
3.	Total No. of ST women in SHGs	1,41,510
4.	Total No. of Minorities in SHGs	1,30,351
5.	Total No. of others in SHGs	11,37,988
6.	Total No. of women of all categories	17.66 lakhs
7.	Total No. of Groups having Bank Accounts	1,10,912
8.	Total savings of the members	414.84 crores
9.	No.of Groups who have taken loan from different banks	87,005
10.	Total loan amount	458.05 crores
11.	Total No. of Groups who have been given Revolving Fund	1.00 lakh
12.	Total Revolving Fund Released by the Government	50.00 crores
13.	No. of Groups who have saved from Rs. 75,000/- to 1.00 lakh	1,017
14.	No. of Groups who have saved more than 1.00 lakh	310
15.	The total cost of the project from starting to here is Rs.	101.62 crores

Progress of Stree Shakthi Scheme in Pavagada Taluk

Details of Self Help Groups under Stree Shakthi Scheme in Pavagada taluk are depicted in the following table - 2.

Table - 2

Annual wise details of SHGs under Stree Shakthi Scheme in Pavagada taluk 2002-03 to 2006-07

			No. of Women of SHGs				
Sl. No.	Year	No. of Self Help group (SHG)	Total No. of SC women in SHG	Total No. of ST Women in SHG	Minorities	Others	Total No. of Women of all Categories
1.	2002-03	3003	8599	732	844	37902	48107
2.	2003-04	4493	12528	1264	1188	60287	75267
3.	2004-05	4493	12528	1264	1188	60287	75267
4.	2005-06	4493	12528	1264	1188	60287	75267
5.	2006-07	5392	14702	1571	1365	72096	89734

Source : Women & Child Development Department, Pavagada taluk.

The data regarding the performance of the scheme in Pavagada taluk indicates that there is a progressive trend in formation of SHGs. Even in SC/ST women also we can notice the higher trend in the formation of groups. This show that awareness among women is gradually increasing. During 2002-03 there were 3003 SHGs, then it has been gradually increased to 5392 SHGs.

The savings are actually carried out by the Self-Help Groups. The animator of the group collects the money and deposit in the banks in the name of the group. The savings also can be given weekly and fort nightly to enable them to save the nearer amount then and there itself. Here most of the respondents are in the Rs. 30-50 savings group. It is heartening to note that all the borrowers save some amount of money.

The Government will give a revolving fund of Rs.5000/- to each group which has maintained savings at least for six months. The numbers will start loan activities by using the savings of the numbers and the revolving fund. The Supervisors and Assistant child development project officer will regularly examine and get ensured that the numbers are repaying the loans in time and money is not misused in any manner.

Table - 3
Annual wise Financial Details of SHGs under Stree Shakthi Scheme in Pavagada taluk 2002-03 to 2006-07

Sl. No.	*Year*	*No of Groups who have started saving*	*Savings accumu-lated (Rs. In lakhs)*	*No. of Groups taken loan from the bank*	*Total loan Amount taken from bank (Rs. In lakh)*	*Revolving Fund Released by Govt. (in lakhs)*
1.	2002-03	3003	522.52	1367	250.41	44.25
2	2003-04	4493	891.68	2150	511.07	161.91
3.	2004-05	4493	1560	3281	669	225
4.	2005-06	3281	1676	3281	846.42	7714
5.	2006-07	5392	2251.25	4359	895.35	34.00

Source : Women & Child Development Department, Pavagada taluk.

Of the total 80 groups, 48 groups are of size 10-15 and 32 groups are of size 16-20. The percentage of 10-15 size groups to the total groups constituted is 60% and the percentage of 16-20 size groups to the total groups constituted is 40%. These figures are presented here below in the table - 4.

Table - 4
Size wise distribution of SHGs & % to the total

Sl. No	*Size of the Group*	*No. of Groups*	*Percentage to Total*
1.	10-15 members	48	60.00
2.	16-20 members	32	40.00
	Total	**80**	**100.00**

Source: Field Survey.

Of the above 80 random sampling beneficiaries of the programme from eight taluks of Pavagada taluk, 64 beneficiaries have been engaged in agriculture and allied activities, 4 beneficiaries have taken up rural cottage industrial activities and 12 beneficiaries have been involved in small business activities. In the table - 5 presented here below the activity wise beneficiaries of SHGs according to the three broad classification of income generating activities.

Table - 5
Activity wise Beneficiaries of SHGs under Stree Shakthi Scheme in Pavagada taluk

Sl. No.	*Income Generating Activities*	*No. of Beneficiaries*	*Percentage of Total Beneficiaries*
01	Agricultural & Allied activities	64	80
02	Rural Cottage Industrial Activities	04	05
03	Small Business Activities	12	15
	Total	**80**	**100**

Source : Field Survey.

Reasons for seeking benefit from the programme

Of the 80 sample beneficiaries of SHGs under the study, 56.25% beneficiaries have taken assistance from the programme for starting the activity and this is the major reason given by the beneficiaries of SHGs. For the 21.25% beneficiaries, the intention is to expand the scale of activity is another major reason for taking the assistance from the programme. The third major reason given by the 12.5% beneficiaries for taking the assistance from the programme is that the attraction of low interest on loans. And the fourth reason given by the 10% beneficiaries for taking the assistance from the programme is to avoid taking loans from intermediaries. The details can be seen in the table - 6.

Table - 6
Reasons for seeking benefit from the Programme

Sl. No.	*Reasons*	*Beneficiaries*	*Percentage*
1.	To start economic activity	45	56.25
2.	To expand the activity	17	21.25
3.	To avail of low interest finance	10	12.50
4.	To eliminate intermediary	8	10.00
	Total	**80**	**100.00**

Source: Field Survey.

FINDINGS OF THE STUDY

Based on the analysis and discussion in the economic empowerment of kadu golla women through stree shakti programme - a case study in pavagada taluk, the following findings have been drawn:

1. In Karnataka, Self - Help Groups under Stree Shakthi Scheme have managed an ideal scenario and provide a way for reducing poverty that simultaneously improves the capacity of its members on many levels. They are grounded in participatory decision - making, which creates a sense of ownership among the members. They are very different from many other poverty alleviation / human development programmes which evolve with a top - down system of decision-making and distance from the people most affected by these decisions for the purposes of presenting an alternative approach to sustainable development.
2. In terms of Self Help Groups under Stree Shakthi Scheme, Karnataka State has 130000 total No. of SHGs, 20.00 lakhs total No. of women in SHGs, No. of Groups taken loan from the different banks are 98,133 and total loan amount taken from bank

is 5962.60 lakhs among the districts in the State (at the end of December - 2007).

3. SHGs have potentiality to tackle the poverty and they can be an important weapon for poverty alleviation in Pavagada taluk of Tumkur district.
4. The study shows that there is an increase in the level of income and assets of the rural women of SHGs and reduction in the level of poverty as a result of intervention of micro finance by SHGs.

POLICY IMPLICATIONS

The following suggestions have been offered for the better implementation and effectiveness of the women development programmes.

1. It is important to note that most of the women beneficiaries are illiterate. Hence, the beneficiaries need to be educated about the formalities to be fulfilled in obtaining the necessary finance. The bank staff should help the uneducated women in getting their credit sanctioned from the banks. If the beneficiaries are educated they can get loans easily from the banks.
2. While loaning to Self - Help Groups right time, right person and right purpose should be kept in mind and the process of loaning should be more easy and convenient for the women beneficiary.
3. The problem of promoting livelihood among SHG member is becoming increasingly important because of the need to create livelihood and employment opportunities for higher incomes in the rural areas. We believe that the problem of rural migration, which is a cause of concern, could among others be addressed through this intervention

References

Mayoux, L (1998) Women's Empowerment and Microfinance Programmes: Approaches, Evidence and

Ways Forward. Discussion Paper. Milton Keynes: The Open University.

Jonathan, Morduch, (1999). The Micro-Finance Promise. Journal of Economic Literature, XXXVII: 1156-1614.

Ghatak, Maitresh and Timothy W Guinnane (1999). The Economics of Lending with Joint Liability: Theory and Practice, Journal of Development Economics, 60: 95-228.

Ledgerwood, Joanna (1999), 'Microfinance Handbook, An institutional and Financial Perspective, Sustainable Banking with the Poor' The World Bank, Washington D.C.

Yunus, Muhammad (2000), 'How Donor Funds Could Better Reach and Support Grassroots Micro credit Programmes: Working towards the Micro credit Summit's Goal and Core Themes,' The Bangladesh Development Studies, Vol XXVI, June-September, Nos. 2 & 3.

4

Role of Micro-Finance and Its Impact on Socio-Economic Development of Women in Karnataka

Shivanand Nari

Introduction

Micro-finance has, in recent times, come to be recognized and accepted as the new development paradigms for alleviating poverty through social and economic empowerment of the poor. With focus on empowering welfare programmes within the country and else where, have shown that the key to its success lies in the participation of community based organisations at the grassroots level. The empowerment through group process can be highly effective; ultimately empowerment must lead to change the individual level and not in terms of control over extrinsic resources, but also greater authority and autonomy in decision making assertiveness etc. People participation in credit delivery, recovery and linking of formal credit institutions to borrowers through the intermediation of Self Help Groups have been recognized as a supplementary mechanism for providing credit support to the rural poor.

Micro-finance is aimed at providing the rural and urban poor especially women, with savings, credit and insurance facilities to set up or expand income-generating activities and to improve household income security. The micro-finance programmes are expected to alleviate poverty and empower the poor. This expectation is rooted in the limited success of government policies pursued since independence in alleviating poverty in India, where about 24 per cent of the world is poor. A strong rural economy presupposes that the rural people must have reasonable access to sufficient livelihood support systems. The emphasis on credits mechanism is to trigger agricultural growth and rural development.

Microfinance implies providing the poor with savings, credit and insurance facilities to set up or expand income generating activities relating to agriculture, allied activities and non-farm Sector, and thereby, increases household income security. A group of about 15-20 members provide Microfinance services. The members periodically contribute savings, which are used to build a savings fund that can be revolved among the members. The members are encouraged to borrow from the savings fund thus created to meet their consumption and short-term production needs. Since this fund, built entirely on the savings of members is normally insufficient to finance income generating activities involving larger amounts of start-up capital, the micro- finance groups are linked to formal banks to obtain bulk loans for on-lending to group members.

Objectives of the Study

1. To examine the existing institutional credit facilities and strategies in Karnataka.
2. To study the extent of influence and support of micro finance institutions in implementing

microfinance programmes for upliftment of the poor.
3. To suggest measures to strengthen micro-credit programmes in the state.

Results and Discussion

Group lending activities are first started in the Southern states of India such as, Andhra Pradesh, Kerala, Karnataka and Tamilnadu; while West Bengal and Orissa have joined later. Though, Micro finance programmes are mostly organised by Non-Governmental Organisations (NGOs) in India, National Bank for Agriculture and Rural Development (NABARD) launched a Bank Self help group (SHG) linkage programme in a small way in 1992. The idea of introducing the programme emanated mainly from the successful experiences of the institutions in other countries. The linkage programme under NABARD aims to reach those outside the network of formal credit, improve living standards of poorer sections of rural society and achieve high deposit- credit mobilization and recovery of loans.

Karnataka, a pioneer in SHG-Bank Linkage Programme and a recognized laboratory for Micro-Finance Innovations, continues to maintain its leading status in promotion and credit linkage of SHGs. While the NGOs and Women and Child Development Department (WCDD, GOK) have been actively involved in promotion of a majority of the SHGs in the state, all the banks have taken the responsibility of linking these groups with the formal banking system. Over a period of time, some of the RRBs and Co-operative Banks in the state have developed the skill in promoting SHGs on their own and assumed the mantle of Self-Help Promoting Institutions (SHPIs).

The SHG-Bank Linkage Programme registered its progress in the state of Karnataka by leaps and bounds during the year 2003-04.While as many as 1,88,477 SHGs have been promoted by different SHPIs in the state, the cumulative credit linkage by various agencies crossed an impressive one lakh SHGs by 31 March 2004.

Model-wise SHG-Bank Linkage in Karnataka

The NABARD identified three models of credit linkage of SHGs with banks in Karnataka showed the following trend as on 31 March 2004:

Table - 1
Model wise SHG-Bank Linkage in Karnataka, 31 March 2004

Model	*Description*	*No. of SHGs Credit Linked*	*%*	*Bank Loan (Rs. Million)*
1	SHGs formed and financed by Banks	48,528	47	1,425.73
2	SHGs formed by NGOs and formal agencies, but directly financed by banks	33,347	32	819.26
3	SHGs financed by Banks through NGOs	21,991	21	591.19
	Total	**1,03,866**	**100**	**2, 836.18**

Source: SHG Bank linkage programme Karnataka 2003-04 NABARD

Agency-wise SHG -Bank Linkage

As on March 2004, 3838 branches of 58 banks participated in the SHG-Linkage programme. The broad category -wise number of these banks, total branches participated and their percentage share to the total achievements is indicated below. The data are presented in Table - 2 explaining the SHG-Bank Linkage progress of the Commercial Banks in Karnataka.

Table - 2
SHGs Linked by Commercial Banks in Karnataka

Year (As on 31 march)	*No of SHG's Linked*	*Bank Loan (Rs. In lakh)*	*Refinance (Rs. In lakh)*
1995	316	42.85	45.00
1996	718	100.15	93.00
1997	391	63.00	64.00
1998	583	91.27	90.00
1999	966	176.34	173.00
2000	1855	543.99	191.10
2001	1566	434.40	396.00
2002	8030	974.24	119.12
2003	6562	2113.34	35.75
2004	14925	5687.34	8.26
Total	35912	10227.38	1215.23

Source: SHG Bank linkage programme Karnataka 2003-04 NABARD

REGIONAL RURAL BANKS (RRBs)

In Karnataka, 13 Regional Rural banks particularly Grameena Banks have provided loan to 38,631 self help groups the end of March 2004.The highest number of SHGs has been linked by Malaprabha GB (2981), in the state, followed by Cauvery GB(2087).The other RRBs showing significant increase were Tungabhadra GB,Krishna GB and Kalpataru GB. SHG - Bank Linkage Physical and Financial Progress of Participating Regional Rural Banks in Karnataka are provided in Table - 3.

Table - 3
SHG's linked by RRBs in Karnataka

Year (As on 31 march)	*No of SHG's*	*Bank Loan (Rs. In lakh)*	*Refinance (Rs. In lakh)*
1995	340	46.10	37.00
1996	318	44.93	52.00
1997	364	95.62	94.00
1998	506	127.92	126.00
1999	889	198.77	195.00
2000	2318	486.86	364.00
2001	3599	647.50	644.00
2002	4945	1374.00	997.49
2003	10194	3026.59	2444.78
2004	15158	4898.99	3969.72
Total	38631	10947.28	8923.99

Source: SHG Bank linkage programme Karnataka 2003-04 NABARD

COOPERATIVE BANKS: All the 21 DCCBs in the state have involved themselves prominently in the SGH-Bank Linkage Programme upto March 2004.The major contributors were Hassan, Bidar, Dakshina Kannada, Tumkur and Mandya DCCBs in that order. The amendments made by the DCCBs in the Cooperative Societies Act have enabled the SHGs to become members of PACS and avail loans. Table - 4 narrates the Progress of SHGs Linkage by Cooperative Banks in Karnataka.

Table - 4
SHG's linked by Co-operative Banks in Karnataka

Year (As on 31 march)	*No of SHG's Linked*	*Bank Loan (Rs. In lakh)*	*Refinance (Rs. In lakh)*
1997	5	0.50	0,50
1998	49	13.00	13.00
1999	147	54.75	53.50
2000	845	144.05	103.50

Year (As on 31 march)	No of SHG's Linked	Bank Loan (Rs. In lakh)	Refinance (Rs. In lakh)
2001	2844	364.50	364.00
2002	5438	1374.90	1104.08
2003	8390	2021.35	1593.02
2004	11605	3373.58	2112.24
Total	29323	7346.63	5343.84

** Started participating in SHG-Bank linkage from the year 1996-97
Source: SHG Bank linkage programme Karnataka 2003-04 NABARD

One of the main objectives of Grameen Banks in the state is the starting of micro-finance institutions across the districts. In Karnataka, there are 27 districts and in all the districts DCBs are giving finance to self-help groups. According to the NABARD report 2003-04 the DCBs have been highly successful in its banking service to the poor as well as in its poverty alleviation programmes.

SHG -Bank Linkage programme in Karnataka was started in 1992-93 with Linking 114 SHGs and providing bank loan of Rs.5.73 lakhs. As on March 31st 2004, 103866 SHGs are credit linked and Rs.28521.29 lakhs Bank loan is granted and also refinance of Rs.15483.06 lakhs is granted. The progress of SHG -Bank Linkage programme year wise and district wise has been provided in Table - 5.and Table - 6 respectively.

Non-Government Organisations are the backbone of microfinance system. As noted earlier, NGOs have popularised the concept of microfinance in Karnataka. Most of them have introduced microfinance as one of the activities in their overall programme aimed at the development of the marginalised sections consisting of landless and marginal farmer households belonging to depressed castes of dalits, etc. In the micro-finance programmes sponsored by the government, promotional agencies of NABARD and external funding agencies, NGOs are preferred organisations to implement the programme

Table - 5

SHG Bank linkage (1992-93 to 2003-04) in Karnataka

Year	*No. Of SHGs credit linked*	*%of annual growth rate*	*Bank loan (Rs in Lakh)*	*%of annual growth rate*	*Refinance (Rs in Lakh)*	*%of annual growth rate*
1992-93	114	-	5.73	-	5.73	-
1993-94	51	-55.26	5.51	03.84	5.51	-3.84
1994-95	481	843.14	77.71	1310.34	70.71	1183.30
1995-96	1046	117.46	145.08	86.69	145.08	105.18
1996-97	760	-27.34	159.12	9.68	159.12	9.68
1997-98	1138	49.74	232.19	45.92	228.10	43.35
1998-99	2002	75.92	429.86	85.13	422.28	85.13
1999-2000	5018	150.65	1054.81	145.38	649.00	53.69
2000-2001	8009	59.61	1714.00	62.49	1404.00	116.33
2001-02	18413	129.90	3475.39	102.76	2229.00	58.76
2002-03	25146	36.57	7249.50	108.60	4073.55	82.75
2003-04	41688	65.78	13960.37	92.74	6090.22	49.53
Total	103866		28521.29		15483.06	

Source: SHG Bank linkage, Karnataka 2003-04 NABARD.

Table - 6
SHG-Bank Linkage District wise in Karnataka upto 2004(Rs. million)

DISTRICTS	1992-2002	Cumulative Bank loan disbursed up to 2002	2003	Bank loan disbursed during 2002-03	2004	Bank loan disbursed during 2003-04	Total No. of SHGs as on March 31st2004	Cumulative Bankloan disbursed up to March 31 2004
1.	2	3	4	5	6	7	8	9
Bagalkot	349	4.81	381	3.58	576	19.79	1306	28.18
B'lore Urban	228	4.06	312	3.31	1152	41.12	1692	4849
B'lore Rural	367	14.66	201	6.68	304	16.87	872	38.1
Belgaum	742	16.92	937	31.49	1480	61.99	3159	110.4
Bellary	3406	49.63	1073	43.47	1774	61.99	6253	155.09
Bidar	3571	75.11	2026	47.52	1577	81.61	7174	204.24
Bijapur	586	12.43	550	20.76	518	17.33	1654	50.52
Chamaraj nagar	1122	36.75	626	18.58	877	37.7	2625	93.03
Chika magalore	368	8.9	182	8.39	664	20.74	1214	38.03
Chitradurga	3708	54.01	1548	58.33	1842	59.4	7098	171.74
D.kannada	4922	95.4	3087	92.84	6925	217.71	14934	405.95
Davanagere	559	15.95	249	3.63	577	11.5	1385	31.08
Dharwad	874	18.94	366	11.02	795	20.89	2035	50.85

1.	2	3	4	5	6	7	8	9
Gadag	250	6.45	172	4.19	527	11.69	949	22.33
Gilburga	1051	23.99	1532	53.71	1993	46.76	4576	124.46
Hassan	1916	36.7	2072	41.81	2941	87.59	6929	166.1
Havery	408	9.26	321	3.21	618	19.44	1347	31.91
Kodagu	409	5.09	283	9.14	682	18.98	1374	33.21
Kolar	2072	32.99	1190	32.42	1553	40.24	4815	105.65
Koppal	381	9.14	250	3.75	605	6.38	1236	19.27
Mandya	993	12,29	1060	21.67	1891	52.45	3944	86.41
Mysore	2722	47.08	1091	39.51	2601	85.61	6414	1722
Raichure	782	15.17	427	8.22	831	18.42	2040	41.81
Shimoga	2109	56.69	646	27.22	1033	82.18	3788	166.09
Tumkur	1853	17.01	1865	41.31	2943	79.74	6661	138.06
Udupi	1033	26.65	1956	81.23	3427	134.57	6416	242.45
U.kannada	251	9.11	743	7.96	982	43.36	1976	60.43
Total	37032	715.9	25146	724.95	41688	1396.04	103866	2836.18

Source: Progress of SHG Bank linkage in INDIA 2003-04 NABARD,

due to a number of factors. First the quality in the formation and consolidation of groups were considered to be superior in these programmes as compared to government programmes. Second, the micro-finance groups formed by them had the potential to adopt the strategy of micro-finance as an instrument of poverty alleviation and empowerment. Third, the NGOs introduced incentives and mechanisms to facilitate the participation of members in micro-finance programme.

Microfinance sector of India is unmatched because of both its large size and diversity of institutions operating in the field. Having crossed the stage of formative years more under an informal framework the microfinance sector is now looking forward to a conducive and an appropriate regulatory environment to grow further. Since SHGs are mostly unregistered local groups, lack of legal framework does deter many grass root bankers from the concept as a major methodology for continuous lending. There is a need for establishing an apex Organisation with some required statutory powers for microfinance at the national level, which should work for advocacy of microfinance and also for networking among NGOs banks and governments.

Microfinance programs are costly because of the small size of their loans and because banks cannot operate them with their traditional mechanisms and overhead structures. Strategies must be devised to minimize processing costs, increase staff productivity, and rapidly expand the scale of micro enterprise portfolios. Incentives to staff for improving their performance in SHG-bank linkage banking need to devised in order to encourage linkage banking without compromising on the quality of linkage. Also, incentives to SHGs for encouraging them to maintain good group health need to be devised.

SUGGESTIONS

Some valuable suggestions are drawn from the experience of the present study.

1. SHGs may be permitted to issue fixed deposits certificates, Cash certificates and other savings oriented instruments may be under the authorizing of the concerned lead bank in the respective district.
2. SHGs to become more meaningful and purposeful should be constantly guided by NGOs with regard to their activities, especially the purposes for which the loans are sanctioned.
3. Literacy programmes including awareness programmes may be taken up seriously by NGOs, Banks, SHG Federation's and Voluntary Organizations as this component alone can bring success for any socio-economic welfare in the State.
4. Banks and NGOs should provide training to the members of the SHGs in different filed especially in income generating activities.
5. The Banks in the rural areas may be asked to liberal to SHGs with regard to amount of loan with lower interest that can be lent to SHGs.

References

Fisher, Thomas and M. S. Sriram (2002).'Beyond Micro-Credit: Putting Development Back into Micro-Finance'. New Delhi: Vistaar Publications.

Ghate, P.et.al. (1992) Informal Finance: Some Findings from Asia, Oxford University Press, and Hong Kong.

Jayaram B. (2001) " Microfinance Restospect and Prospect" NABARD, Mumbai.

Karmakar K.G (1999) " Rural Credit and Self Help Groups; Micro-Finance Needs and concepts in India" Sage Publication, New Delhi.

Khandker, Shahidur (1998),'Fighting Poverty with Microcredit: Experience in Bangladesh'. Oxford: Oxford University Press.

Koontz, H. (1972), "The systems approach and decision making in Banks: Management McGraw Hill Book Company, New York.

Krishna Gupta (1994) " Credit Planning and Management " Arihant Publishing House, Jaipur.

5

Impact of Primary Agricultural Cooperative Societies on Rural Community – A Case Study of Mysore District

Mahadevaswamy M.S.

Introduction

Cooperative undertakings have long been accepted as an alternative to the private and public sector enterprises in India in organizing key economic activities, especially where people of small means are involved. The cooperative societies have direct contact with the member agriculturists and various other sectors of the economy. Hence it would not be an exaggeration to state that the success of the cooperative movement in general and credit structure in particular depends to a very large extent on the success of the Primary Agricultural Cooperative Societies. Cooperative societies have an important role to play in the process of economic development of India.

The main principle of Gandhian approach is to setup a system of village self-sufficiency. In this regard, the hypothesis of Gandhiji was establishment of gram swaraj in the country side which means the complete independence of the Indian villages. The ultimate goal of Gandhian planning was to make Indian villages fully independent. Mahatma Gandhi often used to say that the real Indian was to be found in the villages, not in the cities and towns.

Agriculture is the only basis we have for feeding humanity. If our agriculutre is unsustainable, then we, as a species, are unsustainable. It is time that we come together again to put farming first, Gandhiji had realised the importance of cooperative banks and their role in shaping the path of history and progress of agriculture sector. He spared no effort to drive home the fact that agriculture is most important and equal in all respect, especially his concern for rural development and uplift of the rural deprived class those who are engaged in agriculture and its allied occupation. Gandhiji is known to be one of the people who encouraged agriculture and agro-based business. He was marked as a rare promoter of agriculture co-operatives and self-sustainability in agriculture.

For more effective functioning of cooperatives, government should recognise that cooperatives are private sector enterprises which are formed and managed by their members and which are not subject to intervention by government authorities in their internal management. In the light of this recognition revision of cooperative legislation should be taken up as a mater of priority. The powers vested in government to direct and supervise cooperatives should be critically reviewed. The overall aim should be to give autonomy to cooperatives. It will be appreciated that rural economy is the weaker sector of the national economy and even in the rural economy, a major segment is not only weak but in a miserable state. This weakness is mainly responsible for the backwardness of the rural areas. Cooperatives seem to be the only hope to inject strength and accelerate the growth of rural economy and ensure the development of the rural areas in the country.

The cooperative organization in our country has developed and spread its activities and functions in all spheres of economy like agriculture, poultry, dairy, fisheries, handlooms, banking, sugar, spinning, consumer cooperatives and what not?. That is why this sector has emerged as an important and vital sector of our economy. The cooperatives have 207 million members embracing 100 percent villages and 67 percent of household in its fold in the country.

Today the India's cooperative scene presents a mixed picture. On the one hand, the cooperative movement has grown, membership has increased, it has become more diversified, there has been great deal of regional dispersal and there are numerous examples of cooperatives in India's landscape where it has made spectacular achievements. On the other hand, a large number of cooperatives are languishing, and considering the number of cooperatives is languishing, and considering the number of weak elements in the society, such elements cannot legitimately be said to belong to the cooperative fold.

One marked change in the cooperative movement that has surfaced in recent years is that several cooperatives have become big and more cooperatives have started making departures from the practice of cooperative principles enunciated by International Cooperative Alliance (ICA), particularly in raising capital by use of joint stock company methods. They had challenged the relevance of the existing principles, particularly limited interest on capital which they considered as the devil of the peace hampering the growth of the movement.

Objectives of the Study

The following are the main objectives of the study.

1.To examine the performance and growth of primary agricultural cooperatives in Karnataka.

2. To evaluate the impact of primary agricultural cooperatives in development of agriculture in Mysore district.

3. To offer suggestions for the further improvement of the role of cooperatives in the development of community in each and every nook and corner of the society.

Methodology of the Study

The study is based on both primary and secondary source of data. This study is confined to Mysore district of the Karnataka State. To gauge the impact of primary agricultural cooperative societies on farming community in Mysore district 30 farmers have been interviewed. The secondary data has been collected from Cooperative Societies, Mysore district, Cooperation Journals and District Statistical Outline, Mysore district. The data has been collected up to 2006-07.

Results and Discussion

The history of cooperatives in India could be traced back to as early as 1891, when the first cooperative society was started in Punjab for controlling the common land of the village. However, the first official step to formalize the cooperative organization was taken in July 1901 and it got its final shape in 1904 when the first Cooperative Societies Act was passed. The Cooperative Credit Societies Act 1904 was restrictive in its scope as it permitted only primary credit societies and kept non-credit and federal societies out of its purview. The Cooperative Societies Act of 1912 removed many of these short comings and served as a model for subsequent Acts passed by various Governments when Cooperative Societies became a transferred subject under the constitutional reforms of 1919.

The promotion of cooperatives has been accepted as a part of the state policy in the development of various economic activities, particularly those providing support to agriculture. This was the strong policy recommendation of the Rural Credit Survey Committee of 1954. The policy led to state partnership in the share of cooperative law

1955 appointed by the Government of India suggested a number of modifications in the cooperative legislation. For giving effect to the concept of the state partnership and accordingly various State Cooperative Societies Acts were amended which in effect also strengthened the government control on the cooperative institutions.

In Mysore district cooperative movement has undoubtedly lent unflinching support to the needy and common man. Cooperation never failed to assist agriculture in a vary big way which is the main occupation in the district. Primary agricultural credit cooperative societies and milk producers cooperative societies are the back bone of the cooperative movement in Mysore district. Taluk agricultural cooperative marketing societies have thrived and created history, the performance of some of these institutions is really an unparalleled. Business development programme for cooperatives has been successfully implemented in the district. Besides PACs, some women multi purpose cooperative societies and a house building cooperative society have embanked upon banking activities in a big technology women society have started functioning and their performance is really encouraging. A district level horticultural producers cooperative society is in existence for the last ten years which has been successful in processing fruits grown by farmers and in helping them in getting a good price for the produce. Comparative growth of cooperative societies in the district for the last five years details are furnished in table – 1.

At present there are 1449 Cooperative Societies are functioning to cater the needs of the community thereby enhancing the life style in the society in Mysore district. The data clearly show that there is an increasing tendency in different Cooperative Societies in the district. This is actually a healthy development in the cooperative movement in the district. Loans sanctioned by the cooperative credit societies in Mysore district during 2002-03 to 2006-07 details are furnished in table- 2.

Table - 1
Comparative growth of cooperative societies in the district for the last five years

Types of cooperative Societies	*2002-03*	*2003-04*	*2004-05*	*2005-06*	*2006-07*
DCC Bank	01	01	01	01	01
PACs	245	200	230	223	225
PCARD Bank	07	07	07	07	07
Credit Cooperative Societies	48	49	13	13	15
Cooperative Union	01	01	01	01	01
TAPCMs	07	07	07	07	07
Processing Cooperative Societies	-	-	01	01	01
Live Stock Cooperative Societies	04	07	06	05	03
Co-operative Milk Union	01	01	01	01	01
Milk Producers Cooperative Societies	649	683	691	706	722
Lift Irrigation Cooperative Societies	-	-	12	11	06
Fishers Cooperative Societies	17	20	20	21	22
Weavers Cooperative Societies	35	24	21	20	18
Industrial Cooperative Societies	-	-	23	19	17
Consumers Cooperative Societies	92	89	80	70	69
House Building Cooperative Societies	36	34	37	37	35

Types of cooperative Societies	*2002-03*	*2003-04*	*2004-05*	*2005-06*	*2006-07*
Labour Contract Cooperative Societies	05	03	-	-	-
Multipurpose Cooperative Societies	-	-	24	23	25
Student Cooperative Societies	-	-	07	06	05
Mahila multipurpose Cooperative Societies	-	-	27	24	24
Tailoring Co-operative Societies	-	-	01	01	01
Water Consumers Cooperative Societies	28	33	19	40	43

Source: District Registrar Office, Cooperative Department, Mysore.

Table- 2
Loans Sanctioned by the Cooperative Credit Societies in Mysore district

Particulars	*Type of loans*	*2002-03*	*2005-06*	*2006-07*
Loans given by agricultural credit cooperative societies	Short-term	7295	6329	2328
	Medium-term	16843	18	-
	Total	24138	6347	2328
Liquidated cooperative societies	Credit	6	9	11
	Non-credit	165	143	110
	Total	171	152	121
Non-credit cooperative societies	Marketing	7	8	8
	Housing	36	36	27
	Milk	271	249	241
	Others	308	290	579
	Total	622	583	855

Particulars	*Type of loans*	*2002-03*	*2005-06*	*2006-07*
Credit cooperative societies	Agricultural	230	243	237
	Non-agricultural	89	107	112
	Total	319	350	349
Other cooperative banks		77	236	235

Source: Mysore District at a glance.

Now let us explain the performance of primary agricultural cooperative credit societies in Mysore district, in terms of number of societies, total membership, total borrowers, share capital i.e., from members and from government, funds of societies, deposits, borrowings, total profit and total losses. The details of these particulars are depicted in table- 3.

Table- 3
Details of Primary Agricultural Cooperative Credit Societies in Mysore District

Particulars		2006-07
No.of Societies		226
Total Membership		156301
Total Borrowers		33243
Share Capital	From Members	732.46
	From Government	202.59
Funds		419.64
Deposits		1577.66
Total Borrowings		5293.04
Total Profit		351.91
Total loss		59.90

Source: Assistant Registrar of Cooperative Union, Mysore district.

The success of credit institutions and the prosperity of cultivators mainly depend on productive utilization of agricultural finance. Misdirection of loan reflects adversely on the character of the cooperative institution and ultimately results in the stopping of the flow of credit to cultivators even for productive purposes. Proper end use of credit is more important than the provision of adequate credit itself. Proper utilization of loan is one of the prime factors in the filed of rural finance to boost-up production.

Once the credit is used for unspecific purpose, it's not only results in low production and indebtedness of the farmer, but also leads to the vicious circle of poverty. The diversion of loan to unproductive purpose has an equally adverse effect on the lending institution, that the recover of the loan become difficult and this result in decreasing the lending capacity of the bank.

Loans from Primary Agricultural Cooperative Credit Societies in Irrigated Area

In Mysore district nearly 58.11% of the loan has been sanctioned to all the three types of farmers against their requirements, remaining 41.25% of the loan is considered as credit gap. In case of small farmers 49.10 percent of loan has been sanctioned remaining portion of the loan considered as credit gap. Whereas 47.9 percent and 68.75 percent of the loan has been sanctioned for medium and big farmers respectively. In the case of big farmers credit gap is little compared to the small and medium farmers. In other words, major portion of the requirements of the big farmers have been fulfilled compared to medium and small farmers. The details are furnished in the table- 4.

Table- 4

Loans from the Primary Agricultural Cooperative Credit Societies in Irrigated Area 2002-2007

Types of farmers	*No of farmers*	*Required*	*%*	*Sanctioned*	*%*	*Credit gap*	*%*
Small	10	224000	100	110	49.10	104	46.42
Medium	10	365000	100	175	47.94	195	53.42
Big	10	560000	100	385	68.75	175	31.25
Total	30	**1149**	**100**	**670**	**58.15**	**474**	**41.25**

Source: Field study, Mysore.

In the case of non-irrigated region it says that only 41.22 percent of the loan has been sanctioned, remaining 58.78 percent of the loan considered as credit gap. In case of small farmers only 45.12 percent of the loan has been sanctioned, whereas in case of medium farmers it is 45.97 percent. And nearly 37.56 percent of loan has been sanctioned in case of big farmers. It is clearly shows that medium farmers get more loans compared to small and big farmers, but big farmers compared to small farmers get less loan. The details of loans sanctioned from the PACs in non-irrigated area since 2002 to 2007 are furnished in the table- 5.

Table- 5
Loans Sanctioned from the Primary Agricultural Cooperative Credit Societies in Non-Irrigated Area - 2002 to 2007

Types of farmers	*No of farmers*	*Required*	*%*	*Sanctioned*	*%*	*Credit gap*	*%*
Small	10	195	100	88	45.12	107	54.87
Medium	10	235	100	108	45.97	127	54.04
Big	10	386	100	145	37.56	241	62.43
Total	30	816	100	341	41.22	475	58.78

Source: Field Study, Mysore.

End use of Loans in Irrigated Area

Normally farmers use loan for several purposes, such as purchase of seeds, fertilizers, pesticides, bullock carts, land improvements, digging well, pump sets, paying labour charges and other purposes like paying old bets education, house hold utensils. The details of end use of loan in irrigated area in Mysore district are depicted in table- 6.

Table- 6
End use of Loans in Irrigated Area

Particulars	*Small*	*%*	*Medium*	*%*	*Big*	*%*
Seeds	42000	22.22	49	24.37	88	20.41
Fertilizers	47000	24.86	46	22.88	86	19.95
Pesticides	33000	17.46	31	15.42	25	5.8
Land improvement	21000	11.11	20	9.95	51	11.83
Pump set	-	-		-	26	6.03
Labour	39000	20.63	37	18.40	96	22.27
Others	7000	03.70	18	8.95	59	13.68
Total	189000	100	201	100	431	100

Source: Field Study, Mysore.

It has been observed that, in case of small farmers 22.22 percent of the loans are used for purchasing of seeds, whereas 24.86 percent of loan is for purchasing of fertilizers, 17.46 percent for pesticides, 11.11 percent for land improvements, 20.65 percent for labour and for other purpose 3.70 percent of loan is used. In the same way, in case of medium farmers 24.37 percent of loans are used for purchasing of seeds, 22.88 percent for fertilisers, and 15.42 percent for pesticides, 9.9 percent for land improvements, 18.40 percent for labours and 8.95 percent for other purposes.

In the case of big farmers 20.4 percent of loans is used for purchase of seeds, 19.95 percent for fertilizers, 5.8 percent for pesticides, and 11.83 percent for land improvements, 6.03 percent for pump sets, 22.27 percent for labour and 13.68 percent for other purpose.

End use of Loans in Non-Irrigated Area

In Mysore district, in case of small farmers 13.03 percent of the loan is used for purchasing of seeds whereas, 15.57 percent for fertilisers, 14.75 percent for pesticides, 14.75 percent for land improvements, 15.57 percent for labours and 21.31 percent for other purposes. In the case of medium farmers 25.37 percent of the loan utilised for purchasing of seeds, 10.44 percent for fertilisers, 11.10 percent for pesticides, 8.95 percent for land improvements, 15.65 percent for labours and 28.35 percent for other purposes.

In the case of big farmers in Mysore district, 13.13 percent of the loan is used for seeds, 13.63 percent for fertilisers, and 15.65 percent for pesticides, 18.68 percent for land improvements, 14.64 percent for labours and 24.24 percent for other purposes. The details of end use of loans of PACs in non-irrigated area in Mysore district are presented in table- 7.

Table- 7
End use of loans of Primary Agricultural Cooperative Credit Societies in Non-Irrigated Area in Mysore district

Particulars	*Small*	%	*Medium*	%	*Big*	%
Seeds	22000	18.03	34000	25.37	26000	13.13
Fertilizers	19000	15.57	14000	10.44	27000	13.63
Pesticides	18000	14.75	15000	11.19	31000	15.65
Land improvement	18000	14.75	12000	8.95	37000	18.68
Pump set	19000	15.57	21000	15.67	29000	14.64
Labour	26000	21.31	38000	28.35	48000	24.24
Total	122000	100	134000	100	198000	100

Source: Field Study, Mysore.

On the basis of these two tables we can easily say that the farmers in non-irrigated area used more loans to other purposes like for education, paying old debts, marriage etc., compared to the farmers in irrigated area.

Repayment Performance of Primary Agricultural Cooperative Credit Societies

It is very interesting to say that, no farmers were found irregular in repayment of the loans availed from the PACs in Mysore district, it means all the farmers in Mysore district i.e., small, medium and big are regular in repaying the loans to the PACs. The details of loans obtained from the beneficiaries regarding repayment of PACs in the district are furnished in the table- 8.

Table- 8
Repayment performance of Primary Agricultural Cooperative Credit Societies in irrigated area in Mysore district

Types of farmers	*No of farmers*	*Regular*	*Irregular*
Small	10	10	0
Medium	10	10	0
Big	10	10	0
Total	**30**	**30**	**0**

Source: Field Study, Mysore.

With concerned to non-irrigated area the situation is different; we may find irregular cases in all the types of farmers in Mysore district. In case of small farmers 50 percent of them are regular in repayment the loans to the PACs. Whereas remaining 50 percent of them are irregular in repaying the loans to PACs in the district. In case of medium farmers, 70 percent of the farmers are regular re-payers. And in the case of big farmers, 80 percent of the farmers are regular in repayment the loans, remaining 20 percent are irregular in the district. The details regarding repayment furnished in the table- 9.

It is observed that the purpose of the loan taken is agriculture and consumption loan in case of the marginal and small farmers and in case of the medium and large farmers it is agriculture and business. In concluding remarks we can say that access to organized credit facility is very high in case of the medium and large farmers and it is less in case of their counterparts like marginal and small farmers. Therefore the marginal and small farmers trying to get loans from the money lender who have been exploiting them to a greater extent.

Table- 9
Repayment position of the Primary Agricultural Cooperative Credit Societies in Non-Irrigated Area

Types of farmers	*No of farmers*	*Regular*	*Irregular*
Small	10	5	5
Medium	10	7	3
Big	10	8	2
Total	30	20	10

Source: Field Study, Mysore.

Major Findings of the Study

1. It has been observed that, in case of small farmers 22.22 percent of the loans are used for purchasing of seeds, whereas 24.86 percent of loan is for purchasing of fertilizers, 17.46 percent for pesticides, 11.11 percent for land improvements, 20.65 percent for labour and for other purpose 3.70 percent of loan is used.

2. In the same way, in case of medium farmers 24.37 percent of loans are used for purchasing of seeds, 22.88 percent for fertilizers, and 15.42 percent for pesticides, 9.9 percent for land improvements, 18.40 percent for labours and 8.95 percent for other purposes in Mysore district. Hence under study the role of cooperative banks in advancing agricultural sector is quite satisfactory.

Policy Implications

The analysis of data and the researcher observations reveal that there are some lacunae for the development of agriculture through cooperative credit institutions. Therefore, few suggestions have been made to promote agriculture through cooperative credit.

1. PACS have to train and educate the farmers regarding the utilization of loan in a proper way and to adopt modern and scientific method of cultivation so as to enable the farmer to repay his loan amount within the stipulated period of time out of his earnings.
2. The prompt repayers should not be deprived by delaying the issue of loan and at the earliest possible not exceeding a week after receiving his loan application, loan has to be sanctioned.
3. Loan is usually sanctioned before the sowing of karif season and not for rabi. But in some cases loan is required for second crop also which has to be considered by PACS and sanction the loan depending upon the prevailing conditions.

References

Mathur B.S., (1983)Cooperative In India, Himalaya Publications, Bombay Revised Edition.

Sanjibkumar Hota and Vinod Sharma (2001) "Cooperative Credit: Revamping Needed", Yojana, Vol.45 July 2001.

Thanikodi. (1998) "Central Cooperative Banks in India – Problems and Remedies" The Cooperator, Vol.42. No.12.

Memoria &Saxena, (1974)Cooperative In India, Himalaya Publishing House, Bombay.

Misra, R.V (1998) Cooperatives for Empowerment of People, The Cooperator, Vol.37(5) Nov. P.195-197.

Mohanan .W (1972) Cooperative Overdues and Small Farmers, Indian Cooperative Review, Vol.13 (3):241-249.

Nakkiran .S, (1971) Problems Of Urban Cooperative Banks In India, Anmol Publications, Ajmeer.

Nair.T.G (1976) Deposit Mobilization by Cooperatives in India - A Review, Indian Cooperative Review, Vol.13 (3):241-249.

Anegundi (1998) Problems Of Urban Cooperative Banks In Karnataka, Sapna Book House, Bangalore.

Nakkiran.S ., (1986) "Cooperative Banking in India", Rainbow Publishing House, Coimbatore.

George.P.T, Mohanan N and Rajgopal (1985) Status of Cooperative Movement in India, NIRD, Memio.

Patnaik Surendra (1999) Cooperative Banking in India, The Cooperator, Vol.37(5), Nov.P 171-182.

6

Dimensions of Female Agricultural Wage Rates in India

Ziaulla

INTRODUCTION

The objective of this study is to analyse the patterns of female agricultural wage rates in India and on the basis of analysis and discussion suggestions have also been made to further effective improvement of agricultural wage rates for the female. Women are the molders and builders of any Nation's destiny. They play a significant role in any economy. They are considered as the backbone of the rural economy. Most of the women perform various types of work for their livelihood and agriculture is considered as the biggest unorganised sector, where large numbers of rural women take part actively. About 75 percent of the Indian female population is from rural families, who belonged to the small and marginal farmers and landless agricultural labourers (Census of India). Though women's primary responsibility is indulging in domestic work, greater emphasis is laid on women's earning in the form of money by working outside the four walls. In India, a significant proportion of the population is below the poverty line and it is a fact that labour force participation will increase with poverty, a large proportion of rural women are under a pressure to participate in the labour force.

Results and Discussion

Women do work under testing conditions, where men are relatively better disposed. Both with regard to ploughing and harvesting men could operate with machines or drought animals, whereas women, in all their activities has to exert their physical strength, at times in knee deep water under the scorching sun. The working hours too vary and women work at least 6 hours more than males, and working day accounts for nearly 15 hours in the peak season both in the filed and at the home, put together. Sprays of fertilizers, is done both by men and women. But men do the work with sprays, whereas women is entrusted the work which could be done with hands. Moreover, women working under these testing conditions have no facilities like rest periods, shelters sheds, crèches for keeping suckling babies, and even first aid. These facilities are unheard of in this area, as there is no union to represent their sufferings. These unknown and unacknowledged beings are responsible to keep the economy at a steady pace and helped the Nation to occupy a significant place in the World.

Types of Female Labourers in agriculture

There are two types of female labourers in Indian agricultural practices i.e., casual and contract gang labour. Casual labour is known as Dinaguli that means wage is for a day. This is an important segment of the hired labour market in India as well as in the study area. The labourers are hired for a certain, for a day, a week or more. This type of labourers are engaged in sowing, manuring, weeding, threshing, transplanting and harvesting etc., and they always be ready to work for any employer, who preferred to pay the current market wage. The labour receives the payment weekly i.e., on bazaar day or in intervals. Both land-less and small and marginal holdings landed households hire themselves out as casual labours.

The other type of labour hiring system prevalent in the study area is contract gang labour. This practice has got a significant place in the labour market, which is locally termed as "Guttige" who work in employers field in a day where there is no stipulation of time and a group of labourers also work in a similar way that are known as gangs. In the study area a group of families form this gang and work together as a labour force. The payment is fixed on size of land, nature of work and crop, and distance from home. Payment will be generally made only in cash especially on bazaar day.

Characteristics of female agricultural labourers

Before any attempt is made to evolve at a rational policy for improving the living conditions of a female agricultural labourer, who belong to the lowest socio-economic strata of the society. It is essential to know the distinguishing features of female agricultural labours in India.

- Female agricultural labourers are especially village dwellers.
- Generally they are unskilled workers carrying on their agricultural operations in traditional ways.
- The bargaining power and position of female agricultural labourers in India is very weak.
- Female agricultural labour is the most exploited class of people in India.
- Female agricultural labourers work as casual and contract gang labour. The nature of employment, wage and the employer-employee relation differs across these groups.
- In some parts of India, Female agricultural labour

are found to be migratory, that is moving in search of jobs especially at the time of sowing and harvesting in near by areas.

The association of women in agriculture is an age-old practice. The 1991 census data indicates that 43.6 percent of women are working as agricultural labourers 34.5 percent are cultivators, but it is increased to 50.35 and 41.51 respectively in 2001 census. The details are furnished in Table - 1.

Table - 1
Distribution of female workers in India (1951 - 2001)

(in thousands)

Year	*Total female population*	*Cultivators*	*Agricultural Labourers*	*Industry and service*	*Total female workers*
1951	173543	18368	12694	9477	40539
		(45.3)	(31.3)	(23.3)	(100)
1961	212467	33103	14171	12128	59402
		(55.7)	(23.9)	(20.4)	(100)
1971	263900	9266	15794	6238	31298
		(29.6)	(50.5)	(19.9)	(100)
1981	321357	14932	20768	9273	44973
		(33.2)	(46.2)	(20.6)	(100)
1991	402813	22871	28833	14485	66189
		(34.5)	(43.6)	(21.9)	(100)
2001	495738	41299	50093	8083	99475
		(41.51)	(50.35)	(8.14)	(100)

Source: *Towards Equality: Report on the Committee on Status of Women, Government of India, Ministry of Social Welfare, New Delhi.*

Though rural farm labourers work under severe limitations, whereas their contribution towards agricultural production and development is noteworthy. Apart from the job they do outside the household, the unpaid activities in the domestic sphere go unnoticed and un-rewarded.

Women work force outside the four walls is obviously larger in rural areas than in urban India. Women in rural areas help to grow at least about 50 percent of the World's food. They work in all aspects of cultivation including planting, weeding, harvesting, sowing, threshing, etc.

According to the census reports, there is an increased participation of rural women in economic activities besides doing household duties. Though participation of women in agriculture, contribute a lot for the economic growth and progress of the country, their problems are shown least concern.

In India female agricultural labourers are not homogeneously distributed all over the country, their percent varies in different areas due to demographic, technological, ecological and sociological reasons. This may be clearly seen from the following table.

Table - 2
Distribution of Female agricultural labourers in different states in India - 2001

Name of the State	*Total agricultural labourers*	*Female agricultural labourers*	*Percent of the Female agricultural labourers*
Andhra Pradesh	11850113	7191188	60.68
Assam	2509526	437630	17.44
Arunachalpradesh	171565	7972	4.65
Bihar	7205937	4652672	64.57
Gujarat	5721030	2515045	43.96
Haryana	2376211	543088	22.85
Himachalpradesh	1266666	37288	2.98
Jammu& Kashmir	940081	50760	5.40
Karnataka	6854752	3455460	50.40
Kerala	1925009	505086	26.24
Maharashtra	12695748	6121358	48.21

Name of the State	*Total agricultural labourers*	*Female agricultural labourers*	*Percent of the Female agricultural labourers*
Madhyapradesh	8669974	3769434	43.48
Manipur	381802	55895	14.65
Mizoram	118377	5293	4.47
Orissa	4200930	2390685	56.90
Panjab	1749465	363685	20.79
Rajasthan	8496356	1449004	17.05
Sikkim	91543	8322	9.10
Tamilnadu	7175171	3897586	54.32
Uttarpradesh	11799397	5184385	43.94
West Bengal	5821973	2244803	38.55

Source: Provisional Population Totals, paper 3 Census of India,2001.

Table - 2 reveals that, distribution of female agricultural labourers in India, among all the states Bihar has the highest female agricultural labourers i.e., 64.57percent to the total agricultural labourers in India, and followed by Andhra Pradesh with 60.68 percent. The lowest female agricultural labourers are seen in Himachalpradesh, Mizoram and Arunachalpradesh with 2.94percent, 4.47 percent and 4.65 percent respectively. Karnataka has got fifth place in relation to having female agricultural labourers in India i.e., 50.40 percent to the total agricultural labourers.

The agricultural women workers are subjugated, subordinated and exploited by the social forces, the responsibility of which rests with the male members of the family, landlords, enforcing authorities and policy makers. Ignorance, illiteracy and abject poverty crushed these neglected and isolated lot whose sorrowful melancholy did not reach the ears of gregarious social animals around.

In the agricultural sector which absorbs the largest proportion of India's workforce both male and female while differentials exist between wages paid to male workers in different agricultural operations. More ever differentials exist within the scheduled castes, scheduled tribes and non-scheduled population. Women laborers constitute about 39 percent of the total agricultural labour force, but they receive relatively low wages than men even for the work of similar nature. It is often argued that since women do less labour work than men, they receive lower wages than men. However, the available data for various states show that such wage discrimination exists even for similar type of work performed by men and women.

Table- 3 presents the data on growth rates of wages in rural male and female workers involved in rural agricultural and non-agricultural occupations. It is clear from the data that the non-agricultural wage rate in all year is greater than the agricultural wage rates.

Table - 3
Real wage rates of males and female laborers in agriculture and non-agriculture in rural India

Year	*Agriculture*		*Non-agriculture*	
	Male	*Female*	*Male*	*Female*
1974-75	3.26	2.26	5.09	2.34
1977-78	3.76	2.67	6.2	3.02
1983	4.63	3.46	7.27	3.78
1987-88	9.46	7.05	11.0	7.99
1993-94	21.35	15.33	32.48	17.45
1999-2000	40.14	28.38	64.92	56.13

Source: Various Reports of Rural Labour Inquire Committees.

The all India picture is some what different between 1974-75 and 1999-2000. Male agricultural real wage rates increased from 3.26 rupees in 1974-75 to 40.14 rupees in 1999-2000. Female agricultural real wage rates have also increased from 2.26 rupees in 1974-75 to 28.38 rupees in 1999-2000. In the year 1974-75 for agriculture workers for male was 3.26 rupees and female was 2.26 rupees a clear difference of 1 rupee can be seen. Now for non-agriculture workers for male in the same year was 5.09 rupees and for female was 2.34 rupees, a difference of wearing 3.5 rupees can be seen between male and female group. The real wage rates in both in agricultural and non-agricultural occupations have been increasing over time.

Table - 4 presents the data on wage rates for male and female laborers in agriculture for 16 major states during 1977-78 to 1999-2000. Now we have male and female in both agriculture workers and non-agriculture workers wage rates. This wage rates have been taken across 16 major states and whole India. Beside the male and female agriculture workers and no-agriculture workers of 16 major states of India are have wage rates of whole of India. There are wage rates for male and female across 16 major states of India namely, Andhra Pradesh, Bihar, Gujarat, Haryana, Himachal Pradesh, Jammu and Kashmir, Karnataka, Kerala, Madhya Pradesh, Maharashtra, Orissa, Punjab, Rajasthan, Tamil Nadu, Uttar Pradesh and West Bengal. Here the male and female wage rates of the 16 major states given above are have divided in 4 periods, via 1977-78, 1987-88, 1993-94 and 1999-2000. These four periods are of two types i.e., pre-reform period and post-reform period.

From 1977-78 is called pre-reform period and period from 1993-94 to 1999-2000 is called post-reform period. There has been a vast difference in the agriculture wage rates from pre-reform period to post-reform period for both male and female workers. The wage rates for male workers from pre-reform period to post-reform period have a vast increment. As well as the wage rates for female workers also has an vast increment in the wage rates and a sudden increment can be deserved at the last year i.e., 1999-2000. Hence here we can observe this, that difference of wage rates across different states of India for both male

Table- 4

Real wage rates of male and female laborers in agriculture by major states

States	*Male labourers*				*Female labourers*			
	1977-78	*1987-88*	*1993-94*	*1999-00*	*1977-78*	*1987-88*	*1993-94*	*1999-00*
Andhrapradesh	3.44	8.87	19.12	39.8	2.36	6.12	13.61	26.49
Bihar	3.52	9.02	10.93	36.1	3.15	8.02	14.78	30.96
Gujarat	4.1	9.32	20.06	38.81	3.62	9.11	19.17	33.27
Haryana	5.79	10.35	30.54	60.04	4.87	7.51	24.22	53.28
Himacal Pradesh	6.05	13.75	30.95	63.52	4.11	12.47	28.08	56.79
J&K	6.16	11.04	35.4	85.91	4.46	7.5	25.58	Nil
Karnataka	3.14	8.46	19.2	40.32	2.12	6.04	14.13	27.21
Kerala	6.87	18.29	43.18	94.52	4.67	13.52	29.88	62.22
Madhyapradesh	2.73	7.67	17.04	30.01	2.18	6.74	14.29	25.44
Maharashtra	3.17	9.16	19.54	37.67	1.99	6.01	12.17	24.34
Orissa	3.11	7.89	16.3	28.69	2.35	9.34	12.09	22.31
Punjab	7.3	15.99	41.98	63.57	4.62	9.14	38.82	73.98
Rajastahn	4.48	6.69	27.66	51.66	3.16	9.14	22.6	39.12
Tamil Nadu	3.89	9.82	25.11	52.36	2.35	6.18	15.09	30.48
Uttarpradesh	3.59	13.14	21.59	38.29	2.64	6.99	16.57	29.05
West Bengal	4.26	11.85	24.2	43.45	3.73	10.71	19.57	37.03
All India	3.79	9.46	21.52	40.58	2.67	7.05	15.33	28.57

Source: GOI(1998 and 2003).

and female workers are increased. The wage rates for this period of time has been also categorised for both scheduled caste and scheduled tribes and other caste people for both male and female workers group.

It has been seen that among all the states than two North Western States, i.e., Punjab, Haryana and Kerala from South consistently maintained a high average level of real wages throughout the period under review. As for the wage rates of male workers the highest average for the 1999-2000 was reported from Kerala followed by Jammu & Kashmir and Punjab in that order. Relatively low level of real wages has all along been reported, especially for the period. Until 1977-78 from the states of Madhyapradesh, Orissa, Karnataka, Andhrapradesh and Uttarpradesh.

The same picture emerge in the case of wage rates of women workers given in table-4. It has been observed that Punjab, Kerala and Rajasthan in that order showed highest average of wage rates. On the other hand, Orissa reported the lowest wage rates again through the period.

In the year 1977-78 workers wage rate for Andhrapradesh male was Rs.3.44 and female was Rs.2.36. here a difference of Rs. 1.08 can be observed. In the year 1999-2000 for male was Rs.39.8 and female was Rs.26.49 here difference of Rs.13.31 can be observed. The real wage rates in various seem to correspond very closely to the output per worker. The highest absolute level of real wages is found in the states of Kerala, Punjab and Jammu & Kashmir. The exercises were done separately for male and female wage rates pertaining to four selected years namely, 1977-78, 1987-88, 1993-94 and 1999-2000. Some important differences in real wage trend women workers as compared to those of male workers. First, real wages increased in all states without exception during 1977-78 to 1999-2000. Secondly, the magnitude of increase in real wages is much higher in the case of women workers.

It has been found the real wage rates for male and female were found to be higher for others as compared to SCs/STs. The wage rates for male and female laborers were lower in the case of agricultural occupations as compared to that of non-agricultural occupations. The rates for male were found to greater as compared to that of female labourers belonging to SCs/STs and other; involved in both agricultural and non-agricultural occupations. It has also been observed that wage rates for both male and female laborers registered increasing trends. The increase was quite faster in the case of male and in the case of non-agricultural occupations. There has been a considerable regional variation in the wage rates for both male and female in agricultural and non-agricultural occupations. Such regional variation in the wage rates is closely associated with the growth of agriculture and diversification of employment away from agriculture in favour of non-agricultural occupations and educational status.

SUGGESTIONS

On the basis of analysis and discussion some suggestions have been made to further effective improvement of wage rates among female agricultural labourers in order to empower the women. Following are the suggestions of the study;

1. Awareness among female agricultural labourers should be created so that they can form an organisation, through which they can bargain to reduce or resolve the problem of wage difference in agriculture in particular and in rural area in general.
2. Policy makers should take consideration of the interests of female agricultural labourers at the time of framing policies for the development and welfare of agricultural labourers.
3. The law enforcement agencies must play a crucial role in implementing laws related to agricultural labourers like equal pay for equal work.

4. Creation of awareness among the masses about the benefits of government programmes and government should reserve some projects or part of the project mainly for female workers of rural area.
5. Minimum wage rate should be fixed. And at the same time there is very much need to increase the female literacy rate for the shake of benefits of the women workers.

References

Indira Hirway (1986) Wage Employment Programmes in Rural Development, Oxford & IBH Publishing Co.Pvt.Ltd, New Delhi.

Government of Karnataka, Manpower Profile Karnataka, 2000 - 2006. Manpower and Employment Division, Bangalore.

Devdas.R.P (1972) Role of Selected Farm Women in Agricultural Operations, Indian Journal of Home Science, Vol.6. No.1.

Varma Shashi (1982) Women in Agriculture: A Socio-Economic Analysis. Concept Publishing Co. New Delhi.

Jha Shailendra (1990) Agricultural Labour: Problems and Present Positions. Deep and Deep Publications, New Delhi.

Sarap Kailash (1989) Trends in wage rates and living conditions of agricultural labourers in Orissa, Man and Development, Vol.II, No.3, Sep.pp.113-123.

Subah Singh Yadav and Gujar Ram Kumar (1993) Poverty Alleviation and Employment Generation. Concept Publishing Co. New Delhi.

7

Problems and Prospects of Co operative Sector Under Globalization Regime - A Study in Karnataka

Sreenivasaiah, K.N.

Introduction

An attempt is made in this paper is to analyse the problems and prospects of cooperative sector in Karnataka. In India cooperatives were set up in response to the prevalence of exploitative interests. From this perspective, maximizing the welfare of the members and serving the economic ends were the responsibilities of these institutions. In independent India, the cooperatives took up and successfully shouldered the responsibility as institutions to purvey credit for agricultural and rural development. In every nation cooperatives have played an active role in the empowerment of rural areas. Cooperative have contributed their might in the development of economies all over the world. In India, cooperatives are playing a major role in filling the gap left by the public and private sectors. The cooperative movement was strengthened by the combined efforts of Sardar Vallabhbhai Patel, Jawaharlal Nehru and Lal Bahadur Shastri.

Co-operatives have treated the path, where no public and private sector could reach and worked in empowering the rural masses at the grass roots level to help themselves as well as the nation. The Government of India played a major role by emphasizing on the co-operative sector development right from the First Five Year Plan.

Co-operative movement in modern days is built on voluntary co-operation where in individuals make a deliberate choice to so-operate in some aspects of their lives. Co-operation is the free and voluntary association of people to create an organization which they democratically control, providing themselves with goods, services and a livelihood rather than profiting from others, with an equitable contribution of capital and accepting a fair share of the risks and benefits generated by the joint activity. To sustain their endeavour, they must develop the individual society and build a solidarity relationship with other co-operators and like-minded people. Cooperatives have been successful and they have reformed the market place where they have become strong enough in their respective fields.

In the beginning of this century, the Indian farmers were heavily indebted to the moneylenders, and were steeped in poverty and misery. The Indian Government felt that if the farmers were provided with cheap and adequate finance, they would be able to improve their output. The only way to provide such credit, it was thought, was through co-operative credit societies in rural areas for the purpose of providing cheap credit or loan to farmers. The Co-operative Credit Societies Act, 1904 was passed by the government and rural credit societies were passed by the government and rural credit societies were formed.

The co-operative movement started in India in 1904 by the enactment of co-operative societies Act 1904. For the needs of the members its establishment on their financial status freely, self-help based on mutual help theory without the interference of the members, but beginning by govt., govt. views, programs all these are mandatory. Now these institutions are seen as govt. institutions. Similarly govt. has considered as sub branches for the implementations of schemes. For the profit and their freedom, independence, development going along with work and its control.

We can see the co-operative movement in different fields like agriculture credit society, marketing dairy, joint farming, irrigation, cottage, sugar industrial godowns, consumers etc,. Co-operative movement in India started in 1904 and was amended in 1912. It is the spread of this cooperative, no reorganization of this co-operative movement gained movement untill1930. But in 1934 the act of Reserve Bank the credit department established in agriculture, village credit societies.

In 1942, the British Government enacted the multi-unit cooperative societies Act, 1942 with an object to cover societies whose operations are extended to more than one state. The impulses of the Indian freedom movement gave birth to many initiatives and institutions in the post independence era in India and armed with an experience of 42 years in the working of multi unit cooperative societies and the multi-unit cooperative societies Act, 1942, the central government enacted a comprehensive Act known as multi state cooperative societies Act, 1984, repealing the Act of 1942.

The co-operatives are the preferred instrument of socio-economic development. Their content the national economy of the country is very significant. In the wake of declining role of public various limitations of private sector, relevance of cooperatives is achieving greater heights. In the environment of capitalistic form of society, cooperatives must succeed to provide opportunities and deprived section of society for their socio-economic development. Government is also providing policy support for the development of cooperative sector in the country.

Co-operative institutions have played a vital role in

the Socio-economic development of the country, particularly in the rural areas and in agriculture and allied sectors. It is our firm belief and conviction that the Co-operative institutions will continue to play a key role in the economic development of country and will become more relevant in the changing economic environment of Liberalization and Globalization.

Karnataka stand 3rd in co-operative movement in the country after Maharastra and Gujarat. Co-operative movement is wide spread in the developmental sectors like credit, marketing, consumers, silk industry, dairy, fishery, horticulture, sugar, house building, constructions of godowns etc.

The Co-operation in Karnataka has gained momentum and this is evident following table. Highlights of the registered growth of societies are as follow

Table - 1
Growth of Co-operative Movement in Karnataka

(Rs. in lakhs)

Year	*No. of societies*	*Membership (actual)*	*Share capital*	*Working capital*
1905-06	5	386	0.11	0.14
1925-26	1603	92292	35.52	112.38
1950-51	5190	501281	138.74	690.90
1975-76	22713	5945009	12543.00	91637.00
2000-01	29930	16167000	147316.00	2119867.65
2004-05	32764	20100000	174295.00	2521411.00
20005-06	32577	20500000	191700.00	2647500.00
2006-07	32997	20800000	195300.00	2698000.00

Source: Govt. of Karnataka, Dept of cooperation, Annual report 2006-07

The cooperative movement in Karnataka was originated in the region of Mysore Royal Family by their advent patronage of co-operation. Mysore was the first princely state to conceive the idea of co-operation as an important instrument of rural development even before it was though the officially and seriously in British India. the beginning was made in 1894 by the association of land lords into agricultural banks of work strictly on co-operative principles not for the purpose of earning any profit divisible among its members, but for the purpose of obtaining money by their own united credit and lending it according it to the actual requirements of each members, the extent of the others have confidence on him. However, they did not survive long due to low rates of interest, insufficient capital, insufficient management and inadequate supervision.

In 1904, when the first cooperative Act was passed the first ever cooperative society was formed in Kanaginahal village of Dharwad district since the passing of Mysore cooperative regulation Act in 1905, on the lines with Indian Co-operatives Act of 1904. The cooperatives in Karnataka have progressed along with the Indian cooperative movement. By this development in cooperation need for a central financing society were felt soon and the Bangalore Central Cooperative Bank was organised and it started lending actively in 1909-1910.

Decadal Growth of the Cooperative Societies in Karnataka since 1961 - 2001

Recognizing the prominent position of the state in the cooperative sector, the Institute of Cooperative Management was founded in Bangalore (1962). In 1990, the National Agricultural and Rural Development Training Institute were founded at Bangalore to train the bank and cooperative sector officials. The decadal growths of the cooperative societies in Karnataka since 1961 details are presented in table.

The above table clearly shows that there is a mixed tendency in the cooperative movement in the state of Karnataka since 1961 to 2001. The total number of societies in the state increased during the 1960s, 1970s and 1980s at 2.66%, 19.15% and 8.31% respectively. During the 1990s,

Table- 2
Decadal growth of the cooperative societies in Karnataka since 1961 - 2001

Particulars	*1961*	*1971*	*1981*	*1991*	*2001*
Primary Cooperative Agricultural & Rural Development Banks	118	170	177	177	177
Primary Agricultural Credit Societies	7107	8775	8871	4350	4388
Grain Banks	1027	851	844	151	123
Urban Banks	NA	210	239	223	313
Employees and other Cooperative Credit Societies	NA	766	1594	1599	2913
Marketing Cooperative Societies	259	207	192	189	177
Special Commodity Marketing Cooperative Societies	NA	62	144	340	135
Processing Cooperative Societies	29	40	69	32	101
Farming Cooperative Societies		144	499	595	242
Milk Supply Cooperative Societies	70	617	2577	6291	8253
Live Stock Cooperative Societies	NA	63	90	73	241
Irrigation Cooperative Societies	35	63	225	564	1421
Fisheries Cooperative Societies	70	123	193	272	375
Consumer Cooperative Societies	395	1302	1541	1650	1502
Housing Cooperative Societies	350	920	1309	1606	1274
Weavers Cooperative Societies	621	798	831	726	410
Industrial Cooperative Societies	1064	1835	1892	1001	891
All other types of Cooperative Societies	1388	1355	1368	1439	3305
Societies under liquidation	277	2175	4408	4158	3823
Total	14954	19431	23159	25083	29930

Source: Registrar of Cooperative Societies in Karnataka, Bangalore.

the growth of cooperative societies accelerated to 13.12% per annum. It can also be said that Milk Supply Cooperative Societies and Irrigation Cooperative Societies have been increased gradually from 1961 to 2001 also i.e., from 70 to 8253 societies and 35 to 1421 societies respectively.

Type of Cooperatives in Karnataka

All types of cooperatives exist in Karnataka, agricultural credit cooperatives, input supply cooperatives and processing and marketing cooperatives over the entire agricultural sector in the state. Industrial, housing and cooperative banks have spread in the urban areas. However, the share of each type of cooperatives in the sole cooperative sector is brought out in the following diagram.

Table - 3
Type of Cooperatives in Karnataka

Sl. No	*Type of Cooperatives*	%
01	Agricultural Credit Cooperative Societies.	18
02	Non-Agricultural Cooperative Societies	11
03	Milk Cooperatives	31
04	Marketing Cooperative Societies	3
05	Housing Cooperatives	6
06	Women Cooperatives	4
07	Industrial Cooperatives	6
08	Consumers Cooperatives	6
09	Others	15
	Total	100

Source: Registrar, Cooperative Societies, Govt. of Karnataka.

As can be seen in the above diagram, milk cooperatives dominate this scene with 31% share. Agricultural credit cooperatives are the second largest constituents with 18% share. Non-agricultural credit cooperatives have 11% share. The traditional, long standing consumer, marketing and industrial cooperatives have lost the ground with negligible share each has in the entire cooperative sector in the state.

Growth of Cooperative Societies in Karnataka

Growth of cooperative societies in Karnataka almost since the inception of the cooperative movement has been traced and presented in Table - 3. Perusal of the table reveals that the vital parameters of cooperative societies have been growing at healthy rate. Membership increased around 35 percent during the last three decades was at a higher rate prior to that. Similarly, the share capital also rose, but the rise was not consistent. It was high with 30% during 1905-06, 1910-1920 and 1950-60. In recent years, the rate had decreased below 10 percent, and in the last decade, the increase in share capital was 12.03%. The same trend is seen in the case of working capital, where the increase was less than 30% in the decade ending 1906, 1910 and 1961. In the recent decades, the working capital of cooperatives societies had come down below 10 percent, but in the last decade, the working capital of societies increased by 18.07 percent per annum.

From the foregoing, it is amply clear that vital parameters of cooperative societies in Karnataka, has been registered a consistent rate of growth, though the high rate of growth recorded during the earlier periods of the cooperative movement were not sustained in the later decades. The present level of membership of cooperative societies stands at 1.83 crores with a share capital of Rs.1342.26 crores and a working capital of Rs.166621.57 crores.

Table- 4
Growth of the Cooperative Movement in Karnataka

(Amount in lakhs)

No	*Year*	*No.of Societies*	*Membership*	*Share capital*	*Working capital*
01	1905-06	5	386	0.11	0.14
02	1910-11	111	9043	2.31	3.71
03	1920-21	1500	92,121	34.34	81.97
04	1930-31	2213	1,37,615	48.88	189.32
05	1940-41	1956	1,43,370	53.08	271.77
06	1950-51	5190	5,01,281	138.74	690.90
07	1960-61	14871	24,33,000	1,738.39	10,340.91
08	1970-71	19437	43,45,000	8,235.00	12,336.00
09	1980-81	23159	82,89,000	17,570.00	1,26,128.00
10	1990-91	25083	1,18,00,000	43,108.00	3,15,833.00
11	2000-01	28343	1,83,23,000	1,34,226.60	16,62,157.55
12	2006-07	32454	1,95,35,000	1,54116.00	18,70,123.12

Source: Registrar of Cooperatives, Govt. of Karnataka, Bangalore.

Table- 5
Decadal View of Share Capital and Working Capital

Years	*Share Capital*	*Working Capital*
1970-71	8235	52336
1980-81	17570	126128
1990-91	43108	315833
2000-01	***134226.6***	***1662157.6***

Source: Registrar of cooperation, govt. of Karnataka.

Table- 6
Decadal Growth of Membership

Year	*Membership*
1970-71	4345000
1980-81	8289000
1990-91	11800000
2000-01	**18323000**

Source: Registrar of cooperation, Govt. of Karnataka, Bangalore

District Wise Spread of Cooperatives in Karnataka

The growth of cooperative societies in Bangalore division shows that Kolar district registered a growth of 5.15% per annum, followed by Bangalore district with a growth of around 2 percent per annum. The growth was negative in Chitradurga and Shimoga at 7.29% and 5.03% respectively. In the Bangalore division, Bangalore Urban has the highest number of societies of 1880, followed by Bangalore Rural (1377). Most of the societies in Bangalore city showed a decline during the last five years. The sole exception was other non-credit societies which increased by 24.94% per annum. A similar pattern of growth is seen in Bangalore rural as well. Kolar had a growth of 81% in non-credit cooperative societies, 162 of processing cooperative societies and 80 of weavers' cooperatives. Milk cooperatives grew at the rate of 6.31% per annum to 1244, which constituted the bulk of the societies.

Shimoga shows a decline in the number of societies. The decline was primarily is milk societies. There was a 7.17 percent decline in the number of housing cooperative societies. The number of milk societies decreased in Tumkur to 473 a decrease of 4.31% per annum. The number of PACs has also decreased by 2.15% per annum.

Cooperative societies had increased in Belgaum and Bijapur districts, and in Dharwad growth had declined. Belgaum had the largest number of cooperative societies, numbering 3387, which was followed by Bijapur at 2070 and Dharwad 1882. The largest numbers of societies were employees' credit societies (512), Milk cooperative society (514) and PACs (526). The number of irrigation societies had declined at the rate of 7.13% per annum. Processing societies and special commodity marketing societies had shown over 15 percent growth per annum. The number of most of the societies declined in Bijapur district. Urban banks had increased in the district at 13.76% per annum. The details can be seen from the Table-7.

Table - 7
District-wise Growth of Cooperative Societies in Karnataka

District	Consumer CS 2006-07	Consumer CS Growth %	DCC/ Apex/ SLDB/ Fed 2006-07	DCC/ Apex/ SLDB/ Fed Growth %	Farming 2006-07	Farming Growth %
Bangalore	380	0.44	22	7.22	0	-
Bangalore	24	-1.59	9	-	5	0.00
Chitradurga	14	-27.93	1	-18.77	11	5.85
Kolar	41	-4.47	1	18.77	1	-18.77
Shimoga	44	-9.09	1	-28.08	5	24.65
Tumkur	59	-3.05	1	-18.77	2	-34.69
Belgaum1	80	3.54	2	-38.30	17	-9.17
Bijapur	100	-1.18	2	-6.70	4	-37.96
Dharwad	63	-13.53	1	-18.77	10	-26.19
Uttar Kannada	-	-	1	-28.08	-	-
Chikmagalur	24	3.62	1	-18.77	3	-10.91
D.K	41	-11.14	3	-40.89	5	4.56
Hassan	37	5.76	1	38.30	3	-27.23
Kodagu	15	21.48	1	-18.77	3	-
Mandya	57	3.04	1	-12.94	1	-34.29
Mysore	152	-6.72	3	-17.81	10	36.41
Bellary	148	1.60	1	-18.77	9	1.18
Bidar	16	1.30	1	-18.77	2	0.00
Gulbarga7	9	-1.35	1	18.77	5	-2.21
Raichur	44	-1.63	2	-6.70	5	-0.77
Total	1518	-4.00	55	-13.26	101	-19.88

Source: Registrar of Cooperatives, Bangalore.

Dharwad showed a decline in the number of societies and a general decline in every society. The sole exception was other non-credit cooperative societies which increased at the rate of 1013% per annum. All the districts of Mysore division showed an increase in the number of societies.

it was the highest in Kodagu at 4.76 percent followed by Chickmagalore (3.65%), Dakshina Kannada (2.80%), Mandya (2.76%) and the lowest in Mysore at 0.26% per annum.

In Kodagu the increase in the number of cooperative societies was contributed by other non-credit cooperative societies (21.04%) and special commodity marketing societies (45.41%). The growth of societies in Chickmagalore was due to the growth in milk societies (3.39%), fishery societies (7.57%) and weavers societies (16.23%). There are 1329 cooperative societies in Dakshina Kannada. The growth in the number in the district was due to contract labour societies, irrigation societies, and fishery societies, general purpose marketing societies, other non-credit societies and urban banks.

In Hassan district, there were 1006 cooperative societies of which milk societies and PACs were the largest. Both these societies registered only a moderate growth of around one percent per annum. State had development banks, employee's credit societies and farming societies registered a decline during the last five years ranging between 17-38% per annum.

There were about 1372 cooperative societies in Mandya district, again dominated by PACs (210) and milk societies (666) while the number of milk societies increased, the PACs remained constant. The number of societies in Mysore which numbered 1912 was dominated by housing (103), milk (640) and PACs (240). None of these societies registered any significant increase during the last five years.

Gulbarga division had relatively larger number of cooperative societies. Bellary with 1823 societies, registered at 20.02% per annum. In Gulbarga district also the number grew by 5.87 percent per annum. The major societies in Bellary district are consumer (148), milk (390) and PACs (164). Significant growth rates in PACARD banks (10.20%), urban banks (70.08%) and weaver cooperative societies (36.43%). In Bidar also milk and PACs dominate the scenario. However the number of milk societies is declining by 4.21%. In percentage terms, the biggest increases are seen in special commodity marketing societies (67.03%), urban banks (29.73%) and weaver cooperative societies (17.61%).

Table - 8
District-wise Growth of Cooperative Societies in Karnataka

District	*Milk CS 2006-07*	*Milk CS Growth %*	*PACs 2006-07*	*PACs Growth %*	*PCARD 2006-07*	*PCARD Growth %*
Bangalore	286	3.29	41	-3.10	3	0.00
Bangalore	874	4.26	155	0.13	8	0.00
Chitradurga	69	-19.53	215	-0.28	6	-7.79
Kolar	1244	6.31	203	1.11	10	-1.89
Shimoga	249	-3.55	230	1.54	8	-4.36
Tumkur	473	-4.31	236	-2.15	10	0.00
Belgaum	514	-2.18	526	3.82	10	0.00
Bijapur	273	-4.40	409	0.17	10	-1.89
Dharwad	225	-16.84	530	6.50	9	-11.94
Uttar Kannada	-	-	160	0.38	-	-
Chikmagalur	141	3.39	113	0.45	8	0.00
D.K	326	3.17	170	0.90	14	11.84
Hassan	473	1.03	169	1.22	8	0.00
Kodagu	24	4.36	73	0.00	3	0.00
Mandya	666	3.19	210	-0.10	7	0.00
Mysore	640	1.63	240	-2.22	11	0.00
Bellary	390	19.96	164	-0.42	13	10.20
Bidar	222	-4.21	171	0.12	5	0.00
Gulbarga	180	8.67	233	0.09	10	0.00
Raichur	152	0.08	180	-4.12	8	-2.33
Total	7421	0.43	4428	0.45	161	-1.88

Source: Registrar of Cooperatives, Bangalore.

Table - 9
District-wise Growth of Cooperative Societies in Karnataka

District	*Weavers 2006-07*	*Weavers Growth %*	*Women 2006-07*	*Women Growth %*	*State 2006-07*	*State Growth %*
Bangalore	38	0.48	43	-1.19	1880	2.04
Bangalore	20	7.19	13	5.92	1377	2.33
Chitradurga	56	2.59	25	-3.84	650	-7.29
Kolar	63	75.90	63	8.54	1943	5.15
Shimoga	5	-5.25	18	3.66	725	-5.03
Tumkur	21	-6.56	28	-	1238	-1.07
Belgaum	132	-0.10	79	5.72	3387	3.46
Bijapur	83	12.95	98	31.82	2070	2.92
Dharwad	35	20.45	80	7.51	1882	-6.07
Uttar Kannada	-	-	-	-	0	-
Chikmagalur	6	16.23	13	6.15	477	3.65
D.K	5	-8.97	12	-20.59	1329	2.80
Hassan	7	13.79	-	-	1006	0.15
Kodagu	-	-	19	1.02	360	4.76
Mandya	7	-2.45	-	-	1372	2.76
Mysore	11	-17.20	61	0.00	1912	0.26
Bellary	66	36.43	41	3.36	1833	20.02
Bidar	18	17.61	-	-	764	1.09
Gulbarga	24	5.32	154	11.65	1382	5.87
Raichur	16	7.45	53	121.74	999	2.40
Total	**613**	**0.26**	**800**	**5.65**	**26586**	**1.32**

Source: Registrar of Cooperatives, Bangalore.

Gulbarga district has a large number of consumer cooperative societies, irrigation societies, housing societies, milk societies, other non-credit societies, PACS and woman's societies all of which are growing at a healthy rate. The comparison of societies in Bidar is similar to that of Gulbarga. Urban banks and woman cooperatives have registered very high rates of growth.

Levels of Cooperative Development

After independence, and particularly after 1951, the Reserve Bank of India, the highest monetary and banking authority in the country, took great interest in the cooperative movement. It wanted to expand and strengthen the movement. RBI was influenced by the slogan: "Cooperation has failed, but cooperation must succeed". RBI adopted three guiding principles in the reorganisation of rural cooperation viz:

1. The State government should participate in the cooperative movement at all levels;
2. The should be full cooperation between credit and other activities such as cultivation, marketing, processing, and so on; and
3. The cooperative movement should be run by adequately trained and efficient men who are fully aware of the needs of the farmers.

According to RBI, our farmers could be provided with adequate and cheap finance only through the cooperative societies. the State Government should participate in the cooperative movement financially as well as otherwise. It should subscribe to the share capital of the cooperative societies and banks at all levels. In this way, the cooperative credit societies will be financially strengthened and will be enabled to land extensively to the farmers. The state should also participate in the organization of marketing and processing of agriculture produce.

Conclusion

It may be concluded from the following that the

cooperative movement, which was launched to solve the problems of weaker sections of society. In our opinion there is a greater necessity of evaluating, whether this motto has been achieved or not. The cooperative credit societies have got some success the distribution of term loans, but these credit societies are unable to fulfill the growing demand of small and marginal farmers due to it adverse growing policy. It has been noticed that the cooperative movement has been misguided with its target hunting g programmers no doubt cooperative movement has covered many of the areas and different sections of people, but the statistical data does not reveal the real state of affair and closes scrutiny would show that the position is not satisfactory at our expectation in many part of the state this is evident the fact that in case of non-agricultural, non-credit societies are defunct and to have confined themselves to the government statistics, that type of societies are organized by wasted interested lack of service motive , lack of sacrificing, lack of loyalty , lack of awareness, illiteracy and corruption are the common feature of the Indian cooperative movement. There has been wide spread erosion in the values of cooperative and which leads to the growth of chine effects. Thus pulling the members away from their appreciation of their own cooperatives, participation of member in the affairs of their cooperatives has been not mush enhancement of participation is based on the awareness and education of members about role and objectives of the cooperatives.

References

Agarwal,R.D.,(1977), Cooperative management, principles policies and Practice, (Pune,VMNICM)

Ansari,A.A (1990), Cooperative management patterns, Anmal publications, New Delhi.

Baken, Hendry,H., and Marvin schars, .(1937), the economics of cooperative marketing , Newyork: Mc Graw Hill

Bedi, R., theory, histrtoy and practice, International publishing house Meerut.

Benerjee, J., (1961) Cooperative movement in India Navjeevan printing works Pvt., Ltd., Culcutta.

Bhagavathi prasad, Mohan Mishra and Sanjay Kumar varma (2008), "Power of Cooperative Networking", The Cooperator, January, Vol.45, No7, Published by National CooperativeUnion of India, Delhi.

Bhat Ramachandra and Rao, Aruna (1982) , "The Evaluation and Growth of Primary Agricultural Credit Societies in Karnataka", Indian Cooperative Review. Vol. 19(3):251-263.

Chowbey, B.N., "Principles and Practice of Cooperative Banking in India, Asian Publishing House, New Delhi, 1968.

Chamola, S.D. and Ramesh Hasita, (1980), "Trend Analysis of Primary Agricultural Credit Societies in India", Indian Cooperative Review, Vol. 17:310-316.

Chattopadhtay, B.C., (1985), Rural development planning in India, S. Chand and Co., Delhi.

Daratri, S.D., (1968), Role of cooperative e credit in agriculture Development, Orient Longman, Madras.

Desai, R.G., (1968), Farmers societies and agricultural development: Chugh publications: Allahabad.

Hajela, T.N., Principles Problem And Practice Of Cooperation, Agarwal And Indian Cooperative Review, Vol.13 (3):241-249.

8

Social Security Schemes and Socio-Economic Development of Depressed Classes – A Study in Karnataka

Umesha, C.

INTRODUCTION

Social security measures help a man to face the contingencies. When such contingencies arise, it is difficult for him/her either to work or get work and support himself/herself and the family. Social security thus provides a self-balancing social insurance or assistance from public funds, or a proper combination of both. Due to the physical incapacity to work during any contingency, any effective scheme of social protection must take care of workers income and medical care. Social security in some countries is applied to all governmental programmes planned to maintain income; in other countries, it mainly applies to social insurance programmes; in some others, it covers a variety of health and welfare services. Thus, the coverage of social security is dynamic. Though social security programmes vary from country to country, their three major characteristics are: they are established by law; they provide some form of cash payment to individuals to replace at least a part of the lost income that occurs due to such contingencies as unemployment, maternity, work injury, invalidism, sickness, old age and death; the benefits or services are provided in three major ways: social insurance, social assistance or public services.

Karnataka is predominantly rural and agrarian. About 66% of the population live in rural areas. Nearly 71% of its working force is engaged in agriculture and allied activities that generate 49% of the state's income. Over 70% of the cultivable area in Karnataka are based on rain-fed farming. The annual rainfall in the state varies roughly from 50 to 350 cm.

Karnataka is one of the states with the most disparity between urban and rural areas. Some of the reasons offered for Karnataka's rural poverty are most notably, poor land and irrigation quality, non-diversified rural economy and the vast rural-urban gap in terms of social services such as education and health. The state has attempted eradication of poverty via several poverty alleviation schemes. The latest intervention in eradicating poverty is via SSIs. These women groups are encouraged to save money. The government steps in with revolving fund as well as bank credit. This method is found to be the most effective in delivering rural credit as well as eradicating poverty.

Poverty in Karnataka

Karnataka's performance in reducing poverty on the income dimension during the 1990s compares favorably with all - India performance (Economic Survey 2001-02 : P. 139) Between 1973-74 and 1990-2000, the percentage of population below the poverty line declined from 54.47 to 20.04 in Karnataka against a decline from 54.88 to 26.10 percent at the national level. In rural Karnataka, the decline is form 55.14 to 17.38 and in urban areas from 52.53 to 23.62 per percentage. Poverty reduction seems to be more pronounced in rural areas despite the fact that income per workers in the primary sector has been Lowest in 1980-81 and 1990-91 and growth rate negligible compared to growth in the Secondary and Tertiary Sectors. This could be due to increase in employment opportunities (including those for marginal workers), through labours productivity has remained low. With increase in the number of marginal workers, some increase in family income has also been realized. (Table - 1).

Table - 1

Poverty Ratio in Karnataka: Below the Poverty Line in Percentage.

Year	*Rural*	*Urban*	*Total*
1973-74			
Karnataka	55.14	52.53	54.47
India	56.44	49.01	54.88
1977-78			
Karnataka	48.18	50.36	48.78
India	53.07	45.24	51.32
1983-84			
Karnataka	36.33	42.82	38.24
India	45.65	40.79	44.48
1987-88			
Karnataka	32.82	48.42	37.53
India	39.09	38.20	38.86
1993-94			
Karnataka	29.88	40.14	33.16
India	37.27	32.36	35.97
1999-2000			
Karnataka	17.38	25.25	20.04
India	27.09	23.62	26.10

Source: (a) Government of India: (b) Human Development in Karnataka 1999 PP: 90

Poverty & Levels of Living : Socio - Economic Groups

The previous Economic Survey Reports have highlighted the state's achievements in poverty reduction relative to the average all - Indian performance. From the perspective of policy choice, implementation and monitoring, it is important to know economic profile of the population by different occupational and social categories, their relative importance and their differential participation in the growth process. One such profile could be measures of levels of livings as given by monthly per capita consumer expenditure, incidence of poverty and relative inequality in levels of living. Relative importance of each occupational / social group for policy choice could be assessed with reference to its relative size, that is, its percentage share in total population.

In the State of Karnataka for the welfare of the people who are destitute, handicapped and the elderly have no support, hence several social security programmes are being implemented time to time. For the welfare of the handicapped, the financial assistance provided has been enhanced to Rs. 100/- per month from January 1998. In 2001-02 Rs. 36.87 crores were distributed to 3.19 lakhs beneficiaries and gradually it has been increased to 4.01 lakh beneficiaries during 2007-08. The details of the scheme is presented in the Table -2.

Table- 2
Progress of Financial Assistance to Physically Handicapped

Year	*Year Expenditure (Rs.Lakhs)*	*Beneficiaries (000's)*
1980-81	200	50
1990-91	1425	242
1991-92	1490	266
1992-93	1212	276
1993-94	1531	280
1994-95	1913	289
1995-96	2614	300
1996-97	2421	304
1997-98	2431	311

Year	*Year Expenditure (Rs.Lakhs)*	*Beneficiaries (000's)*
1998-99	3486	318
2001-02	3687	319
2002-03	3938	301
2003-04	4049	314
2004-05	4716	318
2005-06	5481	345
2006-07	5790	352
2007-08	6619	373
2008-09	6970	401

Source: Director of Treasuries, Govt. of Karnataka.

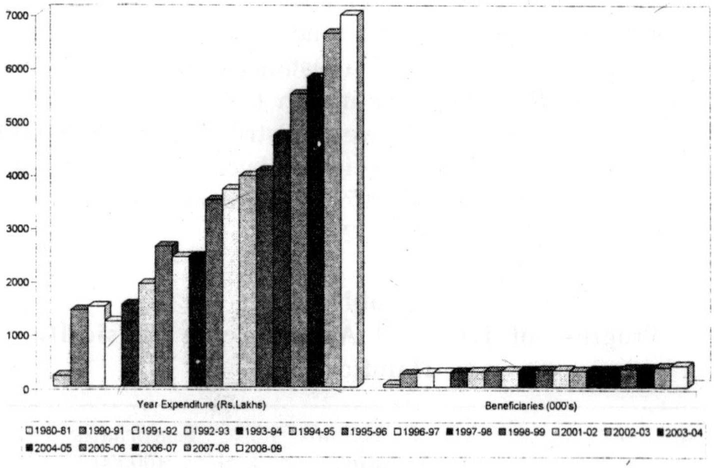

A scheme of providing old age pension to elderly persons of over 65 years age without any means of support has been enhanced to Rs.100/- per month from January 1998. In 2002-03 old age pension was paid to 4.20 lakh elderly persons. In 2003-04 Rs.25.68 crores were distributed to 4.36 lakh persons upto the end of September, 2004. During 2008-09 nearly 5.33 lakh were benefited. The details of old age pension scheme in Karnataka is resented in the Table 3.

Table - 3
Old Age Pension Scheme in Karnataka Since 1980-81 to 2006-07

Year	*Expenditure (Rs.Lakhs)*	*Beneficiaries (000's)*
1980-81	125	312
1990-91	3047	507
1991-92	3617	552
1992-93	3637	509
1993-94	3530	503
1994-95	3503	496
1995-96	3979	496
1996-97	3753	492
1997-98	3635	493
1998-99	4946	491
2001-02	4666	487
2002-03	4830	420
2003-04	5154	436
2004-05	5657	437
2005-06	5517	458
2006-07	6070	469
2007-08	6570	495
2008-09	8185	533

Source: Director Treasuries, Govt. of Karnataka.

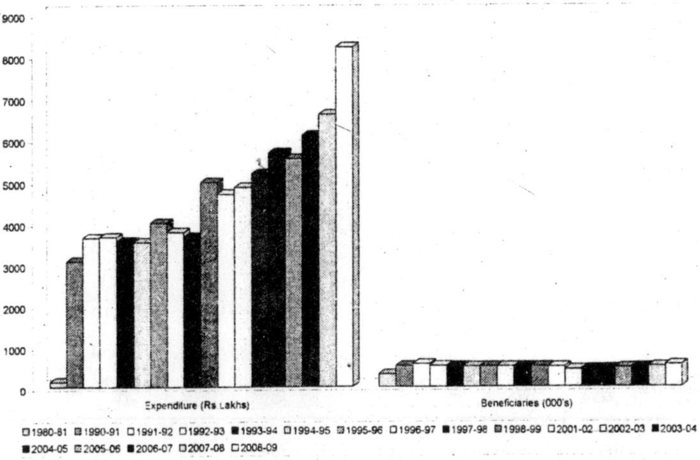

The Table clearly shows that expenditure towards old age has been gradually increased since 1980-81 to 2008-09, whereas the beneficiaries have not been benefited. This might be due to lack of awareness regarding the benefits of the schemes.

A programme of providing financial assistance to destitute widows is being implemented since 1984. The financial assistance provided has been enhanced to Rs. 100/- per month from January, 1998. In 2000-01 Rs. 64.48 crores were distributed to 5.31 lakh beneficiaries. In 2001-02, crores were distributed to 5.62 lakh beneficiaries, then it has been increased to 6.76 beneficiaries in 2007-08. The details may be had from the following table.

Table - 4
Destitute Widows Scheme of Karnataka

Year	Expenditure (Rs.Lakhs)	Beneficiaries (000's)
1990-91	2366	427
1991-92	2300	469
1992-93	2631	482
1993-94	2336	485
1994-95	2237	495
1995-96	4181	508
1996-97	4040	523
1997-98	4190	528
1998-99	5876	546
2001-02	6085	545
2002-03	6448	531
2003-04	6856	567
2004-05	6747	578
2005-06	7688	604
2006-07	8365	613
2007-08	8237	634
2008-09	5961	676

Source: Director Treasuries, Govt. of Karnataka.

Destitute Widows have benefited much from the scheme implemented by the Govt. of Karnataka. Year by year expenditure as well as number of beneficiaries have been increased i.e., during 1991-92 Government had provided Rs. 2300 lakhs then it has been increased to Rs. 6085 lakhs during 2001-02. During 2008-09 it was Rs.5961 lakhs.

Distribution of Sarees and Dhoties

A scheme for providing sarees and dhotis at subsidized rates to green card holders is being implemented since October 2nd 1985. The beneficiaries covered under the programme are landless agricultural labourers, village artisans, small and marginal farmers, beneficiaries of old age and widow pensioners and plantation workers. The programme is also extended to families who are living in slums. In 2001-02, Rs. 5.41 crores have been spent and 24 lakh beneficiaries covered. An amount of Rs. 12.5 crores has been allocated for 2001-02 to cover 24 lakh beneficiaries. As at the end of October 2007, 0.7 lakh beneficiaries have been covered and expenditure it has been increased to 450 thousand (Table - 5).

Table - 5
Progress Under the Scheme of Distribution of Subsidized Sarees And Dhotis

Year	*Expenditure (Rs.Lakhs)*	*Beneficiaries (000's)*
1990-91	406	37
1991-92	680	31
1992-93	428	28
1993-94	422	21
1994-95	1002	30
1995-96	1425	32
1996-97	1738	36
1997-98	959	30

Year	*Expenditure (Rs.Lakhs)*	*Beneficiaries (000's)*
1998-99	728	13
2001-02	1263	24
2002-03	541	11
2003-04	1250	20
2004-05	255	6
2005-06	300	4
2006-07	341	5
2007-08	300	5
2008-09	450	7

Source: 1. Karnataka Handloom Development Corporation.
2. Department of Women & Child Development , Bangalore.

Maternity Allowance Scheme

Under the National Maternity Benefit Scheme, a lumpsum amount of Rs.500 is payable in the duration 2-8 week before delivery for the first and second child for three months covering pre natal and postal period from August, 1998. In 199899, Rs.1.56 crores were spent during which about 45 thousand beneficiaries were covered. In 1999-2000, Rs.3.10 crores have been spent covering 61,948 persons. In 2000-01 approximately Rs.3.10 crores were spent covering 62,000 beneficiaries. After 2001 maternity allowances have been changed gradually year after year up to 2008-09 the data has been given in table. Year wise expenditure and the beneficiaries covered are given in Table - 6.

Table - 6
Progress Under the Scheme of Maternity Allowance

Year	*Expenditure (Rs.Lakhs)*	*Beneficiaries (000's)*
1990-91	246	82
1991-92	232	77

Year	*Expenditure (Rs.Lakhs)*	*Beneficiaries (000's)*
1992-93	242	81
1993-94	232	77
1994-95	227	76
1995-96	214	70
1996-97	210	72
1997-98	275	80
1998-99	156	45
2001-02	310	62
2002-03	358	72
2003-04	323	64
2004-05	204	40
2005-06	175	34
2006-07	226	40
2007-08	275	55
2008-09	295	68

Source: Department of Women & Child Development , Bangalore.

Welfare of the Scheduled Castes and Scheduled Tribes in Karnataka

Various schemes for improving the socio-economic conditions of Scheduled castes and Scheduled tribes are being implemented. Important ones are;

A. Welfare of Scheduled Castes .

For the well fare of the scheduled castes community the Karnataka State Government has implemented many developmental programmes in recent past. Among them some of the important welfare measures as a social security measure are in the following way;

- Financial assistance of Rs.8,000 and Rs.10,000 is being provided to scheduled caste students pursuing M.Phil and Ph.D courses respectively.

- Rs.5000 incentive money is being paid to those SC students who secure within the first three ranks in graduation and post-graduation levels during the academic year.
- One time assistance of Rs.50,000 is being sanctioned to students studying in IIM/IISC/IIT.
- Financial assistance to the SC students who take up higher studies in foreign universities to a maximum of Rs.10.00 lakhs for entire course with an annual assistance of Rs.3.50 lakhs.
- An amount of Rs.20.86 lakhs have been spent for all the above programmes covering 36 candidates in the state of Karnataka.
- Under Navachetana Scheme certain reputed institutions/private organizations are imparting training to scheduled caste educated unemployed youth in different trades and in computer to enable them get employment or be self-employed. During 2006-07 Rs.28.48 lakhs have been spent on 306 students as against a provision of Rs.84.25 lakhs to train 2070 SC students.
- Prize money is being awarded to encourage the SC students who secure first class in first attempt in public examination. During 2006-07 Rs.52.25 lakhs have been spent on 5792 students as against a provision of Rs.74.89 lakhs to cover 7625 SC students.
- 164 women welfare centres are running in 27 districts. Children in these centres are being provided with mid-day meals. During 2006-07 Rs.338.02 lakhs have been spent as against a provision of Rs.484.12 lakhs to cover 6366 SC boys and girls.
- Distribution of free houses to the scheduled caste families is being implemented in the State under SCP. The scheme is implemented by the Rajiv Gandhi Housing Corporation to construct houses for SC families living below poverty line. Rs. 40

crores has been proposed to construct 20000 Ambedkar houses during 2006-07. Rs.20.00 crores has been spent during 2006-07 to cover 10,000 beneficiaries.

- Scheduled caste widows and unmarried women are trained in various crafts through 57 centres in the State. During 2006-07 Rs.36.25 lakhs have been spent as against a provision of Rs.51.41 lakhs to train 1180 women.

B. Welfare of Scheduled Tribes

For the welfare of the STs also government of Karnataka has been implemented many welfare measures time to time. Among them some of the important welfare measures are in the following manner.

- Financial assistance of Rs.200 per parent is being provided to encourage the parents of the children belonging to the Primitive Tribal Groups to send their children to the pre-matric schools.
- Free houses to the scheduled tribes families are being distributed in the state. During 2008-09 Rs.500.00 lakhs have been released to Rajiv Gandhi Housing Corporation for this purpose.
- Under Navachethana Scheme, certain reputed institutions/private organizations including information technology are imparting training to scheduled tribe educated unemployed persons in different trades. During 2008-09 Rs.11.74 lakhs has been spent covering 485 beneficiaries.
- The most important criticism of the social security measure undertaken by the government is their totally insufficient coverage. A Majority of the people continue to remain outside the ambit of social assistance and social insurance schemes.
- India does not have an integrated scheme of social security. On account of this reason, there is considerable overlapping of schemes and similar benefits are being disbursed under various schemes.

This results in wastage of effort and money. The social security schemes are woefully inadequate in relation to the demand for them by the beneficiaries.

- In consonance with the commitment to faster social sector development under the National Common Minimum Programme (NCMP), the Central Government has launched new initiatives for social sector development during 2007-08. Substantial progress was also made on the major initiatives launched in earlier years.
- Under a new scheme called "Aam Admi Bima Yojana" (AABY), launched on October 2, 2007, insurance to the head of the family of rural landless households in the country has provided against natural death as well as accidental death and partial/permanent disability. This cover is Rs.75,000 on death due to accident and permanent disability due to accident, Rs.37,500 in case of partial permanent disability due to accident and Rs.30,000 in case of death of a member, prior to terminal date.
- In the State of Karnataka for the welfare of the people who are destitute, handicapped and the elderly have no support, hence several social security programmes are being implemented time to time. For the welfare of the handicapped, the financial assistance provided has been enhanced to Rs. 100/- per month from January 1998. In 2001-02 Rs. 19.61 crores were distributed to 3.06 lakhs beneficiaries and gradually it has been increased to 4.01 lakh beneficiaries during 2008-09.

Policy Implications

In the light of our findings and observations some suggestions are made about effective functioning of social security schemes in the development of the weaker sections. The suggestions are listed as follows:

1. The review of the social security schemes in India suggests that there is a need to widen their coverage so that a majority of the people who continue to be outside their ambit are brought within it. There is a need to bring a qualitative improvement in the security provided, introduce unemployment insurance and bring about are integration among the various social security schemes.
2. The various social security schemes are in operation in India to provide adequate cover to the workers against contingencies but these are not said to be adequate. Much more schemes required in this direction by the central and state governments.
3. The employers should come forward and contribute liberally to social security schemes introduced by the governments.
4. Whatever schemes introduced by the governments are only for workers of organized sectors. There is no such scheme for workers in unorganized sector.
5. There are many pitfalls in our social security measures such as no proper administrative machinery to carry out the schemes. There is hardly any coordination in the planning and the legislation". The Government should provide reasonable protection to weaker sections from all ills.

Conclusion

Social security is now generally understood as protection provided by the society to its members through a series of public measures against the economic and social distress otherwise caused by the stoppage or substantial reduction of earnings due to sickness, maternity, injury, occupational disease, unemployment, invalidity, old age death etc. There are several social security programmes implemented by the Central Government for the destitute, disabled and the elderly.

References

Agarwar D.R. (1998), Labour Problems, Social Welfare and Security, Forward Book Depot Delhi.

Amartya Sen (1991) Social Security in Developing Countries, Clarendon Press, Oxford.

Badagaiyan, S.D. (1986) "Class and Ethnicity: Chhotanagpur in the 19th Century", in K.L. Sharma (ed) Social Stratification in India, Manohar Publications, Delhi.

Banerjee, Biswajit and J.B. Knight (1991), "Caste Discrimination in India Urban Labour Market", Journal of Developing Economics, Vol. 7, pp. 277-307.

Bergmann,B.R.(1974) "Occupational Segregation, Wages and Profits when employers discriminate a by race or sex", Eastern Economic Journal, Vol.1 No.2, pp.103-110.

Beteille, Andre (1974), Six Essays in Comparative Sociology, Oxford University Press, Delhi.

Bhatia, Mukhmeet (2000), "Chotanagpur Tenancy Act: Pluging the Loopholes", Bulletin of Bihar Tribal Welfare Research Institute, January 2000.

Bina Agarwal (1990) Social Security and the Family: Coping with Seasonality and Calamity in Rural India. Clarendon Press, Oxford.

9

Commercial Banking in the Development of Mysore District Economy - With Special Reference to Small Scale Industries

Venkatesha, J.N.

INTRODUCTION

Banks play a very important role in our economy. Many economists and progressive bankers have stressed the importance from time to time. Today, Indian banking system has evolved into a powerful instrument for planning economic growth. The success of economic development depends mainly on the extent of mobilization of the resources and their investment with operational efficiency. Indian banking system, after nationalization, has brought about a speedy transformation of the entire economic structure. Very few attempts have been made to examine the entire range of its working in a changing socio-political environment. At this stage of growth-oriented changes, it is essential to make a fresh appraisal of the Indian banking system. The concept of Indian Banking System has changed and a perspective analysis of needs and deeds in the background of planned economic development has been made in this study.

Social welfare is the prime consideration of any country and therefore, social considerations call for the expansion of banking sector and liberalization of the credit policy. Money or finance is a necessary input for any developmental activity. Banks were the vast reservoirs of funds and they are endowed with inherent capability of generating credit many times. The economy of any country or any state or a region of a state within the country needs a lot of financial capital for its development. The sate with backwardness needs more funds than is ordinarily required.

Commercial banks in India were urban-biased, profit-oriented and generally not responsive to the requirements of the community. The branch network had a strong urban bias with consequent inadequate coverage in all the rural areas consists of the banks had increased but bulk of the increase was accounted for by the urban branches. At the same time the bank lending were urban-oriented and concerned mostly with organized industry and trade. Hence, the result was that the other sectors of the economy depended up on non-institutional agencies for their requirements of finance. The banking facilities were also beyond the reach of the unorganized and allied sectors of the economy and also of the vast number of economically weaker sections of the society. All this resulted in lopsided development of the banking system.

But the late sixties witnessed a sea change in Indian banking since commercial banks were expected to commit themselves to the development of the country and not to function as business concerns only. Earlier the banks were not much interested in the task of economic development, particularly of the rural branches were used as agencies for collecting funds for investment in the industrial sector in the urban centers. The agricultural sector had been remained neglected and the banks did not owe any social commitments. 76 percent of the population of the country was classified as rural and 50 percent of it was living below the poverty line.

After the historic nationalization of the commercial banks, the performance of the Indian commercial banks up to 1975 in respect of branch expansion, deposit mobilization inter-alia, had been hailed as unprecedented and without parallel. However, there was a widespread apprehension that the dispersal of banks to the rural areas according to the norms of branch expansion was not achieved. The mobilized deposits from rural branches were not achieved. The mobilized deposits from rural bank branches were not utilized for the upliftment of the rural economy. In other words, it was alleged that rural bank branches had been utilized as conduits to direct the rural deposits into urban/metropolitan region.

Objectives of the study

The specific objectives of the present study are the following:

2. To evaluate the performance of commercial banks in the development of Mysore district economy and how commercial banks have played a significant role in providing assistance to the development of small scale industries in the district.
3. To offer suggestions for the further improvement of the role of commercial banks in the development of district economy.

Methodology of Data Collection

A planned approach has been employed for data collection so that the facts that are near to reality and free from aberrations are elicited for impact evaluation. The sources of secondary data for the study are; existing literature and data in websites, various publications of Central, state especially State Level Bankers Committee, Bangalore and Institutional Finance Department and other sources like books, magazines, newspapers, reports, articles, seminar papers published by universities and research institutions.

Results and Discussion

Mysore is the second largest industrial district of the state of Karnataka. State Bank of Mysore, having the largest number of branches in the district is the lead bank of this district. The bank also its zonal office in Mysore city guiding all its branches in Mysore and in the contiguous eight districts. Further, a specialized Small-Scale Industry branch (SSI Branch- first of its kind in the bank) was also opened in Mysore city in the year 1993, to improve the bank's coverage of industries in this area. The details of bank branches, total deposits, total advances and credit deposit ratio has been depicted in the table- 1.

Table - 1
Banks details in Mysore District

Sl. No	*Taluk*	*Commercial Banks*	*Grameena Banks*	*Total Deposits (Rs.in lakhs)*	*Total Advances (Rs.in lakhs)*	*Credit Deposit Ratio*
01	H.D.Kote	03	12	5697	6558	115.11
02	Hunsur	11	07	15169	11802	77.80
03	K.R.Nagar	08	10	10829	9115	84.17
04	Mysore	142	22	412231	296465	81.45
05	Nanjangud	13	11	14717	19211	130.54
06	Periyapatna	09	07	13642	16186	118.65
07	T.Narasipura	10	09	9756	9220	94.51
	Total	196	78	482041	368557	76.46

Source: Lead Bank Office, Mysore.

The government is indicating to promote Mysore

district as the alternate industrial hub to Bangalore and their Department of Industries and Commerce has already recommended acquisition of additional land of around 3,900 acres for industrial purposes in the district. Accordingly, the targeted outlay of funds under the credit plan for every year is around Rs.34.03 crores. In spite of all these efforts, the industrial growth in the district has been sluggish. Further, the growth of industrial advances of the bank, in this region has not been proportionate even to the level of industrial development.

In this background, it was felt that a study to review the position of banks in lending to SSIs in Mysore district is absolutely necessary. Hereunto, an attempt is made to ascertain the bank market share in lending to SSIs. This study further tries to analyze the strengths and weaknesses of the banks in this area. As a corollary to this, an attempt has also been made to understand the industrialization plans of the district and to arrive at the causes for many of the existing units becoming sick. It presumed that this study would help the operating functionaries in drawing the required data to formulate strategies in improving the bank market share.

The scope for the growth of industries in this district and the causes for its sluggish growth, till now, were discussed with the Joint Director for industries and Commerce, the Assistant General Manager, KSFC and the President of Hebbal Industrial Estate, Mysore. With this as the base, bank's position was reviewed with the data made available by Lead Bank department. In this process, some inferences regarding the strengths and weaknesses of the banks have been drawn and a few suggestions have been made to improve the position in this important area of operation.

Table - 2
The Industrial Scenario of Mysore District/ Mysore City Vis-a-vis Banks Status

Particulars	*Mysore District*	*Mysore City*
No. of industrial estates	07	03
No. of industrial sheds	544	460
Total no. of industrial units	20710 (Including 123 medium & large scale industries)	-

These figures indicate that the large and medium scale industries in Mysore district are very few.

Table- 3
Number of units under different types of industries in the SSI sector in Mysore district

Sl.No	*Types of industries*	*Number*
01	Food & Beverages	3796
02	Textiles	4034
03	Forest	2894
04	Paper	568
05	Rubber & Plastic	355
06	Chemicals	1159
07	Leather	613
08	Glass & Ceramics	633
09	Gen. Eng	2266
10	Electrical & Electronics	450
11	Coir	202
12	Repairs & Service	460
	Total	20587

Source: DIC, Mysore.

Figure-1
Types of Industries

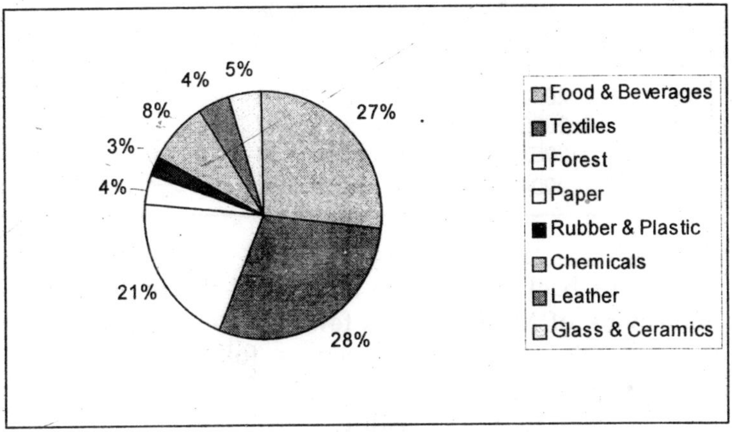

This indicates that textiles, food and beverages, forest and general engineering industries are more predominant in Mysore district in the same order of merit. The total investment in the SSI sector in the district is approximately about Rs.22,295 lakhs and it employees about 1,04,120 skilled, semi-skilled and unskilled laborers.

The total outlay of funds for the growth and development of the SSI sector as per the district credit plans for the last five years and the achievement thereof is stated in the table, except in the year 1995-96, the achievement of the district as a whole under the SSI sector has exceeded the targeted figures.

Table- 4
Target and achievement of SSI sector in the district (Rs.in crores)

Sl. No	*Year*	*Target*	*Achievement*
01	1995-96	32.72	22.62
02	1996-97	32.85	46.45

Sl. No	*Year*	*Target*	*Achievement*
03	1997-98	37.65	42.35
04	1998-99	27.08	17.58
05	1999-00	25.92	16.31
06	2000-01	26.51	16.79
07	2001-02	26.59	17.21
08	2002-03	28.87	18.09
09	2003-04	29.54	19.26
10	2004-05	30.42	20.57

In this background, the target and the performance of State Bank of Mysore and a few other major public sector banks in the district has been as follows:

Table - 5
STATE BANK OF MYSORE
(Rs. In Crores)

Sl.No	*Year*	*Target*	*Achievement*
01	1995-96	10.35	7.02
02	1996-97	12.62	16.59
03	1997-98	14.60	12.32
04	1998-99	9.72	4.46
05	1999-00	5.73	3.58
06	2000-01	6.78	4.05
07	2001-02	7.56	5.21
08	2002-03	8.01	6.58
09	2003-04	8.57	6.89
10	2004-05	9.98	7.24

State Bank of Mysore has 47 branches in Mysore district and 28 branches in Mysore city, which also includes a specialized SSI branch. However, the bank has not achieved the target in so far as financing SSIs is concerned except during the year 1996-97. The bank is also loosing its market share in this crucial credit area. The market share, which had risen to 36% during 1996-97, has dropped down to 26% by March 1998. This has been further reduced to 22%

while accepting the target for the year 1999-2000. Though during 1998-99, SBM market share went up by 1% point, for Canara Bank, SBI and Vijaya Bank there has been a steep dip.

The performance of SSI intensive branches in Mysore city, which includes Mysore main, Market branch, Metagalli, Visveswaranagar, VV.Market, Yadavagiri etc., also has not been encouraging. The exposure to SSI sector by these branches was at Rs.26.06 crores as on 31-12-97 has gone up by a meager Rs.1.19 crores taking exposure to Rs.27.25 crores as on 1998.

Further, it is surprising to note that the bank's budgetary allocation for advances under the SSI sector in Mysore district for the year 1998-99 is only Rs.3.50 crores as against a targeted growth of Rs.9.72 crores as accepted under the district credit plan. This mismatch, though it is learnt happens in all the yeas, needs to be corrected at the Lead Bank Department, Zonal office and with the DIC who prepares this estimates in so much so all the other major players have achieved their targets by playing their figures low. The specialized SSI branch has an outlay of Rs.5.40 crores to the SSI sector.

Table- 6
CANARA BANK- Target and Achievement
(Rs.in crores)

Sl. No	*Year*	*Target*	*Achievement*
01	1995-96	1.11	3.13
02	1996-97	1.77	1.96
03	1997-98	1.16	3.67
04	1998-99	1.09	1.66
05	1999-00	1.56	1.61
06	2000-01	1.35	1.40
07	2001-02	1.49	1.52
08	2002-03	1.65	1.72
09	2003-04	1.78	1.83
10	2004-05	1.80	1.93

Table- 7
SYNDICATE BANK - Target and Achievement
(Rs.in Crores)

Sl. No	Year	Target	Achievement
01	1995-96	0.41	1.09
02	1996-97	0.51	0.62
03	1997-98	0.74	0.79
04	1998-99	0.68	1.96
05	1999-00	0.71	1.02
06	2000-01	0.79	1.23
07	2001-02	0.81	1.35
08	2002-03	0.92	1.58
09	2003-04	0.89	1.29
10	2004-05	0.95	1.51

These two banks viz., Canara Bank and Syndicate Bank, which have 19 and 19 branches respectively, in the district, have exceeded the targeted figures in all the years. However, it can be seen that the targeted growth itself has been too less for these banks. It is surprising to note that Canara Bank, which has 19 branches including a special SSI branch, has never set a target beyond Rs.2 crores.

Table- 8
STATE BANK OF INDIA - Target and Achievement
(Rs.in crores)

Sl. No	Year	Target	Achievement
01	1995-96	0.74	0.34
02	1996-97	1.24	0.10
03	1997-98	1.22	0.72
04	1998-99	1.15	0.41
05	1999-00	1.29	0.52
06	2000-01	1.35	0.65
07	2001-02	1.42	0.70
08	2002-03	1.50	0.72
09	2003-04	1.52	0.80
10	2004-05	1.60	0.86

Table- 9
VIJAYA BANK - Target and Achievement
(Rs.in crores)

Sl. No	*Year*	*Target*	*Achievement*
01	1995-96	0.90	0.42
02	1996-97	1.86	0.69
03	1997-98	0.66	1.65
04	1998-99	0.80	0.21
05	1999-00	0.95	0.35
06	2000-01	1.00	0.75
07	2001-02	1.21	0.86
08	2002-03	1.25	1.00
09	2003-04	1.29	0.98
10	2004-05	1.32	1.02

State Bank of India and Vijaya Bank which have about 9 and 16 branches respectively, have shown very poor growth under the SSI sector. It is worth mentioning here, that SBI has a specialized SSI branch in Mysore city. Further, the target set for these banks under the SSI sector has been far less when compared to that of State Bank of Mysore.

Table- 10
Comparative figures of the major banks in the district with regard to financing the SSI sector

Year	*SBM*	*CANARA*	*SYNDICATE*	*SBI*	*VIJAYA*
1995-95	67	281	263	46	46
1995-96	131	111	121	8	79
1996-97	84	316	105	59	251
1997-98	55	152	287	4	26
1998-99	61	148	299	8	15
1999-00	60	145	198	10	19
2000-01	52	123	158	12	27
2001-02	65	198	201	41	165

Year	*SBM*	*CANARA*	*SYNDICATE*	*SBI*	*VIJAYA*
2002-03	71	158	256	58	195
2003-04	98	165	178	62	187
2004-05	58	102	196	75	190
% Market share under advances					
1995-96	15	18	3	18	4
2004-05	17	13	5	19	5
% Market share under SSI advances					
1995-96	26	10.5	7	2.2	6
2004-05	27	10	12	2.5	1.25

The data furnished above in respect of the district as a whole and the performance of SBM vis-à-vis the other major banks of the district with regard to SSI sector implies:

Though the growth of the SSI sector in Mysore district has been sluggish the district has been achieving the targeted levels in so far as the credit exposure is concerned. The sluggish could be for various reasons as stated below:

(1) Lack of entrepreneurial and professional skills. It appears that many of the entrepreneurs prefer to venture at nearby Bangalore on account of the options and opportunities available there.

(2) Non-existence of large-scale industries in good number to absorb the produce of these SSIs.

(3) High cost of transportation making these SSIs in competent in as far as the price is concerned.

(4) Historic sickness in the industries in the area causing a psychological impact on the upcoming units. The closure of established companies like M/S Java India Ltd., M/S Mahindra and Mahindra, M/S Aravinda Parimala works etc., has had a direct bearing on the new units and the existing dependent units.

(5) General recession in the industrial sector and especially in the automobile industry. A large number of SSIs in Mysore City are in the line of producing parts/ spares for the automobile industries.

(6) The industrial development in Mysore district is fairly recent and as such most of the entrepreneurs are of the first generation facing problems under technology, finance and expertise.

The district has more number of SSIs under the unorganized sector. Food processing and textile industries are the predominant units in the district. Food processing technology though available locally through CFTRI and DFRL, it appears is not tapped by the SSIs for gaining a competitive edge over the large units. Textile units, though large in number, mainly comprise of very small and economically unviable silk reeling, twisting and weaving units. As such the growth of the industry has been slow.

The performance of SBM has been poor when compared to the targets set. Except during the year 1996-97, SBM not achieved the targeted annual growth under the SSI sector. Despite SBM being the lead bank of the district having the largest branch network, it is surprising to note that SBM slowly loosing the market share in as far as SBM branches advances are concerned and especially so in the SSI sector. However there seems to be an upward swing again during the year 1998-99. The reasons for this negative trend could be broadly as stated under:

Major Findings of the Study

Based on the analysis and discussion in the study of commercial banking development in the Mysore District economy, the following findings have been drawn:

1. Lack of entrepreneurial and professional skills. It

appears that many of the entrepreneurs prefer to venture at nearby Bangalore on account of the options and opportunities available there.

2. Non-existence of large-scale industries in good number to absorb the produce of these SSIs.
3. High cost of transportation making these SSIs in competent in as far as the price is concerned.
4. Historic sickness in the industries in the area causing a psychological impact on the upcoming units. The closure of established companies like M/S Java India Ltd., M/S Mahindra and Mahindra, M/S Aravinda Parimala works etc., has had a direct bearing on the new units and the existing dependent units.
5. General recession in the industrial sector and especially in the automobile industry. A large number of SSIs in Mysore City are in the line of producing parts/ spares for the automobile industries.
6. The industrial development in Mysore district is fairly recent and as such most of the entrepreneurs are of the first generation facing problems under technology, finance and expertise.

Policy Implications

In the light of our findings and observations some suggestions are made about effective functioning of commercial banks in the development of the district economy. The suggestions are listed as follows:

1. To reduce the time gap between the supply of credit and demand for credit, the credit should be given within short period. Apart from this, there is an urgent need to streamline the procedures at branch-level and bank-level for the quick disposal of the loan applications.
2. It is important to note that most of the beneficiaries

are illiterate. Hence, the beneficiaries need to be educated about the formalities to be fulfilled in obtaining the necessary finance. The bank staff should help of the uneducated industrialists in getting their credit sanctioned from the banks. If the beneficiaries are educated they can get loans easily from the banks.

3. To reduce the problem of overdues, banks should announce certain incentives in the form of cash discounts etc. The farmers who have cleared the loan may be given rebate on interest and priority in giving loans by the bank. This would result in decreasing the number of defaulters in future.
4. Younger industrialists should be given preference in industrial sector as they have shown better results than the old industrialists. It is perhaps the young industrialists who can run industry on scientific lines. The industrialists who own personal assets of relatively high value have shown more incremental income. Literacy level of the beneficiaries has been found to be positively correlated with incremental income, which brings out those literate industrialists can make more efficient use of bank credit.

References

Kusumakara Hebbar., (1988) "IRDP and Commercial Banks", MysoreEconomic Review, Vol.73, No.10, pp.15-19.

Nand Pandey., (1989) Commercial Banks and Rural Development, Deep and Deep Publications, New Delhi.

Deshpande.V.D., (1989) Reaching the Poor (A work of a voluntary organisation- Shranijivi Janata Sehyak Mandal, Koynanagar, District-Satara, Maharashtra); Sponsored by the Ford Foundation, and coordinated by National Institute of Bank Management, Pune (Mimeo).

State Bank of Patiala (1989) Rural Lending- A Study in Patiala District; vol.II; Head Office, The Mall, Patiala (Mimeo).

Singh Pasricha., (1991) Bank Finance and Rural Development in Punjab : A Case Study of Lead Bank Scheme; Ph.D. thesis ; Department of Business Management; Punjabi University, Patiala.

Kashalikar,U.M.,(1986) "Problems of overdue in the Nationalised Banks: A Case Study", Journal of Shivaji University, Vol.24.

Upadhaya and Kaveri., (1982) " impact of Bank Finance on the Decentralised Sector", Commerce, Vol.145.

10

Socio-Economic Empowerment of Women through NGO Based Micro-Finance –A Case Study in Mandya District

Raghava, D.H.

INTRODUCTION

Micro finance programmes are expected to make a significant contribution to poverty alleviation and empower the members in economic, social and political spheres. NGOs are building social capital in the form of groups that can generate a sound base for their members to develop their credibility as borrowers and encourage financial institutions to develop confidence in establishing a lending relationship with the groups.

With this background, the study seeks to examine the functioning of micro-finance programmes, and analyze economic benefits (improvement in livelihoods and access to resources) and social benefits (improvement in knowledge and participation) of the selected micro-finance members in the specific context of NGO programmes in Mandya district.

Micro finance is needed a very traditional and familiar form of business. Microfinance has turned out to be useful development assistance product. It reached millions of poor people and emerged as a revolution. It is a viable alternative that reached the hitherto unreached for their social and economic empowerment through financial and social intermediation. In microfinance the practice of group-lending contracts with joint liability is widely accepted as a potential innovation or a noble solution for imperfections in rural credit markets to minimize risks in the credit markets. The joint liability between the group members provides incentives or compels the group to undertake the tasks of selection, monitoring and enforcement of repayment in a cost effective manner. This leads to reduced transaction costs, increased volume of transactions and improved accessibility of credit to the poor.

In rural India, there is substantial degree of feminization of poverty on account of an increase in the net population growth rate among the landless agricultural labour households (including SC/ST and other backward classes women), low level of human skills, lack of availability of wage employment opportunities and inadequacy of institutional support to create wage as well as self employment opportunities. This list includes economic factors responsible for feminization of poverty which are much stronger in operation and which function along with socio-cultural barriers and discrimination against women in economic participation.

Objectives of the Study

1. To analyse the extent of influence and support of micro finance institutions in implementing microfinance programmes for upliftment of women.
2. To examine the employment activities of Self-Help Groups under micro credit programmes in the study area.

3. To study the role of NGOs and Self-Help Groups in socio-economic empowerment of women in Srirangapatna and Pandavapura taluks in Mandya district.
4. To suggest appropriate policy measures based on the findings, which emerge from the proposed study.

Methodology of the Study

The present study is an empirical investigation based on sample beneficiaries of microfinance institutions in Mandya district of Karnataka. The present study is based on both secondary and primary data and a systematic random sampling method has been adopted for survey. The primary data has been collected from two taluks of Mandya district i.e., from Srirangapatna and Pandavapura taluks. The sample size comprised of 186 beneficiaries from microfinance activities in the Mandya district of Karnataka State. The present study has selected two taluks in the district for the purpose of primary data collection. To have further clarity, Graphs, pie-charts and diagrams have been worked out.

Analysis and Discussion

Here we have made an attempt to analyse the role of NGOs like Shreyas, MRD (MYRADA) and CDS(Community Development Society) in Mandya district of Karnataka State in catering the needs of the women. These three non-governmental institutions actively participated in improving the livelihood security of women through self help groups in Mandya district. Table - 1 shows the reasons given by the members for Joining the SHGs about 37 percent of them opined that they joined the group of promoting savings and for getting loans. Thirty-one percent of them gave multiple reasons like getting loan, inculcating the savings habit, and welfare of the family. In CDS about one-third reported that they were attracted to the group by the possibility of easy access to the formal credit system and opportunity to raise loans.

Table - 1
Motivating factors-Members perception

Reasons	*MRD*	*CDS*	*Shreyas*	*All class*
For getting loan	2(6)	17(33)	7(7)	26(14)
For promoting Savings habit	2(6)	9(16)	5(9)	16(9)
For availing loan and Promoting savings habit	9(26)	11(21)	49(50)	69(37)
For family's welfare	-	2(4)	-	2(1)
Other reasons	4(11)	4(7)	4(7)	13(8)
Multiple reasons	18(52)	10(19)	31(31)	59(31)
Total	35(100)	53(100)	98(100)	186(100)

Source: Field survey figures in brackets are percentages.

Only two members reported that they joined the group for the welfare of their families about eight percent thought that membership in the group would raise their status in society as one of the reason for joining the group.

Table -2 gives the group-wise age composition of the selected members. It is seen that 62 percent of the selected members were in the age group of 30-45 years, which is considered to be the most productive period in a person's life. The proportions of members in the age group of less than 30years and those than 45 years were 19 each.

Table - 2
Agency-wise distribution of members by age group

Age	*MRD*	*CDS*	*Shreyas*	*All class*
Loss than 30 years	6(17)	12(23)	17(17)	35(19)
35-45 years	22(63)	33(62)	61(63)	116(62)
Above 45 years	35(100)	53(100)	98(100)	186(100)
Total	35(100)	53(100)	98(100)	186(100)

Source: Field survey Figures it brackets as percentages.

As per the Census Report 2001, the average family size to the district is 6.49. During the field survey we have observed that majority of the Muslim families were having more than three children.

Table - 3
Agency-wise distribution of members by family size

Family size	*MRD*	*CDS*	*Shreyas*	*All class*
Less than 3	7(20)	19(19)	18 (19)	35(19)
3 to 5	23(66)	32(60)	60(61)	115(62)
Above 5	5(14)	11(21)	20(20)	36(19)
Total	35(100)	53(100)	98(100)	186(100)

Source: Field survey, Figures in brackets are percentages.

However, among the selected members 62 percent were having a family size between 3 and 5 members and 19 percent more than 5 members in the family. Table-4 shows that all agencies had a fair representation of all the religious groups. It is found that in Shreyas, Christians formed more than two-fifths may be due to the fact that SHGs of Shreyas were formed by reorganizing the credit Union, which and existed earlier. Again, there is a general feeling that though membership is open to all, the members are mostly Christians and that built of the benefits in this agency go to them MRD groups concentrated mainly in Muslim areas have about 43 percent of the selected members belonging to the community.

Since SHG is conceptually targeted to weaker sections. It would be interesting to look at the social status of the selected members. In general, SC/ST families constitute the most variable and economically the most backward among the different communities, SC/ST representation was comparatively high in CDS and in the selected MRD groups. However in MRD and CDS, the majority (53 percent) belonged to the category of OBCs (Other Backward communities) in Shreyas, 60percent of the members belonged to the general category belonging to the forward status of the society.

Table - 4
Agency wise distribution of members by religion

Religion	*MRD*	*CDS*	*Shreyas*	*All class*
Hinduism	12 (34)	17(32)	27(28)	56 (30)
Christianity	8(23)	17(32)	40(41)	65(35)
Islam	15 (43)	19(36)	31(31)	65(35)
Total	35(100)	53(100)	98(100)	186(100)

Source: Field survey Figures in brackets are percentages

Table -5 shows that the members of Shreyas groups were more educated than the members of other groups. Forty-four percent of them had qualifications of SSLC or above. In CDS and MRD, the majority of the selected members (47 percent and 35 percent respectively) were found to have only primary education. Illiterates formed time percent of the membership in the CDS groups. Interestingly, in almost all the groups, women were found to be better educated than their husbands.

Table - 5
Distribution of members by social status

Caste	*MRD*	*CDS*	*Shreyas*	*All class*
SC/ST	-	6(11)	2(2)	8(4)
General	16(46)	19(36)	59(60)	94(51)
OBC	19(54)	28(53)	37(38)	84(45)
Total	35(100)	53(100)	98(100)	186(100)

Source: Field survey figures is brackets are percentages.

Table - 6
Distribution of members by level of education

Education level	*MRD*	*CDS*	*Shreyas*	*All class*
Illiterate/No response	1(3)	5(9)	5(5)	11(6)
Literate	3(9)	4(8)	10(10)	17(9)
Primary	13(37)	25(47)	28(29)	66(35)
High school	7(20)	8(15)	12(12)	27(15)
SSLC	6(17)	8(15)	33(34)	47(25)
Above SSLC	5(14)	7(6)	10(10)	18(10)
Total	15(100)	53(100)	98(100)	186(100)

Source: Field survey Figure is brackets are percentages.

Most of the members were found to be either agricultural laborers or self-employed workers seventeen percent of the members had their own small-scale units, run on self-employment basis engaged in non-agricultural activates (Table - 7) In Shreyas 65 percent of the members remained unemployed, while the corresponding figure in

Table - 7
Group-wise activity status of beneficiaries

Activity status	*MRD*	*CDS*	*Shreyas*	*All class*
Laborer	5(14)	9(17)	7(7)	21(11)
Self employed in Non-agriculture	9(26)	8(15)	15(15)	32(17)
Self employed in Agriculture	1(3)	2(4)	7(7)	10(5)
Salary paidEmployment	1(3)	1(4)	7(7)	10(5)
No occupation no Response	16(46)	30(57)	64(65)	110(60)
Total	35(100)	53(100)	98(100)	186(100)

Source: Field survey Figures in brackets are percentages

MRD was only 46 percent. Two-fifties of the members in CDS groups had some occupation or other, through the returns from them were not up to their expectations. It may be noted that despite the fact that ample funds are available for economic activities. It may be noted that despite the fact that ample funds are available for economic activities 60 percent of the total sample was still not having any occupation.

The major source of income of those households came from the work of the male members, husband, father or others. Table - 8 shown that 62 percent of the members feature of the members of the CDS groups is that for 16 percent among them, spouses had either deceased of were non-working.

Table - 8
Activity Status

Activity status	*MRD*	*CDS*	*Shreyas*	*All class*
Laborer Mason/ others	22(63)	16(600)	58(50)	116(62)
Petty shop	3(9)	1(2)	8(8)	12(6)
Gulf employee	1(3)	-	7(7)	8(4)
Self employee, Govt. employee	3(9)	2(4)	15(16)	20(11)
No employment widow	6(17)	14(26)	10(10)	30(16)
Total	35(100)	53(100)	98(100)	186(100)

Source: Field survey Figures in brackets are percentages.

The share of the employment and the employed together in Shreyas formed 23 percent) which shows that these members had not come inevitably from the 'poor' families, as per the accepted definition of poverty.

Impact of Self Help Group Movement on Women's Social And Economic Status

The membership to a SHG has contributed to significant changes in the lives of women. This was revealed by focus group interactions and field visits in the six towns undertaken for this study. Most of the groups visited could be assessed as successful in social and economic terms. Less than 5% of the SHGs formed under the program can be said to be defunct. Forty percent of the urban poor were covered by NGO based SHGs in the short period that the project was active. The impacts can be looked at as those bringing in economic changes, impact on the social status and political impacts, and the impact of SHGs on the community.

Impact on Economic Status

Increased entrepreneurial skills: NGOs convened a number of Entrepreneurship Development programs for SHG. Members which facilitated the learning of generic skills such as book keeping. This has allowed women to change from being wage workers to being self employed. Women also have gained the option to pursue two or three petty businesses, change from one type of business to another, combine wage employment with small business.

Increased access to credit: The micro credit facility of the SHG has encouraged women to save. They are at ease in their minds as they can avail money when they need, without having to pay any collateral. The most important effect has been the escape from the clutches of the money lenders. Pledging on jewelry has also reduced. The interest on loans has reduced from 120% per annum to 24%. They can request for adjustment in the duration of repayment.

Establishment of businesses: At lest half of the members (15-18- generally) have taken a loan from their SHG to micro-enterprise managed either by the women or by their families. There is an endless list of businesses established in this way, based on small credits of Rs.500 to sell flowers, vegetables and fruits, up to Rs.5,000 to establish petty shops and hotels, food grains, manufacture and sale of processed food products would need investments amounts varying between Rs.5,000 many women see house keeping and child rearing along with earning for the family.

While vesting SHGs, the study found many examples that showed that the women who invested in businesses through their SHGs are better off. One woman visited, lakshmi, a member of Durgamba SHG at Mandya taluk had a save (traditional fabric worn by Indian women) business. At every purchase, she invested Rs.5,000 which the made a profit of Rs.1,300. The advantage in this is her be up with the traders of Mandya who were willing to take back the unsold fabric if any.

Impact on social Status

This study found that the participation in the movement by it self as been an empowering and liberating experience for many of the poor women. The strongest impact has been in terms of self esteem and increased social mobility as many women of urban slums had never attended such a program before. The impacts can be summarized as follows.

(i) Increased mobility: This means a lot to poor women and to those who have been restricted by religious taboo. The visit to the SHG has made women more bold and confident. Earlier, women were more confined to the four walls of the kitchen and some to the work place. They were now found to be able to meet each other and discuss problems.

(ii) Increased exposure: This comes from more interactions with other women. Women stated that they are more enthusiastic and positive about their lives. They understand each other's viewpoints and problems. Interaction with other

women has resulted in building effect of spreading the SHG movement.

(iii) Increased awareness: Awareness on health related issues-personal hygiene, communicable diseases, effects of malnutrition and sanitation-have increased as a result of training programs. More importantly, awareness of the rights of women-as prescribed by the constitution and as prescribed by the religious doctrines-has also increased. The membership in the SHGs has allowed many women to come out of boundaries defined by their male companies or relatives. There are now cases submitted for legal mediation by Muslim women, something never heard of before.

Major Findings of the study

Based on the analysis and discussion in the study of NGO micro finance and socio-economic development of women, the following findings have been drawn:

1. The popular size of the each SHG is around 15 to 20 and 80 per cent of SHGs are covered under this category. About 50 per cent of the SHGs out of 60 surveyed SHGs are borrowed loan from Banks. 63 per cent of the SHGs out of 60 surveyed are promoting income generating activities. About 37 per cent of the SHGs are supporting dairy activities.
2. It is evident that the income of the household increased rapidly and resulted in an acquisition of household assets and thereby leading relatively a better life. After joining the group the status of women has been increased.
3. Majority of the members belongs to agriculture work 32 per cent of the members are agriculture land less labourers and 28 per cent of the members are doing business after availing credit facilities from SHG and Banks.

4. As many as 37 per cent members had their house hold annual income ranging up to Rs. 10,000/-, 36 per cent member household annual income ranging from Rs.10,000 to Rs.20,000. Only 16 per cent members household income ranging from Rs. 20,000 to Rs. 30,000.
5. Nearly 50 per cent of the total members belong to economically poor and belongs to back ward communities. About 36 per cent of the total members belong to SC/ST, as many as 28 per cent OBC and only 16 per cent belongs to minority community.

POLICY IMPLICATIONS

In the light of our findings and observations some suggestions are made about effective functioning of NGO controlled microfinance institutions in the socio-economic development of the women. The suggestions are listed as follows:

1. The NGO sector is increasingly pursuing the financial intermediation as one of the effective tools in meeting their social agenda. In this context, the governments, both at the centre and the states have an equally important role to play in creating conducive policy environment for the growth of this NGO sector as future micro finance institutions. Here, what is required is suitable policy framework, innovative package of services with timely credit.
2. SHGs may be permitted to issue fixed deposits certificates, Cash certificates and other savings oriented instruments may be under the authorizing of the concerned lead bank in the respective district.
3. The Banks may encourage SHGs to open Saving Bank accounts for different purpose say for education, marriage, capital asset purchase etc so that the amounts accumulated in the respective account be utilized for the said purpose only. This

ensures the SHG members to fulfill their social commitments much better.

4. SHGs to become more meaningful and purposeful should be constantly guided by NGOs with regard to their activities, especially the purposes for which the loans are sanctioned.

Concluding Remarks

This study indicates that, the NGO controlled microcredit organisations do not incur lower transactions costs than banks, but they are able to transfer these costs to others - donors and borrowers. We also argued that one important component of high administrative costs was the cost of monitoring so as to ensure regular repayment. The lesson from the microcredit experience is that small scale rural credit is indeed necessary. However, rural credit policy must build on the strengths of the banking system in India as its mainstay. Banks have many advantages over private micro credit organisations as providers of small scale loans. They have advantages of scale; the banking system in India has a reach and spread that NGO controlled microcredit cannot begin to match; banks can cross-subsidize loans; banks are better placed to provide specialized training to their employees in development banking; banks are better placed to coordinate banking activity with development administrations, local governments and SHGs; and banks are better able than private microcredit organisations to offer a wide range of financial services to borrowers. For the state to withdraw from the field and hand over small-scale credit to NGO-controlled microcredit organisations is, in effect, to undermine and weaken a major national asset, the widespread rural banking system.

References

Archana Gupta (2002) "NGOs in Micro Financing - Partners in Rural Development", Kurukshetra, Feb, Vol.50, No.4.

Ackerly, Brooke A. 1995. "Testing the tools of development: Credit programmes, loan involvement, and women's empowerment." IDS Bulletin 26 (3) : 56-68.

Aloysius Fernandez (2002) "Impact of SHG-Bank Linkage Programme in India on Social Indicator and Empowerment of the embers ", National Bank for Agriculture and Rural Development (NABARD), Mumbai.

Basu Kishanjeet, Jindal Krishan (2000) "Micro Finance - Emerging Challenges" Bankers Institute of Rural Development, Lucknow.

De Chandra, Fonseka (1991) "NGOs: Challenges and Future Directions Chiangmai. APDC Reginal Dialogue on GO-NGO Relations in Asia" in partners in rural poverty alleviation - NGO Cooperation, United Nations, New York.

Dadhich, C. L. (2001), Micro finance - A panacea for poverty alleviation: A case study of oriental Grameen Project in India, Journal of Agriculture Economy, Vol. 56, No. 4, July-September, 2001.

David Hulme (2003), 'Is Micro-Debt good for poor people? A note on the dark Side of microfinance,' in Malcolm Harper (ed.)'Microfinance: Evolution, Achievements and Challenges,'ITDG Publishing and Samskriti.

Jayaram B. (2001) " Microfinance Retrospect and Prospect" NABARD. Mumbai.

Jha T.N. (2002),"Microcredit models in Bangladesh", Journal Yojana, Volume 46, February.

11

Progress of Self Help Groups in Karnataka - An Analysis

Prasad

INTRODUCTION

This paper intends to analyse the progress of self help groups in the state of Karnataka and to evaluate the role of self help groups in socio-economic empowerment of women. The rural bankers, NGOs and some government functionaries have done splendid work in the development of self-help groups in the state of Karnataka. The state of Karnataka has been a pioneer in the programme of SHG Bank linkage and is indeed hailed as a laboratory for micro finance innovations. Under the "Stree Shakhi" programme of government of Karnataka, the Department of Women and Child Welfare is actively involved in the promotion of SHGs. On the other hand, the Regional Rural Banks have themselves promoted tens of thousands of SHGs and have credit linked them a commendable service indeed.

Micro- Finance or Micro-Credit for the poor and women has received extensive recognition as a strategy for poverty reduction and for economic empowerment. Increasingly in the last five years, there is a questioning of whether micro-credit is the most effective approach to economic empowerment of the poorest and, among them, women in particular. Development practitioners in India and developing countries often argue that the exaggerated focus on micro-credit as a solution for the poor has led to neglect by the state and public institutions in addressing employment and livelihood needs of the poor. With the onset of structural adjustment programmes in the early nineties, there was a public debate around reduced state spending on social sectors. In a country like India, economic uncertainties, loss of livelihood, inflation, lack of access to natural resources, declining employment, increasing social unrest, natural disaster, etc., make the poor extremely vulnerable. In this context it would be necessary to ensure that the poor are empowered to access development resources and use it to their greatest benefit.

Equitable gains from development on a sustainable basis and ensuring viability of financial services are the key elements in a strategy of poverty reduction by means of credit support to the poor. As micro-finance is seen to be an approach addressing these concerns effectively; it has assumed significance in all the developing countries as an effective tool in fighting poverty.

The National Bank for Agriculture and Rural Development (NABARD) launched the SHG -. Bank Linkage Programme. However, between 1984 and 1985, MYRADA, a non-governmental organization engaged in rural development and based in Karnataka, promoted several co-operatives broke up into small groups, which wee the genesis of the first SHGs, referred to at that time as Credit Management Groups, with a focus on the management of credit. The concept of each member making a saving in the group soon followed, as also the establishment of a system of regular meetings, book keeping and records, and collective decision-making. A pilot study (Puhazhendi and Sai, 2000) gave NABARD the confidence to mainstream the SHG- Bank Linkage

Programme in 1996 as a normal lending activity. The programme then spread rapidly, if unevenly, across the country making it by 2002, the largest micro-finance programme in the world.

Thus, the history of SHG promotion started with NGOs taking the lead in the mid-1980s and the lead passing on to NABARD by the late 1980s. after the SG - Bank Linkage Programme was launched in 1991-92, the very first loans to SHGs in the country were given in Kolar district of Karnataka, by the Vysya Bank, Bangarpet branch to Venkateshwara Mahila Sangha of Muduguli on December 9, 1991 and by the Corporation Bank, Anderson pet Branch to Saraswathi Mahila Sangha of Boduguriki on January 30, 1992. NABARD up scaled the programme in Karnataka by initiating a series of measures that included training of NGO and bank staff, convening regular meetings of all intervening agencies, analyzing reports and providing feedback for changes in operational systems to make them more user-friendly, and launching the first RRB (Regional Rural Bank), the Cauvery Grameena Bank of Mysore district, as an SHG promoting institution (1994-95). In the 1990s, IFAD, with World Bank collaboration and in partnership with the Government of India and six state governments, including Karnataka, launched a similar programme titled Swashakti. This experience encouraged Karnataka to launch a state- wide programme called Stree Shakti (women's power) based on the SHG strategy.

Together, the initiatives of the various stake holders (the government, NGOs, banks) increased SHG coverage in Karnataka significantly. At recent estimates, 40,295 anganwadi workers (of the Department of Women and Child Development), 561 NGOs, eight regional rural banks, 20 District Central Cooperative Banks, and two commercial banks are engaged in SHG promotion. Together, they are estimated to have facilitated the creation of close to 2,24,928 SHGs in Karnataka.

Today there is a scarcely a village in Karnataka where an SHG has not been facilitated. The state government is now the single largest SHG promoting institution. It is important also to note that even in the man government programmes that are not primarily SHG-oriented, SHGs are still included and budgeted for mainly to engage and empower the poor and introduce a measure of equity, where otherwise, the programme may have remained poor neutral.

Broadly, therefore there are three categories of institutions promoting SHGs: the government, financial institutions and NGOs. The promoting institution plays a significant role in the way an SHG develops and functions. The Stree Shakthi Programme, anchored by the Department of Women and Child Development, attempts to focus the attention of members on curbing domestic violence against women, promoting girl child education, preventing child marriage, etc. Up-scaling the number of SHG to 100,000 meant that all activities did not take place as scheduled due to budgetary constraints. SHGs promoted by financial institutions are normally viewed as potential sources of clients. They tend to focus on credit provision, and investment in the institutional capacity building of SHGs is limited. These SHGs hardly ever move into social activism. Of the three broad categories of SHG-promoting institutions mentioned above, financial institutions may have the smallest numbers, but in a way they are the most significant since these initiatives of bankers to become directly involved in SG formation have helped to mainstream the SHG strategy in their priority sector portfolio and to make it a normal lending activity of banks. SHGs promoted by NGOs tend to promote the priorities and agenda of the NGOs concerned and to reflect the organizational and financial strengths as well as weaknesses of the NGOs. Thus, at least in the first two years of formation, they may range between two ends of the spectrum: the one determinedly focused on altering power balances in favour of the poor (mainly poor women) without much attention to strengthening SHG institutional systems and the other focused on building up the SHG as a professionally managed institution with little or no attempt made to influence social issues on which members could focus, leaving it to the discretion of members themselves. The details of SHGs in Karnataka since 1998 to 2006 are depicted in Table-1.

Table - 1
Details of Self - Help Groups in Karnataka

Sl. No.	Year	Group Formed	No. of SHGs taken up Economic Activities	Members covered under SHGs
1.	1998 - 99	2002	895	10638
2.	1999 - 00	3167	910	10936
3.	2000 - 01	5627	975	11002
4.	2001 - 02	6150	1000	12521
5.	2002 - 03	6750	1232	12769
6	2003 - 04	1,11,511	79,895	1664824
7	2004 - 05	1,95,585	1,27,000	2930989
8	2005 - 06	2,24,928	1,98,546	3244909

Source: NABARD Reports, Various Issues.

The above table clearly shows that there is an increasing trend in-group formation, groups taken up economic activities and also members covered under SHGs in Karnataka since 1998 –99 to 2005-06. During 1998-99 there were 2002 SHGs, after 1999 groups formation have been gradually increased up to 2,24,928 in 2005-06. In terms of members covered under SHGs also increased from 10638 in 1998-99 to 3244909 in 2005-06.

The SHGs, as originally conceived, are not just groups that promote savings and provide credit, they are intended to become institutions that promote human development and empower their members. The major objectives of building participatory institutions of the poor such as SHGs is to provide the members with an opportunity and the space to develop a vision/mission, to develop and maintain organizational and financial management systems, to grow in confidence and skills to manage their lives and promote their interests in the in the private and public domains, to establish the linkages required for an institution to function effectively and sustainably, and to support its members to become agents of social change. There is adequate evidence to substantiate the claim that in this process, the members of the SHGs build new relationships, which are more balanced in terms of gender and decision-making and more equitable in resource distribution, within the group, in the home and with other institutions and groups in society. Institutions by themselves do not empower the poor unless they are participatory like the SHGs and adequately provided with capacity-building support. A major assumption on which the SHG strategy is based is that participatory institutions of the poor provide them with the space to develop skills and confidence and to mobilize resources.

Banking institutions in Karnataka as promoting agencies of SHGs lent micro credit for different activities. The details of micro credit lent by banks in Karnataka are presented in the Table- 2.

Table- 2
Micro-Credit lent by Banks in Karnataka (upto 2006)

Sl. No	*District*	*SHGs financed (Number)*	*Amount Lent (Rs.in crore)*
01	Bagalkote	2,803	11.47
02	Bangalore Rural	8,030	53.21
03	Bangalore Urban	3,083	18.81
04	Belgaum	9,675	47.80
05	Bellary	9,796	37.71
06	Bidar	10,449	51.86
07	Bijapur	5,760	19.40
08	Chamarajanagar	5,889	25.86
09	Chikamagalur	3,736	16.37
10	Chitradurga	8,717	34.65
11	Dakshina Kannada	23,901	76.29
12	Davanagere	6,268	32.22

Sl. No	*District*	*SHGs financed (Number)*	*Amount Lent (Rs.in crore)*
13	Dharwad	5,134	21.83
14	Gadag	3,308	14.12
15	Gulbarga	12,279	43.06
16	Hassan	17,374	78.91
17	Haveri	4,797	23.98
18	Kodagu	3,296	12.63
19	Kolar	9,669	42.47
20	Koppal	3,296	12.63
21	Mandya	10,275	44.17
22	Mysore	15,043	69.90
23	Raichur	4,550	16.63
24	Shimoga	7,215	31.57
25	Tumkur	14,682	76.55
26	Udupi	10,042	46.04
27	Uttara Kannada	5,907	28.76
	State Total	2,24,928	994.35

Source: NABARD reports.

The livelihood needs of the poor – The income and basic needs perspective of poverty

Cultivating the habit of regular savings and the ability to access them when required through credit not only reduces significantly the vulnerability of the livelihood base of the poor and their dependence, it also enhances human development. It enables them to borrow for urgent needs instead of going to moneylender, which increases their dependency since he/she is often the one who provides them with labour employment at low wages. This, in turn, gives them a degree of freedom to bargain for better wages and working conditions and enables them to build a capital base which, hitherto was impossible since the exorbitant interest rates demanded by moneylenders siphoned off all surplus. The feel good factor is evident in a group that has been able to save enough in the group to meet with urgent needs. However, the members of the group need to go further if they are to justify the claim that savings empower people. They need to ensure that savings and credit are managed effectively. SHG bank linkage agency wise cumulative participation Karnataka up to 2005-06 details are presented in Table- 3.

Table- 3
SHG- Bank Linkage - Agency-Wise Cumulative Participation in Karnataka up to March 2006

(Rs.million)

Sl.No	Name of the Agency	No.of SHGs	Bank Loan
01	Commercial Banks	38,605	1,006.79
02	Regional Rural Banks	37,087	1,094.73
03	Cooperative Banks	28,174	734.66
	Total	103,866	2,836.18

Source: NABARD Report.

The above table clearly shows that all the financial institutions have provided maximum bank loan to self-help groups. Commercial Banks have provided Rs.1,006.79 million and they have formulated 38,605 SHGs in Karnataka up to 2006. Regional Rural Banks have also played a significant role in providing bank loans to SHGs and even Cooperative Banks also participated in promoting SHGs in Karnataka. Savings made by members are pooled and loaned to one another. SHG members determine the terms and conditions. Loans are provided for all purposes without making the traditional distinction between consumption and income generation. The SHG model provides its members with the space and flexibility to make decisions that are appropriate to each situation. Only private moneylenders lend for such a variety of purposes with minimum fuss and paper work; all financial institutions and government schemes lend only for productive purposes. But it is the life events and emergencies that drive the poor to debt traps. It leads also o the diversion of loans taken from formal organizations/ government into consumption loans, which they are unable to repay.

Table- 4

SHG- Bank Linkage - Physical & Financial Progress of Participating Regional Rural Banks upto 2005-06

(Rs.million)

Name of the RRB	*Cumulative No of SHGs provided with bank loan upto 2005*	*No.of SHGs provided with bank loan during 2005-06*	*Cumulative bank loan disbursed upto 2005*	*Bank loan disbursed during 2005-06*	*Cumulative bank loan disbursed upto 2006*
Bijapur Grameena Bank	824	584	25.47	25.73	51.20
Cauvery Grameena Bank	4,114	2,087	119.81	81.56	201.37
Chikmagalur – Kodagu Grameena Bank	120	136	3.84	4.58	8.42
Chitradurga Grameena Bank	3,248	1,369	95.63	46.50	142.13
Kalpatharu Grameena Bank	1,612	1,875	38.96	75.05	114.01
Kolar Grameena Bank	1,203	865	31.42	22.23	53.65
Krishna Grameena Bank	2,409	1,579	70.32	35.84	106.16
Malaprabha Grameena Bank	2,557	2,981	55.33	88.70	144.03
Netravati Grameena Bank	747	194	20.99	5.90	26.89
Sahyadri Grameena Bank	1,420	332	55.04	26.10	81.14
Tungabhadra Grameena Bank	3,152	2,410	76.55	47.84	124.39
Varada Grameena Bank	219	271	4.51	9.84	14.35
Visveswaraya Grameena Bank	304	475	6.96	20.03	26.99
Total	21,929	15,158	604.83	489.90	1,094.73

Source: NABARD Report.

It must be noted, that apart from their savings, SHG members also credit all the interest earned on loans to the group's common fund. Increased lending has been made possible through accessing loan funds from financial institutions, after the SHG- Bank Linkage Programme was launched in 1991-92. Under this pogramme, there are no subsidies for the asset, yet it has grown, particularly after 1999, and is today the largest micro finance programme in the world. The repayment rates average around 95 percent.

SHG members consider their ability to raise loans from banks and their ability to negotiate with banks directly as a major indicator of increased levels of confidence and self esteem. This provides some insights into SHG member's ability to access finance from mainstream institutions. Many members say that the learnt to sign after joining the group. Although this might seem like a minor achievement to most of us., to SHG members, it seems to be away of gaining acceptance in the 'mainstream' and a source of pride. Many members spoke of how they were previously ashamed to conduct bank transactions, as they used thumb impressions in place of signatures. Only after learning to sign were they comfortable about going to a bank. It was after joining the SHG, that the had gained the confidence of conducting bank transactions on their own, and approaching bank officials for loans.

The credit funds provided under the SHG-Bank Linkage Programme in Karnataka compare favourably with the credit disbursed to SHGs in Karnataka under the Swarnajayanti Gram Swarojgar Yojana. It may be recalled that all the previous loan-cum-subsidy programmes of the Central Government for the rural poor, including IRDP and DWACRA, have been merged under SGSY. The SGSY programme is mainly intended to provide loans to groups. Due to various compulsions, individual beneficiaries are also being included in large numbers but they are not considered the primary target. Hence, Table- 6 shows the loans given to SHGs only.

Table-5

Credit disbursements to SHGs under SGSY and Bank Linkage Programmes

(Rs.lakh)

Year	*Credit-cum-subsidy disbursed to SHGs under SGSY*	*Credit disbursed by financial institutions*
2003-04	4187.91	1714.00
2004-05	7114.86	3475.39
2005-06	3688.87	7249.50
Total	14991.64	12438.89

Source: 1.SHG-Bank Linkage Programme in Karnataka, NABARD.
2.Ministry of Rural Development 2005-06 for SGSY.

Table - 6

Increased knowledge and awareness of SHG members

(Percent)

Particulars	*SHG age category*	*Good Knowledge*
Self-help group concept and approach	< 1 year	35
	3 years old	65
	>5 years	90
Banking Knowledge	< 1 year	40
	3 years old	65
	>5 years	95
Health and Sanitation	< 1 year	60
	3 years old	85
	>5 years	95
Family Planning	< 1 year	50
	3 years old	75
	>5 years	70
Income generating programmes	< 1 year	45
	3 years old	75
	>5 years	95
Common properties management	< 1 year	30
	3 years old	25
	>5 years	70

Source: SHG-Bank Linkage Programme in Karnataka, NABARD, 2006-07. Page.102.

The training provided to the SHGs in the initial year and a half, focuses largely on institution building. Apart from this, members also experience an increase in social awareness through capacity building. The study also analysed whether members felt that their knowledge in these areas had increased and whether and recall. Table indicates that there were significant increases in knowledge and recall as the groups progressed. In all cases it can be seen that member's knowledge (and ability to recall this knowledge) increased with the length of time spent as a group member.

CONCLUSION

People need several cycles of loan to overcome poverty and that some of these loans may be non-productive in nature but are an essential part of the process to climb up the socio-economic ladder. Thus, if a leaking roof is not repaired the income earning produce stored under it will be destroyed, if a broken leg is not treated immediately, the labourer may never be able to work productively again, if land pledged to a money lender is not redeemed, the land itself may be lost forever, if a social event is not appropriately celebrated, friends and relatives may become unavailable in times of need. Similarly, a person may not be able to manage a larger programme right from the beginning but if her and she can manage it much better. The varieties of purposes for which loan age given by SHGs indicate that the SHGs are able to meet this need.

In Karnataka Self-help Groups, managed in an ideal scenario, provide a way of reducing poverty that simultaneously improves the capacity of its members on many levels. It is grounded in participatory decision-making, which creates a sense of ownership among members. This is very different from how many other poverty alleviation/ human development programmes evolve with a top-down system of decision-making and distance from the people most affected by these decisions for the purposes of presenting an alternative approach to sustainable development.

References

Durrant, V.L. and Z.A. Sathar 2000. Greater Investments in Children Through Women's Empowerment: A Key to Demographic Change in Pakistan. Paper prepared for presentation at the annual Population Association of America meetings, March 2000, Los Angles, California.

Gurumoorthy. T.R. (2002): Economic Empowerment Through Self - -Reliance. Social Welfare, Delhi.

King, Elizabeth, M and M. Anne Hill (1993): Women's Education in Developing Countries: Barriers, Benefits and Policies. The John Hopking University Press, Baltimore.

Kumar and Singh (1983) : Role of women in Rural Economy", kurukshetra, Jan. 13.

Lynn Bennet (1982): Women, Poverty and Productivity in India, World Bank, Washington D.C.

Mahajan .V.S. (1989): "Women's contribution to India's Economic and social development" Deep and Deep publication, Delhi.

Mathu,r, Deepa (1992) : Women Family and work, Rawat publication, Jaipur.

Everett, Jana. 1991. The Global Empowerment of Women. Summary of the annual conference of the Association for Women in Development, November 17-19, 1989, Washington DC.

12

Performance of Agarbathi Industries in the State of Karnataka - A Study

Narayanamma, P.N.

INTRODUCTION

In this paper an attempt has been made to analyse the performance of agarbathi industries in the state of Karnataka and on the basis of results and discussion some construcitve suggestions have also been made. Karnataka has a viable natural climate and is home for many an industry; large, medium and small industries covering cement, steel, agarbathis, aerospace and procession, engineering etc., Bangalore the capital city of Karnataka known for its climate has been a host to many hitech industries.

Informatics is of the largest industrial estates in the whole of South - East Asia. The city of Bangalore has changed a lot in its character and contents during last two decades. Bangalore district is located in the south eastern corner of Karnataka state and is situated at a height of 916 meters. The city of Bangalore is not only popularly known as Silicon Valley of India but also one of the world fastest growing cities.

The real growth of Bangalore City started after independence. Bangalore a real cosmopolitan city provides scope for all types of business. Karnátaka state has evolved from a basically agricultural economy into an industrial one. In 1993 there were 723 large and medium scale, and 323 small and village industries in Bangalore. Besides there were about 8,00,000 unregistered units spread all over state.

Results and Discussion

The majority of the people in Bangalore district i.e. 84.14% live in urban areas of the district and population of the Bangalore urban generation constitutes 84% of the total population of the district. The composition of the population of Bangalore urban, state and outside the state, presents a mosaic picture of culture. The fast development of the city has also helped the nourishing of a number of slums.

It should be noted that the women belonging to lower socio - economic class, live in slums, their condition of housing are very poor and are uneducated. In Bangalore city these workers are mostly found in the slums of Magadi road, Siddapura, Srirampuram, Jayanagar, Chamarajpet and Mysore City.

The total workers (including main and marginal) in Karnataka increased from 1.49 crores in 1981 to 1.89 crores in 1991 and to 2.35 crores in 2001. The growth of the workforce in the state was 22.29 per cent during the period 1981 - 2001. The proportion of marginal workers increased from 8.65 per cent in 1981 to 17.72 per cent in 2001, thus implying a rise in under - employment. The growth of total workers was faster in Bangalore and irrigated districts such as Mysore, as compared to backward districts like Gulbarga. The total number of unorganised workers in the state rapidly increased from 0.97 crores in 1981 to 1.30 crores in 1991 and to 1.73 crores in 2001.

Table - 1
Structure of work force in Karnataka, Bangalore

Sl. No.	*Particulars*	*Persons Males Females*	*Karnataka*	*Bangalore*
1.	2	3	4	5
	Number of households		10401918	1460697
	Population	Persons	52850562	6537124
		Males	26898918	3426599
		Females	25951644	3110525
	Decennial population Growth rate (1991-2002)		17.5	35.1
	Sex ratio		965	908
	Population of Scheduled Castes (SC)	Persons	8563930	851042
		Males	4339745	435162
		Females	4224185	4158885
	Population of Scheduled Tribes (ST)	Persons	3463986	87018
		Males	1756989	45988
		Females	1708555	45082
	Number of literates	Persons	30434962	4782565
		Males	17661211	2663055
		Females	12773758	2119510
	Literacy rate	Persons	66.6	83.0
		Males	76.1	87.9
		Females	56.9	77.5
	Total workers	Persons	23534791	2566914
		Males	1523355	1986327
		Females	8299436	580587
	Total Non - workers	Persons	29315771	3970218
		Males	11663568	1555048
		Females	17658208	3254168
	Work participation rate	Persons	44.5	39.3
		Males	56.6	58.0
		Females	32.0	18.7
	Type of workers(a) Main workers	Persons	19364759	2378180
		Males	13896845	1878030
		Females	5467914	500150
	b) Marginal workers	Persons	4170032	188734
		Males	1338510	108297
		Females	2831522	80437

1.	2	3	4	5
	Category of Workers(a) Cultivators	Persons	6186932	78439
		Males	4668070	61007
		Females	1518862	17432
	b) Agricultural labourers	Persons	378853	39091
		Males	195324	25045
		Females	188564	16842
	Household industry workers	Persons	795221	57895
		Males	187521	33789
		Females	429	24658
	Other workers	Persons	8597685	2204561
		Males	6859704	1782462
		Females	1700055	5509822

Source: Directorate of Census Operation, Karnataka.

To total number of agricultural laboures (excusing marginal workers) increased from 36.55 lakhs in 1981 to 50.00lakhs in 1991 in relative terms, the proportion of agricultural laboures increased from 24.29 per cent in 1981 to 26.44 per cent in 1991. Two of selected districts (Gulbarga and Mysore) not only had a large proportion of agricultural labourers but also witnessed increasing feminization of the agricultural labour market. In Bangalore and Dakshina Kannada, the workers seemed to be diversifying into non-agricultural occupations. The proportion of agricultural labourers to the total workforce declined in both these districts. The selected districts, thus, provide interesting variations in the indigence of agricultural labour and dependence on farm work for livelihood.

The proportion of construction workers to the total workforce registered a modest rise (from 2.01 to 2.26 per cent during the period 1981 to 2001), such a rise was not uniform across the selected districts. The proportion of construction workers declined in Gulbarga, while it increased in Bangalore, Dakshina Kannada and Mysore districts, where construction activity has been booming. In Bangalore and Dakshina Kannada districts, there was a substantial increase in the case of male construction workers. A faster growth of construction workers can be seen in Bangalore, Dakshina Kannada and Mysore districts, where important cities in the state are located. This indicates the migration of construction workers into the cities.

We do not have secondary data on spatial and temporal variations in the number of domestic workers in the state. Sporadic reports from newspapers and surveys conducted by NGOs have been used to provide some idea on this. It has been stated by the All Karnataka House Maid Workers Association that there are 6,80,000 domestic workers in the state. Another estimate puts the total number of domestic workers in Bangalore city at one lakh. The studies also show that the number of domestic workers is somewhat high in large and growing cities such as Bangalore, Mangalore, Mysore, etc., while it is lesser in cities located in backward districts such as Gulbarga. Most of the workers are reported to belong to depressed castes. (Indian Express, February 23, 2005) (Deccan Herald, May 5, 2004).

Table - 2
Population and Area in Karnataka State and Bangalore

Items	*Karnataka State*	*Bangalore District*
Total Area in Kms	191791.00	8005
Urban Area in Kms	3628.8	424.7
	Population	
Male	3690958	397648
Female	3491142	374892

Source: Census Report, 2001.

The total population of Bangalore district area is 8005 sq.kms, out of which the urban areas in Kms is 427.7. The total population of the Karnataka state as per 1991 census was 450 and in Bangalore district it was 39,48,000 Karnataka state has only one city with more than a million population, namely Bangalore. It is one of the 6th largest urban agglomerations. According to 1991 census among the districts of state, Bangalore had registered the highest density of 2195 persons per sq.km.

The development of industry in Karnataka since independence is impressive. In terms of industrial development, Karnataka was 12th place a decade ago. By 2001, Karnataka occupied fifth place. Investor friendly policies, good industrial infrastructure, natural resources and availability of technical man power, above all, good governance has made Karnataka the most attractive destination for industrial investment from within and outside the country. It is very likely that by 2010, Karnataka will merge as the second most industrialized States in India.

Karnataka has been a pioneer in industry. For several gross now the state has been consistently pursing progressive industrial policies to meet the changing needs of the states economy and industry. Over they last 100 years, the state has the distinction of building a strong and vibrant industrial base, which combines the intrinsic strengths, of large industrial public sector undertakings, large and medium private owned industries and a very wide spectrum of sectors in industry and has outstanding examples of success in the old economy. In recent times, Karnataka has emerged as the knowledge and technology capital of the country making rapid strides in the new economy as well. IT and related industries, biotechnology and strong Research and Development institutions have given Karnataka pride of place in the global market. Karnataka being one among the top 5 industrialized states in the country has achieved substantially in promoting hitech industries in key sectors like Electronics, Telecommunication, IT, Automobiles. Readymade garments witnessed considerable Foreign Direct Investment both in Bangalore and in other parts of the state.

Bangalore has the distinction of being the home for a large number of multi-national companies in knowledge based industries and technology driven sectors and is today recognized as one of the top 10 technological city in the world. The growth in the IT sector has been phenomenal.

Similarly, the growth in other sectors like petroleum and petroleum products, iron-ore and minerals, silk products, jewelry, plastic goods, basic chemicals, pharmaceuticals, cosmetics etc, have been substantial during the post liberalized period and during 2005-2006, state of Karnataka recorded an export performance of Rs. 82,280 crores.

Table - 3
Distribution of Agarbathi Manufacturers (State - wise)

District Name	*No. of Units*	*Investment*	*Employment*
Bangalore Urban	423	194415810.00	2790
Bangalore Rural	204	3646044.00	1734
Belgaum	40	3857555.0	177
Bellary	33	715000.00	120
Bidar	54	396700.00	195
Chickmagalur	90	6521010.00	421
Chitradurga	42	400453.00	152
Kodagu	18	32800.00	112
Dharwad	12	75000.00	35
Gulbarga	357	2150807.00	1693
Hassan	22	633000.00	6268
Karwar	16	142173.00	112
Mangalore	12	412000.00	72
Kolar	16	7878300.00	54
Mandya	88	2393600.00	940
Mysore	42	11389343	585
Raichur	472	129000.00	3664
Shimoga	52	1521099.00	55
Tumkur	29	2472000.00	578

Source : All India Agarbathis Manufacturers Association.

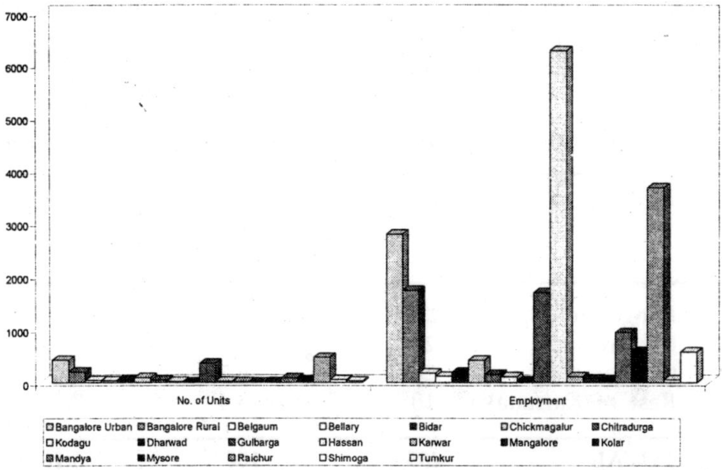

The prominent districts of Agarbathi production are Bangalore, Mysore, Kolar. There is a large concentration of Agarbathi units in and around Bangalore. This is due to commercial importance of the place and availability of good transport facilities. Besides, expansion of Bangalore city has released agricultural laborers to other types of employment. And most these people are un-educated and un-trained, they form a good labour force for Agarbathi manufacture.

It can be seen that 65% of the AIAMA members are from Karnataka, of which, a majority are in Bangalore. The purpose of affiliation is generally to take up causes of the industry and considering the type of members in AIAMA and the number of members in AIAMA, it can be seen that the affiliations form a very small percentage, making it difficult to cover tiny and small units, which do not have substantial numbers in the affiliations. Although the numbers of such units are substantial forming over 90% of the total units in Karnataka. If the small units in Karnataka have to take up causes for their betterment, they certainly have to organize themselves through suitable affiliations either from own members or from among the existing bodies may perhaps change their membership fee structure to enable reach such categories.

Table - 4
Distribution of Aiama Members Unit in Karnataka

	Place	*No. of Units*	*% to total AIAMA units in Karnataka*	*% to total units in India*
1.	Bangalore	238	80.7	52.5
2.	Mysore	27	9.2	5.9
3.	Chintamani	20	6.7	4.4
4.	Rest of Karnataka	10	3.4	2.2
	TOTAL	**295**	**100.0**	**65.10**

Source: All India Agarbathi Manufacturer's Association.

1) Total No. of Aiama Members = 453
2) Total Aiama members form only 8.9% of the total unit in the state.

The Mysore Government distribution of agarbathis as mementos in foreign countries during 1930s acted like a catalyst. The agarbathis were bought from the local reputed agarbathi manufacturers like M.R. Jettappa, Janab Mohammed Yusoof etc. These were liked by distinguished foreigners and demand was thus indirectly created. In 1940s, some pioneers started exporting agarbathis to Srilanka. As the demand for agarbathis increased in Ceylon, the Government of Ceylon took interest in the manufacture of agarbathis. They invited Janab Attar Mohammed Peer of Mysore in 1962 to guide the development of agarbathi industry there.

Our suggestions were made based on the fact that difficulties in getting Jigat, white chips powder and spent wood dust from within the state / country the industry was actively considering offers for the same received from our countries, including Australia.

The entry of multinational and large companies into the agarbathi industry, which has largely remained unorganized, has put pressure on many small and medium agarbathi manufacturers. While many manufacturers have stopped making agarbathis, some others have taken to selling the products of big companies. Small units numbering over 10,000 operate in different parts of the country and the industry turnover has been estimated at over Rs. 1,000 crores, providing employment to over 12 lakh people, directly and indirectly. After liberalization many MNCs have ventured into this sector.

The declining margins in their traditional products such as soaps and detergents and the near stagnant growth of these products over the last few years have forced multinationals and others diversify into agarbathi making. The low cost of entry into the industry has also lured the big companies to build agarbathi brands. "In future, not many of the existing traditional agarbathi manufacturers would be one the scene due to the taxies adopted by the big companies".

In fact, many of the agarbathi manufacturers, with limited resources who cannot counter the big companies. One of the prime reasons for the MNCs to enter this sector was that the agarbathi industry has been growing at an average rate of 10 percent annum, whereas the growth in consumer durables was either stagnant. The demands for the product had been growing by around 20 percent in Northern, Eastern and Western States.

Further, the demand for agarbathi and other products had gone up worldwide with increasing awareness on Indian spirituality and growing popularity of aroma theraby, especially among the youth. India's agarbathi exports touched Rs. 300. The product is being exported to West Asia, Africa, Europe and Southeast Asia. China has emerged as a big market as well as a competitor.

Table - 5
Agarbathi sales by geographic regions and rural / urban sectors (figures indicate percentage of nation wide sales)

Region	*Rural (%)*	*Urban (%)*	*Total (%)*
North	64 (19)	36 (17)	100 (18.3)
South	61 (35)	39 (35)	100 (34.7)
East	64 (18)	36 (16)	100 (17.6)
West	58 (28)	42 (32)	100 (29.5)
All India	61 (100)	39 (100)	100 (100.0)

Source: National Council for Applied Economic Research.

Description of Goods

Oodabathi / Agarbathi is a product which diffuses fragrance, when lighted and which has been in continuous use over centuries, was mainly used in places of religious worship as well as at the residence of nobles. It emitted fragrance since it was manufactured with aromatic leaves, roots, flowers, aromatic oils etc., which gave-out fragrance when lit.

Majority of agarbathis manufactured are of cheap quality containing only charcoal power, low quality sandal wood power with wood gun powder. Agarbathi industry is labour intensive, cottage type of traditional activity in India. The main marketing centers are situated in Mysore and Bangalore in India. It can be taken up in rural areas without any difficulty. It requires only low technology for manufacturing the agarbathis.

Manufacture, Scantier, Packaging, Marketing

Agarbathis are used by many communities in India daily for performing puja. Agarbathis are also used in some of the foreign countries. Hence, demand for the product is good. This industry can be set up with less investment in small areas.

Scenting, Packaging and Marketing

The masala battis or non - scented battis are dipped in a variety of perfumes and then packed with the respective brand names for sale in the market. Sometimes, the marketing is being done a separate agency as per their market reach in each specific region or country. The North - eastern States have ample capacity to set - up Agarbathi enterprises at the community level in rural pockets. This enterprise is capable of creating rural employment and sustainable livelihood opportunity among the community people. The following are the ingredients that are normally used for perfuming 1 kg of rolled agarbathi sticks.

Manufacturing process

Charcoal powder, white chip powder, jigat powder, sandal powder are mixed using water and dough is made. Dough is rolled on bamboo sticks normally. Raw agarbathis can be perfumed either by dipping in perfumed or by spraying the perfumes of the raw agarbathis.

The role of women is changing rapidly in many countries and growing numbers are earning incomes outside the home. For women, earning an income must often be combined with domestic responsibilities for family welfare, children's, care of the elderly, food preparation, and other domestic tasks. Women's contribution to the wider economy is now being given fuller recognition although this recognition has yet to be translated into significant and appropriate forms of support.

SUGGESTIONS

1. The industry is on an unsustainable growth path the availability of key raw materials. The species Mellitus makarantha, the tree source for jigat powder, has declined considerably in south India and is currently being sourced from Uttar Pradesh. In the absence of targeted programmes to augment this species these supplies too will dry up while

demand for jigat is predicted to grow by 50% over the next five years. A 40% increase in the demand for bamboo and 25% for charcoal in the same time frame is also predicted. Supply issues with respect to these are also not being addressed already the industry sources its bamboo splints from the far away North–East. Shortages of raw material could jeopardize the economic viability of the industry and render thousands unemployed or displaced by substitutes. Efforts by relevant state governments to incorporate the raw material needs of the industry into their forestry and social forestry projects are urgently called for.

2. Currently the industry is taxed at multiple levels e.g raw material taxes on bamboo, charcoal, jigat and aromas range between 25 to 90% in addition to which a purchase tax on raw agarbathis and sales tax on the finished produce are levied. There is need to look at the tax structure in to and determine if the burden of taxation is fair or whether it can be rationalized.
3. Different rates of taxation and differing labour law requirements across states creates an anomalous situation. For instance, Karnataka is the only state where the agarbathi industry falls under the purview of the factories act and which consequently has to pay wages some what in lien with minimum wage requirements (wages for home workers have some relationship with and move in tandem with factory wages) and has to provide factory based workers with social security coverage. This along with much lower rates of sales tax in states like Bihar and U.P encourages the industry to migrate to these states to the detriment of the workers cause. A uniform coverage of the agarbathi industry under the Factories Act in all states is called for.

Conclusion

Agarbathis (incense sticks) form part and parcel of the traditional Hindu practice of offering prayers in temples and other places of worship. In modern days, perfumed sticks are also used in houses and in other public places air fresheners and / or mosquito repellents. The demand for agarbathi is increasing both in the domestic and export markets because of the improvement in quality and increase in the types of products. India is the largest producer of agarbathis in the world.

References

Rothboecke, Sandra and Sarthi, Acharya (1999). 'Gender - based Segregation in the Indian Labour Market', *The Indian Journal of Labour Economics,* Vol.42, No.2, October - December, PP.581 - 599.

Sandesara .J.C, 'Industrial Growth in India - Performance and Prospects;, *The Indian Economics Journals,* Vol.30, No.2, 1980, p - 158.

Schultz, Paul (199). 'Women's Changing Participation in the Labour Force', A World Perspective', *Economic Development and Cultural Change,* Vol.38, No.3, April, PP.457 - 485.

Sen Abhijit (1996). 'Economic Reforms, Employment and Poverty', Economic and Political Weekly, Special Number, September.

Sen, A.K. (1990). 'Gender and Co - operative conflicts', in Tinker, Irene (ed), Persistent Inequalities, Oxford University Press, Oxford.

Sethuraman, S.V. (1998). 'Gender, Informality and Poverty: A Global Review of Gender - Bias in Female Informal Employment and Incomes in Developing Countries', (October) (Minco.)

13

Livelihood Security of Women Through SHGs – With Special Reference to Mandya District

Suresha, A.L.

INTRODUCTION

The achievement of SHGs and Government programmes are having a positive impact on the economic empowerment and it increases the role of women in decision making as well as income generating activities. After 2001 which considered as the "Women Empowerment Year" the rate of participation of women in all the sectors has been considered as an important landmark in the economic development. This has changed the fundamental and structural set - up of our economy. At the same time, the changes in the role of women in various sectors started to influence the Micro Finance.

SHGs have helped micro-enterprises set by women as individually and groups. The examples are raising vegetables in the land, ready made garments making, developing horticulture and animal husbandry, cultivation of medical herbs, mushroom cultivation, pot making, stone quarrying, sheep breeding and marketing wool, preparation of pickles, canteens in Government office premises, running a minibus, running public distribution outlets and so on.

The growth of SHGs and bank linkage programme created initially a lot of impression in the minds of feminist as a tool of reducing "gender inequality" and also reducing poverty. Hence forth, this has received a lot of encouragement by the Union Government, State Government, Department of Women and Child Development, NABARD and various Non-Governmental Organizations. But unfortunately in our country, in many conferences held at national and international level, debated for and against about the impact of SHGs on economic development. Therefore it is the right time to make an empirical evaluation of the impact of SHGs on women participation in literacy, decision making, livelihood security etc., in order to achieve the empowerment.

In rural India, there is substantial degree of feminization of poverty on account of an increase in the net population growth rate among the landless agricultural labour households (including SC/ST and other backward classes women), low level of human skills, lack of availability of wage employment opportunities and inadequacy of institutional support to create wage as well as self employment opportunities. This list includes economic factors responsible for feminization of poverty which are much stronger in operation and which function along with socio-cultural barriers and discrimination against women in economic participation.

In general most important rural development programmes or poverty alleviation programmes are land reforms, IRDP (Integrated Rural Development Programmes), basic minimum need programme, national rural wage employment programme (like the erstwhile) NREP, Jawahar Rozgar Yojana, Prime Minister Rozgar Yojana and the present Prime Minister Swarna Jayanthi

Rozgar Yojana have not substantially benefited rural women particularly to enhance their real income and standard of living. From only sixth five year plan (1985) onwards, 30% reservation for women among the total beneficiaries under the rural poverty alleviation programme were provided. This provision undoubtedly has the good intention of providing a social justice to rural women but since the dimension of the problem of feminization of poverty is very huge. Academicians' planners, non - governmental organisation and government felt it alike that the general rural development programmes were insufficient in this regard. Therefore from the early 1990's certain gender specific rural women development programmes are devised and implemented. They are development of women and children in rural areas, Indira Mahila Yojana, Mahila Samakya Programmes (equality through education), Rashtriya Mahila Kosh etc., was implemented. These programmes have the goal of creating self-employment among women both on individual and 'group initiative' entrepreneurship basis. These programmes also aim at socially and politically mobilizing women for achieving other goals of women empowerment. Since the DWCRA could not gain wide support both from Government bureaucracy and Non-Government Organisations it was discontinued. In its place an ambitious programme called SHGs to achieve the same goal is devised and implemented from 1989 / 99 in the middle of 9th plan.

The Ninth Plan (1997 - 2002) documents lay emphasis on the participation of people in the planning process, and the promotion of self-help groups. Empowerment of women is one of the nine prime objectives of the ninth plan. In this context, it is desirable to generate information and analyse to what extent these self-help groups have been able to reduce poverty and vulnerability by; increasing capital/asset formation at the household level, improving household and enterprise incomes, enhancing the capacity of individuals and households to manage risk, increasing enterprise activity within households, expanding employment opportunities for the poor in non-farm enterprises, empowering women and improving the accessibility of other financial services at the community level.

Objectives of the Study

1. To study the role of SHGs in improving the livelihood security of women in Mandya district in order to empower the women.
2. To analyse the impact of SHGs in rising the consumtion level of the women in the case study area.
3. To offer suggestions for further improvement of SHGs to empower the women.

Results and Discussion

The objective of the self-help group is to promote strong and independent women groups who exert control over their own development and that of the community. The women would be equipped with managerial and technical skills through enhanced participation in economic activities. The programme also envisages an enhancement in the capacities of women through the development of training modules and material that can adapt to the local context. With the enthusiastic roles played by the NGOs, the banks, the public and the governments, over a period of one and a half-decade, the SHG approach has transformed into a movement in the rural areas.

Some of the major socio-economic features of respondent women of SHGs include the following;

The study sample of 1000 SHG women include respondents belonging to all age groups. Of the total 1000 SHG women, 181 (18%) women belong to 18-27 years age group; 284 (28.4%) women belong to the age group of 27-38 years, 378 women (37.8%) belong to 38-47 years age group and 100 women (10%) belong to the age group of 47-57 years and 57 women (5.7%) belong to 58 years and above age group. The younger women of 18-27 years of age group in large number have become members of SHGs in Mandya, Malavalli and Maddur taluks, the women of 28-37 years and 38-47 years age group in Srirangapatna, Pandavapura and Nagamangala taluks are members of the SHGs. Further, it may be noted that women of the age group of 38-47 years are participating in large number in SHG activities in all select case study taluks. The ageing is a demographic factor that constrained women participation in SHG activities in Mandya district.

The severity of human poverty of the rural women of Mandya district is further substantiated by how a large number of children of these women are not attending the school (253) and being school drop outs (353), only children of 394 women are attending the schools. That means the illiterate and low literate children of rural women constitute the potential for future supply of casual labour in Mandya district. The lack of income and ignorance about the relevance of education are two factors responsible for the educational backwardness of the rural poor.

The data on access to food by rural poor women and their families reveals that out of 1000 sample women only 495 of them were consuming one ordinary meal; 372 women and their families were able to buy two meals without fruits and vegetable, and 133 families were able to buy the meals with some quantity of vegetables and meat. This means the rural poor women and their families are facing malnutrition due to lack of income. This is a major problem of majority of the rural poor women in Mandya district.

In the case of health care also the access to rural poor women and their families in Mandya district is considerably inadequate. Of 1000 sample rural women, 306 of them have reported not having access to modern allopathic medicine; about 463 women reported to have gained access to rural health after a lot of delay; only 231 of the sample were able to obtain timely health care services whenever they fall ill. Further it is important to note that the Mandya district lags far behind in health care network development.

Table - 1
Consumption Status of Respondents

Sl.No	*Consumption Status*	*Total*	*%*
01	Consuming one ordinary meal	495	49.5
02	Families were able to buy two meals without fruits and vegetable	372	37.2
03	Families were able to buy the meals with some quantity of vegetables and meat	133	13.3
	Total	**1000**	**100**

Source: Field Survey.

Table - 2
Health Care Access to Respondents

Sl.No	*Health Care*	*Total*	*%*
01	Not having access to modern allopathic medicine	306	30.6
02	To have gained access to rural health after a lot of delay	463	46.3
03	To obtain timely health care services whenever they fall ill	231	23.1
	Total	**1000**	**100**

Source: Field Survey.

The rural poor whether men or women ao not have access to institutional credit in Mandya district. Of our sample 1000 rural women, 662, have borrowed loans from local money lenders, 205 from friends and relatives, where as 88 have obtained loans from cooperatives credit societies and banks; 45 from commercial banks. That means 13.3 percent of our sample women had access to institutional source for loans before the introduction of SHG's in Mandya district.

Table - 3
Loan Facilities to Respondents

Sl.No	*Loan sources*	*Total*	*%*
01	Borrowed loans from local money lenders	662	66.2
02	From friends and relatives	205	20.5
03	Obtained loans from cooperatives credit societies and banks	88	8.8
04	From commercial banks	45	4.5
	Total	**1000**	**100**

Source: Field Survey.

The purpose of borrowing loans by the rural poor in Mandya district is spending both for consumption and investment. The consumption purpose includes food, health and education, festivals, marriages and other social activities. Of the 1000 sample rural women, 663 of them have obtained loans to their regular basic needs; whereas the remaining 337 rural women have borrowed loans for the investment purpose like - income generating activities (small and petty trade), purchasing property, house construction, repayment of loans etc., This is the credit / borrowing behaviour of rural poor women before becoming members of the SHG's in Mandya district. The data collected in this regard further reveal that, of the 663 women borrowed for consumption purpose, 309 of them have borrowed loans to buy food, 222 women to spend for festivities and marriage, only 76 spend on health care and 56 to provide educational amenities to their children; (a) Of the 337 rural women, who have borrowed loans to make investments, 175 of them have returned the old loans incurred by their husbands; 99 of them have purchased properties; 24 have spent on acquiring income generating activities and 39 of them have invested in house construction. That means the rural women and their families have lived in perpetuating debt for a long period of time. (b) The 605 rural poor women were defaulters (unable to repay the loans); 278 of such women have repaid the loans by 50% and 117 women have repaid the loans completely. The rural poor women of Nagamangala, Maddur and K.R.Pet taluk are most loan defaulters in our areal sample of the Mandya district, before joining the SHG's formed after 1999.

Findings of the Study

1. An analysis of self-empowerment process reveals that the SHG members have strongly agreed with the recognition in the society due to their association with SHGs. On the other hand, the members are not happy regarding their capacity to take solutions to their family problems.
2. The mobilization of rural poor women for the formation of SHG in Mandya district has been spectacular and highly successful. A large number of rural women have started joining the SHGs particularly after 2000-01 with the availability of more loans on account of the variable and increasing Bank-SHG-Linkage. The attraction of obtaining a sizable amount of loan over Rs. 2,000 up to 10,000 in general. This has acted as a driving force for the poor rural women and also cultivates proper savings habits. Since the ability to borrow directly proportionate to (linked to) the amount of savings made by them with the group.
3. The group membership has provided freedom for rural women to either take up self-employment activities independently as individual or together in a group that means in SHG in effect stand to promote entrepreneurship development among rural poor women both individually and collectively in Mandya district.

4. It is found that individual women member of SHGs working for 5 to 6 days in week are able to earn Rs. 900 to Rs.1,200 per month. The women who do not undertake self-employment activities regularly on daily basis naturally earn less. Very frequently the rural poor women face seasonal unemployment and under employment. The daily wage for rural women in agriculture being Rs. 20-30 the casual manual women agricultural labourer do not earn more than 3 to 5 hundred rupee per month during the agricultural seasons. In this sense the total amount of income earned by the SHG women individually is approximately more than Rs.900- Rs.10,000 per year. Where as a women agricultural labour earn Rs. 3,000 - Rs. 5,000 per annum. Therefore it would be beneficial for rural poor women to join SHGs and take up individual or group entrepreneurship activities than remaining as agricultural labourer.

Suggestions

In the light of our findings and observations some suggestions are made about effective functioning of SHGs in general and Women SHGs in particular. The suggestions are listed as follows:

1. There is a need to reduce the transaction costs for banks as well as borrowers. Banks need to invent new lending products and innovative systems and procedures to reduce the cost of lending to the poor.
2. Bank linkages for SHGs are at present driven more by annual targets than as a system. This is again turning to be like another target oriented government programme where statistics are more enticing than the actual quality of progress achieved. In view of this, banks linkages are to be driven more by passion and zeal than by targets in order to achieve sustainable results.

3. Credible information material should be prepared for the purpose of heralding the role of SHGs in women development. Different forms of communication should be mobilized, and modern information technology may be used to document, validate, and disseminate the experiences of Self Help Groups and their economic impact on development of women. It is preferred that the media messages should also be gender-sensitive. Further, systematic efforts are required to be made for documentation of several innovative micro finance practices being adopted in different parts of India.

References

Bhatt,N and S.Y.Tang (1998) Group Based Microfinance and Economic Development in T.Liou. New York: Handbook of Economic Development.

Bhoumik,K.L(1988),Development of Women and Children, New Delhi: Inter India Publications.

Boserup.E.(1989): Women's Role in Economic Development: Earth scan: London.

Chandrasekhar,R.(ed).,Women's Resource and National Development: A perspective, New Delhi, Gaurav Publishing House.

Charlton, S.E.M.(1984): Women in Third World Development, West View Press, London.

Chawla .A.S.,(1990) Nationalisation and Growth of Indian Banking, deep and Deep Publications, New Delhi.

14

Issues Before Trade Unions in India

Divyathejomurthy, V.

INTRODUCTION

Trade unions are among the major and most influential social institutions in modern societies. They act as agents of labour, and organize large number of workers into a single entity. As collective organisations of workers, they overcome the structural weakness of workers vis-à-vis employers in labour markets. There is long standing debate on the role of trade unions, but there is no dispute over the fact that wherever they exist they have major influence on the wages and other conditions of work. Trade unions exist in all parts of the world, but what a union is and what it does varies from country to country.

Unions have come to occupy a strategic place in the modern industrial organizations. Industrial production, among other things depends upon cordial industrial relations and committed and contended industrial work force. Trade unionism means collective action to protect and improve living standard by people who sell their labour power. Unionism arises wherever and whenever labour is freely brought and sold and occurs because of the dominant bargaining power of buyers of labour power due to their market superiority which enables them to discriminate between sellers and displace them with mechanical power if necessary. Unionism as a global phenomenon has come to occupy a strategic place in almost all modern industrial societies.

Unionists have been almost always a heterogeneous group, ranging from philanthropists to professional experts and revolutionaries not to mention a host of labour racketeers. Result is that trade unions have almost always been found at the centre of controversies. Rarely, attempts have been made to examine the structure and functions of trade unions in the context of rapid changes taking place in the vital sectors of economy and society.

Objectives of the Study: The objectives of the present study are:

1. To review critically the reactions of trade unions to the strains of industrial and general economic development.
2. To examine the functions and growth of trade unions under the regime of globalization in India.
3. To analyse the recent trends in the trade union movement in India.
4. To derive policy implications from unions reactions for structuring a rational labour policy.

Methodology of the study

This study is mainly based on secondary source of data viz., published data about the labour unions in India. Due to time constraint the study could not be able to enquire into primary data. Simple statistical techniques have been used to analyse the data.

Results and Discussion

In India, the differences in the functions of unions are also seen in their affiliation to the state or national federations. The apex of the Indian labour movement comprises a number of central organizations that affiliate individual unions. There are a few non-political federations, but most union federations are explicitly political. The political parties control them and supply them with the upper crust of their leadership. Every central trade union claims to have a unique ideology, though in practice it is not easy to discern much difference between them. The INTUC is inspired by the Gandhian Philosophy, with principles of nonviolence and emphasis on cooperation between employers and employees. The AITUC is the other older of the two communist centres, but it is the CITU, which symbolizes radical Marxism in the Indian labour movement. The HMS with its commitments to socialist ideology lies between the soft line of the INTUC and the radicalism of the communists. The BMS claims to be an independent and non-political union, but in practice it has close links to the Bharatiya Janata Party. The membership of major central trade unions in 1980, 1989 and 2007 is presented in table - 1.

Table - 1
Membership of Central Trade Unions (Millions)

Union	*1980*	*1989*	*2007*
INTUC	3.51	2.69	3.95
BMS	1.88	3.12	6.22
HMS	1.84	1.48	3.34
UTUC(LS)	1.23	0.84	1.37
UTUC	0.61	0.58	0.61
NLO	0.41	0.14	0
TUCC	0.27	0.23	0.73

Union	*1980*	*1989*	*2007*
NFITU	0.53	0.53	0.60
AITUC	1.06	0.94	3.44
CITU	1.03	1.78	2.68
Others	-	-	1.94
Total	12.39	12.33	24.88

Note: Others include LPF (0.61 million members) AICCTU (0.64 million members) and SEWA (0.69 million members).

Source: Ministry of Labour, Verification of Membership of Central Trade Unions.

The Central Trade Union Organisations

The central trade union organisations differ in their influence in different sectors and some of them put more efforts in organizing workers in the informal sector. Table - 2 presents union membership of central trade unions in the formal and informal sectors. In India, the Trade Union Act 1926 recognizes workers right to organize and engage in trade union activities and provides for registration of trade unions. Once a union is registered, it is formally considered a union. The registration status is, therefore, a popular criterion for identification of unions, but it is not a necessary condition. In India, many workers organisations are not registered under the Act, but they perform all functions of unions. The government employee's organisations, for example, are not unions under Act, but on many occasions they have organized strikes and actively bargained with the government for benefits of their members. In the government sector, the railway workers, however, enjoy all trade union rights at par with the other industrial workers and can get their organisations registered under the Act. Another example of unregistered organisations is 'Krishik Sabha', which is an organisation of agricultural labours and small-farmers affiliated to CPI (M).

Table - 2
Membership of Major Central Trade Unions (in '000)

Unions	*Organised Sector*	*Unorganised Sector*		*Total*
		Non-agriculture	*Agriculture*	
BMS	2842 (46)	2037 (33)	1336 (21)	6216
INTUC	2337 (59)	672 (17)	945 (24)	3954
CITU	946 (35)	1622 (61)	111 (4)	2678
AITUC	894 (35)	1078 (31)	1470 (43)	3442
HMS	1816 (26)	866 (26)	656 (20)	3338
UTUC (LS)	324 (54)	303 (22)	746 (54)	1373
Others	712 (24)	789 (20)	2381 (61)	3883
Total	9872 (18)	7368 (30)	7645 (31)	24885

Note : Figures in brackets are percent in total membership.
Source: Verification of Membership of Central Trade Unions.

Union Membership and Union Density

The two indicators frequently used to indicate union influence and union power are union membership and union density. Union membership gives a count of total number of union members in a country or industrial sector. Union density, which is the ratio of actual to potential members, is used to compare levels of unionization across industrial sectors, across countries and over time. The knowledge of the two indicators is important not only for the policy makers entrusted with the formulation of industrial and labour policies, but also important for union leaders and managers to understand their bargaining positions. It is also important for international comparison of union influence. More particularly, comparison of unionization in developing countries has recently become an important subject in discussions on linking trade with labour rights. It is argued that the low level of unionization in developing countries is leading to exploitation of workers and hence there is need strengthen labour rights.

In India, the low level of unionization in most estimates is because of inaccurate estimates of union membership and union density that are based on incomplete data. In India the published estimates on union membership and union density indicate very low levels of unionization. The ILO in its World Employment Report 1997-98 documents trade union density in India to be 5.4 percent of salary and wage earners. Some researchers even compute union density as low as 2 percent of total labour force. They indicate extremely low levels of unionization in India compared to other countries, but it is hard for union leaders, managers, and labour officials to believe that unions in India represent such a negligible percentage of workers.

In fact, plant-level evidence in several studies indicates a high level of union activity in the formal sector. The low estimates are because of inaccurate data on union membership published in the Indian Labour yearbook, which do not include reports from all states in India and include only membership of unions submitting returns. The inaccurate estimates have led to poor understanding of union strength in the country. In this study the estimates include membership data of all the states and membership of all registered unions irrespective of whether they submit returns or not. The results are far different from what is published in the Indian Labour Yearbook. The estimate for 2007, for example, shows presence of 56.7 million union members in the country in place of 6.3 million reported in the Indian Labour year Book.

Union density is defined as the ratio of union members to potential union members. There are some measurement issues in computation of union density. First, there is a dilemma about choice of potential members. The possible choices are: (a) wage and salaried workers; (b) workers in non-agricultural sector; (c) wage and salaried workers in non-agricultural sector; and (d) workers in the formal sector. Depending on what aspect of industrial relations one is interested in, one can use the different choices and

Table - 3
Membership of Central Trade Unions in Major States

State	Wage-employed ('000)	Trade unions							Union of density (% wage employed)
		BMS	INTUC	CITU	AITUC	HMS	Others	Total	
Haryana	2935	140	3	23	53	30	43	293	9.99
Karnataka	9106	23	95	78	19	135	36	387	4.25
Assam	3345	43	336	44	32	51	34	539	16.10
Punjab	3685	265	83	9	183	53	0	593	16.08
Chhatisgarh	3317	204	295	13	32	57	0	600	18.10
Gujarat	8006	163	52	4	16	23	540	797	9.96
Rajasthan	8200	448	25	26	180	237	2	917	11.18
Madhyapradesh	8983	547	223	12	51	17	107	958	10.66
Uttarpradesh	18499	449	304	17	44	190	51	1055	5.70
Kerala	3873	152	71	659	217	134	60	1293	33.38
Tamil Nadu	11172	93	218	255	173	146	625	1508	13.50
Maharashtra	16340	526	448	39	100	410	2	1526	9.34
Jharkhand	3032	301	141	34	117	398	652	1644	54.23
Orissa	4509	462	315	29	143	729	17	1696	37.61
Bihar	9900	366	325	7	865	162	681	2407	24.31
Andhrapradesh	13656	1330	242	207	529	153	0	2461	18.02
West Bengal	10827	137	499	1127	576	251	2311	4901	45.27
All India	147191	6216	3954	2678	3405	3338	5256	24848	16.88

Source: Verification of Membership of Central Trade Unions, 2007.

compute union density. For example, if one is interested in union influence on governments policy, the most appropriate indicator is gross union density calculated as a percentage of union members to the total workforce.

In India there is considerable difference in trade union activity across states. The membership of Central Trade Union Organization and union densities in some major states are shown in the Table- 3. It clearly shows variations in trade union activity across states. In some states like West Bengal and Kerala, workers are more organized than in other parts of the country. The differences are to be seen in conjunction with structural differences of unions across states. Structurally, unions in Gujrat are mostly organized at the enterprise or unit level and not affiliated to any state federation or central organisations (an exception is the textile industry). In contrast, West Bengal has many trade union federations (jute, textile, engineering, plantation) and most unions are affiliated to them. Unionization in the informal sector also varies across states; for example, it is higher in West Bengal than in Gujrat.

Growth and Decline of Trade Unions

In developed countries, there has been progressive decline in union membership, union density, and union popularity in the last three decades. The decline is evident in the time series data of the two indicators for industrialized countries; they show that the declines started in late 1960s and early 1970s. In the newly industrializing countries, union declines started in the 1980s and 1990s (Table-4). In Mexico, labour unions made significant inroads in the seventies, but with economic restructuring in the eighties they started to loose their power. In Korea and Taiwan, unions started to grow in the 1980s and in initial years of 1990s, but then they started to decline. In India, the union membership and union density data do not show similar declining trend in union coverage, but there are clear indications of decline in union power since early nineties.

In India, the absence of reliable union membership data does not allow us to evaluate changes in union membership and union density over the years with considerable accuracy. The main source of data of union membership is those published in the Indian Labour Yearbook. Unfortunately, it only gives membership data of unions that have submitted returns and does not include membership of all unions. An assumption here is that the unions that do not submit their return do not exist, but this is hardly a valid assumption. In practice, majority of the registered unions in India do not submit their returns regularly. Further, the published data do not include data of all the states and some of the major states are always missing. This study computes union membership by using primary data of number of registered unions and average size of unions in different years. In this method of computation, one may object that some of the registered unions may not exist. This is, however, some what compensated as some associations of workers that performs all functions of government employees, organisations of agricultural workers affiliated to CPI (M) and some independent unions like workers committees. The estimates of union membership and union density and their changes overtime are presented in table-5. It clearly shows that both the indicators have steadily increased over the years.

The changes in union membership and union density in India do not indicate decline of the two indicators similar to those seen in the developed countries. There are, however, enough indications of decline of union power in the post-reform years. The state-level data on registration of new unions indicate decline in registration of new unions in the post-reform era. Further, most new unions are in the informal sector. Union membership has increased in the informal sector, but it has declined in the formal sector. The shift of unionization to the informal sector has a major implication, as unions in the informal sector are not as strong as the unions in the formal sector.

Table - 4
Growth and Decline in Trade Union Density

Country	*1950*	*1960*	*1970*	*1980*	*1990*	*1995*	*2000*	*2007*
USA	29	30	28.3	22.8	15.6	14.9	13.5	12.4
Japan	50	NA	34.5	30.3	24.7	24.0	22.2	19.7
Australia	52	50	43.4	46.4	42.7	35.2	24.7	22.9
France	32	19	21.5	17.6	10.2	9.1	9.1	8.3
Germany	35	36	33.0	34.3	30.8	28.9	28.1	22.6
UK	41	42	44.6	44.1	33.5	32.9	29.5	29.7
Denmark	50	58	60.2	76.3	72.5	74.7	75.8	70.4
Sweden	67	71	66.2	78.0	82.9	91.1	81.0	78.0
Italy	-	-	33.4	44.1	33.5	44.1	35.4	33.7

Source: World Labour Report,2007.

Union membership has increased in the informal sector, but it has declined in the formal sector. The shift of unionization to the informal sector has a major implication, as unions in the informal sector are not as strong as the unions in the formal sector. Another indication is that in the post-reform period, there has been growth of non-union firms, and increasingly firms are adopting union avoidance strategies. For example, some employers are promoting workers into administrative/supervisory ranks to take them outside the purview of the Industrial Disputes Act. The loss of job in the public sector through VRS and closures or privatization of inefficient and 'sick' public sector units has also contributed to decline in union power and union membership in the organized sector. All these have led to decline in union power.

The decline of union power is also evident in the increase in income inequality and in growing variations in employment practices. In advanced industrialized countries, increases in earnings inequality in the 1980s and 1990s coincided with the decline in union density and

Table - 5

Growth of Registered Trade Unions in India

Year	*All Workers*	*Wage-employed*	*Number*	*Union submitted returns*			*Union membership (in mn)*	*Union density (%)*
				No.of unions	*Membership (mn)*	*Average membership per union*		
1951	140.0	54.6	4623	2556	2.00	781	3.61	6.6
1961	160.2	63.6	11614	7087	3.98	561	6.52	10.2
1971	180.4	70.4	22484	9029	5.47	606	13.63	19.4
1981	240.0	101.7	37539	6682	5.01	808	26.85	26.4
1991	318.0	147.6	53535	8418	6.10	725	41.16	27.9
2001	352.1	160.9	57952	7242	5.60	773	46.92	28.6
2002	369.1	167.6	58988	8872	7.41	835	48.58	29.0
2003	377.6	170.9	60660	7403	7.25	979	49.98	29.2
2004	386.2	174.2	64817	8152	6.41	786	52.60	30.2
2005	394.7	177.6	66056	7253	5.42	747	53.96	30.4
2006	403.2	180.9	66624	6531	5.87	900	54.77	30.3
2007	409.6	183.1	68544	7812	6.97	893	56.72	31.0

Note: Membership as percentage of wage employed workers

Source: Indian Labour Yearbook, NSSO data for various years.

union power. The changes also accompanied growing variations in employment relation practices. In developed countries, since the 1970s, non-union employment has grown rapidly through expansion of non-union subsidiaries, subcontracting, outsourcing, opening of non-union green-field plants, and union de-certification. There has been decentralization of bargaining and more and more issues are now decided at the firm level than at the industry level. In addition, wages are now more closely linked to performance and skill that vary widely across individuals. In India, there have been similar changes. The distribution of per-capita expenditure shows increases in inequality in the post-reform period compared to those in the pre-reform period. There is no aggregated data on distribution of wages for formal-sector workers, but available piecemeal evidence shows growing wage inequality in the formal sector in the post-reform period with increasing wage gaps between managers and workers, and also among blue-collar workers. Increase in wage inequality in the formal sector is also evident in the fact that in overall changes in inequality, the increase is higher in urban sector. The increase in income inequality, increasing variations in wages, decentralization of bargaining, and growing variations in employment practices in India also point towards decline of unions.

India has, by now, gone through more than a decade of economic reforms. Beginning in June 1991, the thrust of the reform was fiscal stabilization and initiation of major structural reforms aimed at deregulation of the economy to induce accelerated investment, growth, employment and hence reduction in poverty. A good number of these original objectives have been realized. GDP growth in 1990s, after initial year of reforms, was higher than those achieved in 1980s. During the subsequent years, the GDP however slowed down. Growth in industrial value added averaged 8.5% per year during 1993-4 to 1996-7. The same fell to 4.8% per year during 1997-8 to 2000-01. Similarly, the annual average growth in value added in agriculture and allied sector fell down from 4.5% to 1.2 % during the same period. Growth in the infrastructure also came down during the period under reference.

Trade Union Movement during 2001

During 2001 the labour movement celebrated 100 years of its existence in India. During the centenary celebrations, various labour leaders narrated in great length contributions made by them and the India Trade Union Movement [ITUM] in the freedom struggle of India. Many of them have, furthermore, been glorifying their contribution in securing trade union rights and other benefits for workers in the organized sector, However, the ground realities show that in the years following India's independence, the ITUM membership has remained stagnant, if not declining. Its activities have been more or less confined to the organized sector, more so to the public sector enterprises - from where over 70% of its membership is drawn. The number of trade unions and their federation has expanded. Further the state ownership on the one hand and trade unions closeness to political parties made not only the unionization work but also made easier securing non-productivity related financial benefits in the public sector establishments. With the onset of the liberalization process that included disbanding of the public sector and the coalition form of government, the ITUM capacity to influence political leadership in securing undue demands weakened, causing the Labour Movement to move from one stage of marginalization to the other. Since the focus of ITUM was the workers in the organized sector, more so those employed in the government-owned establishments, the mass of workforce engaged in the unorganized sector remained not covered by the trade union movement. Consequently, over 90% of the workforce remained unaware of their rights as workers and as such were being exploited by their employers. Most of the times the worker is not even aware of the employer's excesses. Long working hours, under payment, sexual abuse, physical confinements are day-to-day affairs. The workers take these actions of their employer as fate.

The labour laws in India do not make a distinction between the organized and unorganized sector, yet the resources of the government and trade unions are directed mainly towards this section of workforce. The real exploitation of the worker and his/her family takes place in the unorganised sector where unions are conspicuously absent. Of recent, the international pressure and the shift of workforce from the organized to the unorganized sector, etc., have generated renewed interest in the unorganized sector. The government has repeatedly made announcements about its intention to shift the focus of its activities towards workers in the unorganized sector.

The trade unions too are now trying to penetrate the unorganized sector. All the major CTUOs have specific programmes aimed at enlisting membership of workers in the i nformal sector. There are some indications of workers being organized in beedi, construction, fisheries, forestry, homebased workers, etc. industries. However, enrolling a worker as a member can't be a sufficient indictor of unions' functioning / effectiveness. The latest verified figure on the membership of Central Trade Unions in December 1989 was declared in July 1994 by the Government of India. Accordingly five of the Central Trade Union Organizations [CTUO] have been accorded recognition of being national centres of trade unions. These are, the Bhartiya Majdoor Sangh [BMS] having links with Bhartiya Janta Party [BJP] and with a verified membership of 3,117,324 tops the list followed by INTUC [2,706,451], CITU [1,798,093], HMS [1,477,472] and AITUC [923,517]. In addition there are a large number of non-affiliated / independent unions functional particularly in the unorganized sector and private / joint venture companies. Then there are other forms of workers organizations, such as Morcha, labour cooperatives, NGOs, etc. performing the role of promoting workers welfare.

The Indian Trade Union Movement is close to political parties, has a narrow support base, there is a multiplicity of unions, centralized decision making, ad hoc management, obsolete strategies, external and over-aged leaders, personalized and power-oriented leadership, confrontationist attitudes, non-existent second tier leadership, and negligible gender representation.

Major Findings of the Study

Based on the analysis and discussion in the study of trends in trade union movement in India the following findings have been drawn:

1. BMS occupied the top position by doubling its membership from 31.2 lakhs to 62.6 lakhs. The second place was occupied by INTUC. The AITUC stood at the third place by increasing its membership to 34.4 lakhs, followed by HMS associated with socialists like George Fernandes and established by the Praja Socialist Party at the fourth place with a membership of 33.4 lakhs. CITU increased its membership to 26.8 lakhs in 2002 but was still pushed to the fifth place from third.
2. In relative terms, BMS was able to maintain its share of 25 percent in 2002, similar to that in 1989, and stood at the first place, followed by INTUC whose membership came down from about 23 percent in 1989 to about 16 percent in 2002 a relative decline of 7 percentage points. However, AITUC increased its share from 7.8 percent in 1989 to 13.4 percent in 2002.
3. The trade union which registered the biggest fall in its share was CITU which came down from 15.1 percent in 1989 to 10.7 percent in 2002. The Left organisations like CITU and AITUC are baffled by the rise of BMS, a right-wing organisation, to the top position.
4. The five major CTUOs accounted for about 84

percent of the total membership in 1989 their relative share came down to 79 percent in 2002. The space was filled by other CTUOs during the 13-year period.

5. CITU has accused BMS of fudging its workforce figures while conceding that BMS is the largest CTU worth a top position among the central trade unions. It did not spare its fraternal trade union AITUC too from the charge of fudging, even though the verification of membership is done as per the procedure laid down by the Standing Committee. To question the procedure agreed upon just because it has been pushed down the trade union ladder appears to be totally unreasonable. The problem with CITU is that it considers itself the most powerful voice of the Indian working class and is unable to accept its decline.

Suggestions

In the light of our findings and observations some suggestions are made about effective functioning of trade unions. The suggestions are listed as follows:

1. There is a need to undertake a study on the perceptions of the working class about different trade unions.
2. It is also a hard reality that CITU is losing its grip in a number of states and has been pushed down the trade union ladder to the fifth position as against the third position in 1989. CITU should therefore, do some soul searching about whether the labour is fed up with its duplicity on labour issues to have a belligerent attitude in states ruled by the Congress. BJP and other political parties but play a very docile role in Left-ruled states.
3. To avoid violent actions bargaining units should be defined and the area of bargaining be

streamlined. Statutes should give protection and recognition to the bargaining unit.

4. There should be no distinction between private sector and public sector. Matters that can be settled by collective bargaining should not be referred to adjudication.
5. In view of the multiplicity of trade unions, a united front of trade unions should be formed on certain agreed and common programmes.
6. Encouragement should be given to grow proper leadership amongst the workers. Training on trade union activities should be imparted to the organisers.

Conclusion

Result is that trade unions have almost always been found at the centre of controversies. Rarely, attempts have been made to examine the structure and functions of trade unions in the context of rapid changes taking place in the vital sectors of economy and society. Historical evidence shows that there had been a dynamic and dialectical relationship between trade unions and socio-economic environment in which they existed. The manner in which unions have come to respond to challenges of changes in contemporary Indian society raises a number of issues concerning the survival and future of trade unions. The current thinking on unions is; 1) trade unions are on the decline, 2) unions have been consistently loosing membership and the requisite support from employers, government and public at large, 3) unions are loosing their importance and strength as representatives of working class, 4) unions are becoming increasingly incapable of meeting new challenges of modern technology and global economic upheavals. Hence trade unions in the future need to take up creative ventures in order to serve the interests of the working class.

References

Black, John, Greene, Anne-Marie and Ackers, Peter (1997) , "Size and Effectiveness: A Case Study of Small Unions". Industrial Relations Journal, Vol.28, No.2.

Davala,Sarath.E.A (1992) Employment and Unionization in Indian Industry, Friedrich Ebert Stiftung, New Delhi.

Giri.V.V (1980) Labour Problems in Indian Industry, Shiva House, Asia Publication, New Delhi.

Hirsch, Barry T. and Macpherson, David.A (2000) Union Membership and Earnings Data Book: Compilations from the Current Population Survey, The Bureau of National Affairs, Inc., Washington DC.

Mathur (1964) Indian Working Class Movement, Central Book Department, Allahabad.

Mathur,P.S and Papola . T.S (1982) Growth and Practices of White Collar Unionism: A Study of LIC employees Union in Seth N.R 1982, Industrial Sociology in India: A Book of Readings, New Delhi, Allied Publishers Pvt.Ltd.

Karnik. V.B (1966) Indian Trade Unions: A Survey, Bombay, Manaktalas.

15

Dairy Industry in Poverty Alleviation of Rural Areas – A Case Study

Lepakshaiah, S.V.

INTRODUCTION

Dairying is one of the animal husbandry enterprises, which provide employment, and income not only at the stage of rearing of cattle but also at the stage of production of milk products and cattle feed industry. Dairy is the place where handling of milk and milk products is done and technology refers to the application of scientific knowledge for practical purposes. Dairy technology has been defined as that branch of dairy science, which deals with the processing of milk and manufacture of milk products on the industrial scale. But, dairy is an economic activity, which adds income to households. It provides indirect insurance against risks from crops, such as crop failure due to drought or pests. It is pertinent to study how for dairying helps the farm families to get gainful employment. In the light of the above study of the economics of dairying services shall be appropriate.

A micro investigation in Tumkur district has been made to review the existing structure, growth trend in milk production competitiveness of dairy industry, cost of production and level of efficiency in dairying. Study shall also cover income generation capacity of dairying in rural areas and marketing problems of dairying in the district.

Now it is very pertinent to look into the competitiveness and efficiency of dairy industry. And it is therefore high time that a proper assessment and evaluation were made on role of dairy cooperatives in the development of weaker sections in the district in the light of the needs of the fast changing and growing Indian economy. The present study examines the progress and working evaluation of dairy co-operatives in Tumkur district. The main focus is on analyzing the growth and performance of the dairy co-operatives. It is because of the dominant role-played by the dairy co-operatives in the total co-operative sector in the district.

Research Methodology

The study on dairy cooperatives and poverty alleviation is based on both primary and secondary source of data. The primary data has been gathered from Tumkur district of Karnataka. The secondary data has been collected for various sources like., Dairy Cooperative Journals, Rural Development Journals etc., simple statistical techniques has been applied to analyse the data.

Objectives of the study

This study is based on the following objectives

a) To analyze the performance of dairy co-operatives in Tumkur District in terms of growth in number, membership, financial operations and working results.

b) To study the factors responsible for successful working of the societies and find out the reasons for poor performance of the societies.

c) To identity the specific problems faced by the dairy co-operatives in Tumkur district and

d) To make suggestions for the further development of dairy cooperatives on the basis of the findings of the study.

ANALYSIS AND DISCUSSION

Tumkur district is purposively selected for the present study. Since it is the district with dairy development is one of the most important aspects. Nearly 90 percent of the total populations of the district are engaged in agriculture since agriculture is a basic occupation. There is a lot of importance for dairy development in the district, because of the large extent of availability of livestock in Tumkur district.

Dairy development programme is one of the important phenomena with the cattle development. The Government dairies and the rural dairy centers in the district. Milk products in the rural areas and marketing facilities for the milk producers, are important aspects to serve milk and its products to the city in a whole year.

Animals play still a greater role in the management of Indian agriculture. Animals in Tumkur district are predominantly used for ploughing, sowing, harvesting and marketing. Therefore, Animals should also be considered as an element of system of Agriculture in the entire district.

Growth in Membership

The number of dairy co-operatives has grown up from 327 in 2001-02 to 461 in 2007-08. This up trend increase in the number of dairy co-operatives is the positive trend showing the interest of the dairy farmers to set up the dairy co-operatives the last five years the co-operatives grown at the rate of about 8% per annum. This growth rate is more than the average growth rate of dairy co-operatives in India. i.e., 3.4% per annum. The growth of dairy co-operatives can be observed in the following table.

Table- 1
Growth in Membership

Year	*No. of Dairy Co-operatives*	*% increase or decrease*
2001-2002	327	0
2003-2004	343	5
2004-2005	383	12
2005-2006	407	7
2006-2007	429	6
2007-2008	467	8

Source: K.M.F. Harbinger of Rural Prosperity.

Growth in Milk Procurement

There is a rapid increase in the average milk procurement per day in this district. The average milk procurement was 78,021 kilograms per day in 2001-02 and increased to 1,42,714 kilograms per day. There is an increase of 89% over the last 5 years. This is due to the inputs and incentives given by the co-operatives. And interest shown by the dairy farmers on dairying activities.

The total milk procurement was 2.85 million tones and increased to 5.20 million tones in the district during 2001-2002 to 2007-08. The milk procurement showed a tremendous increase in this district.

Table- 2
Average Milk Procurement

Year	*Milk procurement/day*	*% increase or decrease*
2001-2002	78021	0
2003-2004	90484	16
2004-2005	105581	17
2005-2006	119529	14
2006-2007	125198	5
2007-2008	142714	14

Source: K.M.F. Harbinger of Rural Prosperity.

Increase in Average Retail Sales per Day

The average retail sales per day was increased to 1,51,974 liters per day from 1,00,621 liters per day in 2001-02 to 2007-08. The up trend in the average retail sales per day shows the interest shown by the milk consumers of the milk distributed from the K.M.F. Inspite of the computation by the other privet forms, K.M.F has its lion's share in the total market for the milk in the district. It shows an increase of 52% over the five years. It marked an increase of 10.4% of growth per annum in average milk sales per day. This can be observed from the below given table.

Table -3

Year	*Average retail sales per day*	*% increase or decrease*
2001-2002	100621	0
2003-2004	11482	11
2004-2005	121359	9
2005-2006	126084	4
2006-2007	140851	12
2007-2008	151974	8

Source: K.M.F. Harbinger of Rural Prosperity.

Increase in Artificial Insemination (AI) done

The union on of the important input service provides the artificial insemination to the members and non-members of the dairy co-operatives. The quality and efficient service provided by the technicians of dairy co-operatives increased the demand for artificial insemination. The number of artificial insemination done increased from 7,701 to 1,35,635 during 2001-02 to 2007-2008. The artificial insemination done increased at the rate of 8% per annum. This can be seen in the below given table.

Table - 4
Milk Procurement in the district

Year	*Milk procurement/day*	*% increase or decrease*
2001-2002	7701	0
2003-2004	8283	8
2004-2005	9305	12
2005-2006	10260	10
2006-2007	10338	11
2007-2008	11303	9

Source: K.M.F. Harbinger of Rural Prosperity.

Health Care Services

The district milk union sends the veterinary doctors to the primary dairy co-operative regularly to treat the sick milk cattle. The co-operative also organises the special camps to treat the cows and provides vaccination. Besides these facilities first aid as well as foot and mouth vaccinations are given to milk cattle and other cattle of the village free of the cost to protect the cattle from the dreadful diseases.

Employment Generated

Dairy co-operative movement in the district as generated direct and indirect employment opportunities to a large number of unemployed people. A total of 461 of primary milk co-operatives were working in 2004-05. There are more than 146 people employed in various capacities at Bangalore dairy and two chilling centers. About 1038 people employed at village level dairy co-operatives. About 38 route contract vehicles employ 110 people for milk transportation. Besides, the dairy co-operatives provided indirect employment opportunities to more than 5,400 people in the form of milk transportation, veterinary services, milk sales through agents, parlors, booths etc.

Dairy development has maintained its steady development from its beginning in all fronts. The study is expected to know throw some light on the extent of adoption of improve dairy development practices. The investigation might further help to know the most important sources consulted by dairy farmers for getting information on dairy management practices.

Tumkur is an agricultural district and more than 70 percent of people depend on agriculture and dairy farming and 50 percent of the total income is derived form farming and allied activities such as dairy farming, poultry farming etc.

Dairy development activities under Operation Flood programme pertain to providing guaranteed and remunerative market to the rural milk producers and supply of hygienic milk and milk products to the urban consumers. Out of the total milk production 98,489 (in 1997-98) kgs average milk production 70,000 kgs per day (1997-98) in the district. Tumkur district 7th place in the milk production in Karnataka.

Major Findings

The dairy industries in Tumkur district are mainly an income incentive 442 dairies, total membership 139220, total milk procurement 98,489 kgs but this target is not a great achievement. The progress of dairy development naturally helps for more employment generation making rapid development towards global progress.

In Tumkur district it is unanimously agreed that agriculture in the rural sector as well as rural dairy activities for such a vigorous step agricultural an dairy based industries is the best alternative because in this dairy development sector the skills of the rural population clearly match: more over these dairy industries did not require much skilled labour force the rural people successful run the dairy industry.

POLICY IMPLICATIONS

1. Improvement of milch animals breeds, improvement of dairy cooperative activities and administration needs fresh look for the sustainability of dairy farming.
2. Strengthening of dairy activities and allied agriculture sector and improvements of existing and establishment of new milk routes.
3. Improvement of transport facilities (both public and private) and establishment of veterinary hospital and provision of artificial insemination and vaccination facilities timely.
4. Insurance policy for milch animals and provision of dairy training to farmers at regular intervals.

References

Banerjee.G.C (1998) A Text Book of Animal Husbandry, Published by Raju Primlani for Oxford IBH Publishing Company Limited, Daryaganj, New Delhi.

Chand, Ramesh (1995) Live stock in Himachal Pradesh factors affecting growth, composition and intensity, Indian Journal of Agricultural Economy, Vol.50 - July-September.

Jayachandra (1991) Cost Management in Dairy Industry, Published by Discovery Publishing House, New Delhi.

Kiresur V.R (2002) Economics of Milk Production in Karnataka, Agricultural Situation in India. Vol IX, November.

Lokeshwar.R.R (1997) Hand Book of Animal Husbandry - Published by Publications

Chairman's Speech : 28th Annual General body Meeting. 29th June 2002.

Sivachithappa K. (2002) "Dairy Co-operatives and Rural Prosperity" Tamilnadu Journal of Co-operation, May Vol.2 N. 7. pp . 42 to 45.

16

People Participation in Community Development Programmes – A Study in Mandya District

Chandrakala, K.S.

INTRODUCTION

In this paper an attempt is made to analyse the share of the rural poor in the distribution of IRDP/SGSRY benefits. Rural development in India is recognized as a sine qua non for faster economic development and welfare of common masses. Rural development is not merely development of rural areas but also the development of the rural people into self-reliant and self-sustaining modern little communities. Rural development is, therefore, the development of rural areas in such a way that each component of rural life changes in a desired direction and in sympathy with the other components. Besides, rural development also encompasses structural changes in the socio-economic situation in the rural areas in order that human welfare, which is the primary goal of all development, is secured at the earliest. The importance of rural development in a country like India, which is predominantly rural, cannot be over-emphasized. There are more than 50.7 crores of inhabitants living in rural areas, whereas only 15.7 crores of inhabitants live in urban regions. Besides, the sharp incidence of poverty in the countryside rather than in urban areas emphasizes the supreme need for an accelerated rural development. According to latest official estimate, 40.1 per cent of rural population is estimated to live below the poverty line as against 28.1 per cent in urban areas. Unless concrete and time-bound programmes are formulated and executed to deal directly with the problems of rural poverty, the outflow of the rural poor is likely to grow, creating more slums and posing more problems for urban development.

Rural development for a quite long time was equated with just agricultural growth. The ratio hale behind this was that the benefit of growth would trickle down to the poorer communities. In other words, growth in agricultural produce would itself take care of distributional aspect. However, the expected "trickling down" did not actually take place. Much of the hope of 'percolation effect' in India as well as in other developing countries seems to have faltered. In this regard, the following observation of the planning Commission's Task Force on Integrated Rural Development' is pertinent:

> "After careful consideration, we have belatedly decided to talk what might be considered a rather restricted view of the expression 'rural development'. We have chosen to equate it with agricultural development in the widest sense so as to embrace besides crop husbandry, all the allied activities". Here the word 'allied activities encompass not only agricultural but also all types of development activity intended to improve the quality of life in the countryside.

Objectives of the Study

1. To study the impact of community development programmes on change in income and employmnet status of beneficiaries in rural areas of Mandya district;
2. To study the people participation in community development programmes through village panchayaths in the state of Karnataka;
3. To find out problems based on the study and to offer recommendations for better implementation of the community development programmes.

RESULTS AND DISCUSSION

The existing administrative and organizational approach to rural development does not seem to have encouraged the growth of popular interest, awareness and participation in rural development programmes, especially for the rural poor. It is widely believed that there has occurred the growth of 'dependency relations' on the part of the beneficiaries. This, it is argued, has inhibited the building of their capacity for planning and management of rural development mobilization of resources. It is further argued that this has denied the rural poor the full measure of programmed benefits. Thus the need for participatory approach to rural development is emphasized time and again in social science research as well as in official documents, both domestic and international. As the United Nation's Social and Economic Council, in its resolution adopted in 1975, proposed vigorously that governments should adopt popular participation as a basic policy measure in national development strategy and should encourage the widest possible active participation of all individuals and national non-government organization such as trade unions, youth and women's organizations in the development process in setting goals, formulating policies and implementing plans.

For, the sharing of the rural development benefits by

the core rural poor constitutes an important thrust in the overall rural development strategy of minimizing poverty in the countryside. In this connection, attention will be given to the allied issues such as participation by the rural poor in village cooperatives, their organization, etc. It is well-known that there is an important connection between their participation in development institutions and their share in development benefits.

To begin with, it is known that eradicating poverty among the poorest of the poor which is the basis for Antyodaya approach constitutes the major thrust of Integrated Rural Development Programme. This realization came precisely because the earlier Small Farmers Development Programmes, which were initiated during the Fourth Five Year Plan, had benefited only a small segment of the rural population. These programmes were not designed to tackle the problems of landless labourers, rural artisans and such others who constitute the poorest sections. This deficiency was sought to be rectified under the Sixth Plan when the IRDP was introduced throughout the country. This orientation towards the poorest of the poor is important, because the degree of deprivation suffered by those who are just below the poverty line is qualitatively different from that suffered by those who are at the bottom.

In the following pages, the composite profile of the beneficiaries under IRDP in the selected blocks would be presented, and the various related issues would be considered. In terms of caste, it has been generally observed that persons belonging to the scheduled castes, the scheduled tribes and some artisan castes live in stark poverty. Development schemes under IRDP are intended to essentially benefit these sections. In the following table, an attempt is made to segregate the IRDP beneficiaries along caste lines in the selected blocks.

Table - 1
Caste - wise Distribution of Sample Beneficiary Respondents in the Selected Blocks

Name of the Block	*Caste*				*Total*
	S.C	*S.T*	*B.C*	*F.C*	
Holalu	10(16.67)	1(1.66)	25(41.67)	24(40.0)	60
Muthathi	3(5.0)	28(46.68)	14(23.32)	15(25.0)	60
Kesturu	20(33.34)	-	18(30.0	22(36.66)	60

The following profile emerges from the above table.

In Holalu block it is seen that the number of beneficiaries belonging to the scheduled castes and the scheduled tribes is very small. Statistically speaking, 16.67 per cent (10) of the beneficiaries belong to the scheduled castes and only 1.66 per cent (1) of the beneficiaries belongs to the scheduled tribes. It can be seen from the table that sizeable number of IRDP beneficiaries belongs to dominant backward castes and to the persons belonging to forward castes. Numerically speaking, 41.67 percent (25) of the respondents belong to backward castes and 40per cent (24) of the beneficiaries belongs to forward castes.

The same table provides data about the respondents in Kothathi block also, where only 5 percent (3) or the beneficiaries belong to scheduled castes and 46.68 per cent (28) of the beneficiaries belong to scheduled tribes, but 23.32 per cent (14) of the beneficiaries are backward castes and 25 per cent (15) of the respondents belong to forward castes. When we disaggregate the backward caste beneficiaries between prosperous (9 members) and the poorer section (5 members), we find that their share in IRDP benefits combined with the share of the forward caste beneficiaries, look quite substantial. This gains in sharpness when we see that in this block nearly 70 per cent population are tribal, but as beneficiaries under IRDP they stand at only 46.68 per cent (28) as showed above.

It is thus seen that the non-tribal population are the major gainers in IRDP benefits. This compares favourably with the block level official figures for the tribal and the non-tribal population benefited under IRDP /SGSRY from 2003-04 to 2006-07 respectively. These figures are given in the following table.

Table - 2
Distribution of Tribal and Non-Tribal Beneficiaries Under IRDP/SGSRY Between 2003-04 and 2006-07

Year	*Tribals*	*Non-Tribals*	*Total*
2003-04	-	14	14
2004-05	43	110	152
2005-06	105	98	203
2006-07	516	421	937
Total	663	643	1306

Source: Report of the Developmental Schemes, Holalu Panchayati Samithi, Mandya District.

Lastly, in the third block, namely, Muthathi, the caste-wise distribution of the beneficiaries under IRDP/SGSRY is as follows: 33.34 per cent (20) of the beneficiaries belong to scheduled castes and none belong to scheduled tribes, whereas 30 percent (18) of the respondents belong to backward castes and 36.66 per cent (22) of the beneficiaries belong to forward castes.

As was observed in Holalu block, so in Muthathi block, the bulk of the 'backward caste' respondents belong to relatively dominant castes with in the 'backward castes', namely, 'Chetti Balaja' 'Bestaru', etc. Out of the total 18 beneficiaries belonging to 'backward castes', 12 of them (67 per cent) can be categorized as persons belonging to the above - dominant backward castes, whereas only 6 beneficiaries (33 per cent) belong to poor artisan castes.

On the whole, the caste - wise distribution of the beneficiaries under IRDP/SGSRY in all the three blocks presented above, clearly demonstrates that the dominant sections of the backward caste and the forward castes are benefited and the really needy, mostly belonging to scheduled castes and tribes, and some artisan castes belonging to backward castes, are largely deprived.

We now consider the respondents' occupational particulars to understand what occupational group/Groups were receiving the bulk of the benefits under IRDP. Table 3 patterned after the official format, gives particulars of our respondents' occupational background.

The following picture emerges from table Firstly, in Holalu block, the figures in the table show that 8.34 per cent (5) of the respondents belong to the category of non-agriculture labour who are mostly engaged in household industry and some petty business activities, 20 per cent (12) of the beneficiaries belong to agricultural labourers category, 8.34 per cent (5) of them are marginal farmers and 28.33 per cent (17) of the respondents are small farmers, whereas 33.32 per cent (20) of the beneficiaries are medium farmers and 1.67 per cent (1) of them belong to the category of big farmers also.

The above figures of the occupational distribution of the respondents give some interesting results. Although the main focus of the IRDP is to remove poverty among the poorest of the poor, who are mainly agricultural labourers, rural artisans engaged in non-agricultural activities and marginal farmers etc., in actuality, it was found that the programme was helping considerably the relatively better off, namely, medium-sized farmers, small farmers and sometimes few big farmers also. As it was clear in Holalu block, 33.32 per cent (20) of the respondents are found to be medium farmers whose economic position is substantially sound and 28.33 per cent (17) of the respondents are small farmers who are much above the poverty line and 1.67 per cent (1) of the farmers even belong to big farmers category.

Table – 3

Occupational Distribution of the Respondents in the Three Selected Blocks

Name of the Block	*Occupational status*						*Total*
	Non-Agriculture Labour	*Agriculture Labour*	*Marginal Farmer*	*Small Farmer*	*Medium Farmer*	*Big Farmer*	
Holalu	5(8.34)	12(20.0)	5(8.34)	17(28.33)	20(33.32)	1(1.67)	60
Muthathi	7(11.67)	9(15.0)	11(18.33)	13(21.67)	16(26.67)	4(6.66)	60
Kesturu	4(6.66)	19(31.67)	8(13.33)	16(26.67)	13(21.67)	-	60

With regard to occupational distribution of the respondents of Muthathi block it may be observed that 11.67 per cent (7) of the beneficiaries belong to the category of non-agricultural labourers, 15 per cent (9) of the respondents are agricultural labourers, 18.33per cent (11) of the beneficiaries belong to the category of marginal farmers and 31.67per cent (13) of the respondents are small farmers, whereas 26.67per cent (16) of the beneficiaries belong to medium farmers, and lastly, 6.66 per cent (4) of them belong to big farmers category. A considerable amount of leakage of IRD benefits can then be seen. The figures show that the medium farmers (26.67per cent) and big farmers (6.66 per cent) have been benefited to a considerable extent. It was gathered from our discussions with the block level officials that nowhere in the block household survey, which should precede the identification of the beneficiaries, was conducted. IN the absence of comprehensive household survey, block officials were left with no reliable data about the incidence of the poverty among the households in the block. This resulted in the erroneous identification of the beneficiaries to a considerable extent as it was shown above. It was also observed that two panchayat Sarpanches who happened to be large farmers, also got assets under IRDP (One was given poultry unit; and the other got an asset under social forestry scheme).

It can be observed from the table that 6.66 per cent (4) of the respondents belong to the category of non-agricultural labour mostly engaged in semi-skilled household industry and petty business activity; 31.67 per cent (19) of the beneficiaries are agricultural labourers, 13.33 per cent (8) of them are marginal farmers and 26.67 per cent (16) of the respondents are small farmers and lastly 21.67 per cent (13) of the beneficiaries are medium farmers and none of them belong to big farmers.

It can be stated that in the above mentioned block where there is a high concentration of agricultural labourers who constitute 61.10 per cent in the total workforce; in terms of developmental benefits, they are not, however, a sizeable group. The respondents belonging to medium farmers and small farmers, whose economic base is reasonably sound since entire block has extensive irrigation facilities, were found reaping substantial IRDP benefits.

As pointed out above, the excessive emphasis on 'targets' was also partly responsible for the programme not having serious impact on the poverty situation. "It is natural for the planners to pretend that they foresee the future, although it may delude them; and it suits the administrators to use the targets as a measure of staff performance". Because of the overemphasis on the target approach, it was observed by us in our study blocks that the local bureaucracy exceeded the targets of 600 families per year per block without caring for the exact social background of the actual beneficiaries or looking into the aspect of efficient deliveries. Actually this is an all-India situation. This resulted in the dilution of the focus on poorest among the poor and the basic approach has therefore been mutilated. Our study as well s few other studies at the macro-level confirmed this trend.

It is at this point that patron-client relationship by presenting the figures in all the three blocks. In Holalu block, where 57.14 per cent of the panchayati members belong to semi-medium/medium farmer and large farmer category, the IRDP sample beneficiaries belonging to these sections was to the tune of 34.99 per cent (i.e., 21 out of the total 60 beneficiaries). In Muthathi block, the position is in the following manner: 55 per cent of panchayati member belong to semi-medium/medium farmer and large farmer category, whereas the percentage of IRDP beneficiaries coming from these sections was 33.33. In Kesturu block, where 56 per cent of the panchayati members belong to semi-medium/medium farmer large farmer category, the figure of sample beneficiaries under IRDP belonging to these sections of farmers was to the tune of 21.67 per cent. These figures reveal clearly the linkage between social background of the panchayati leadership and actual distribution of benefits under the anti-poverty programme such as IRDP.

Programme awareness is an important condition for its success. In the case of IRD Programme, the various channels of communication are available to the beneficiaries. In particular, the emphasis is laid on peoples' institutions like Panchayat Raj bodies, which by proximity, are easily accessible to the villagers. A majority of the beneficiaries, who live in abject poverty, need reliable information channels to be aware of the programmes. While formulating the questions on the awareness of the programme, our purpose was to see through which sources the beneficiaries came to know about the programme. With regard to the sources of information about the programme, we gathered the following responses from the beneficiaries in the three selected blocks. These are presented in the following table.

Table - 4
Distribution of Beneficiaries and their Source of information about IRDP

Source	*Block*		
	Holalu	*Muthathi*	*Kesturu*
Gram Sabha	-	-	-
VLW/VDO	45(75.0)	40(66.67)	34(56.67)
Village Panchayat	8(13.33)	5(8.33)	16(26.67)
Any other Source	7(11.67)	15(25.0)	10(16.66)
Total	**60**	**60**	**60**

It was found, quite interestingly, irrespective of the blocks studied, village development officer/village level worker was the main source of the communication to the beneficiaries of the Integrated Rural Development Programme. Statistically speaking, 75 per cent (45) in Holalu block, 66.67 per cent (40) in Muthathi block and

56.67 per cent (34) of the respondents in Kesturu block had stated that village development officer/village level workers was their source of information; through them they came to know about the programme.

It can be observed from the same table that no respondent had stated in any of the three selected blocks that Gram Sabha was the source of information about the development programmes. This situation brings out the fact that the Gram Sabha which is an important participatory structure at the village level, has been thoroughly sidelined. Not only as source of the information but also as an institution in identifying the beneficiaries, the Gram Sabha's role had been insignificant, as no Gram Sabha was called for this purpose.

On the whole, it was observed that the Village Development Officer/Village Level Worker continues to be the important source of information for the rural poor as far as the developmental programmes were concerned. This is notwithstanding the fact that the panchayat s which are supposed to function as peoples' organizations and thereby the centre of all developmental activities, were not seem to have performed this role effectively.

Our next enquiry was with regard to whether the selection of the beneficiary had been preceded by a household survey by the Block Development Office. This question aroused almost negative response from all our respondents in all the three blocks. They stated that nothing like household survey, which was supposed to take into account numerous details of household incomes and expenditures etc., had been conducted in their blocks. This finding of our study comes closer to the study by the Planning Commission which observed that "in Andhra Pradesh no household survey as per the guidelines was undertaken. The identification was done on the basis of information collected by the Village Level Workers with the help of the Sarpanch, Patwari etc., This was followed by credit camps organized jointly by banks and District Rural Development Agencies (DRDAs). The village assemblies were not taken into confidence at the time of the selection of the beneficiaries". In the absence of comprehensive household survey, the selection of the beneficiaries was left to the discretion of village-level functionaries exercised within the constraints of the rural power configurations.

The mode of selection i.e., whether the beneficiaries are identified individually or through group meetings, is an important condition for successful implementation of rural development programmes. Hence, when we enquired whether our respondents were contracted individually or through meetings for the asset distribution, a substantial number of our respondents stated that they were contacted individually by the village Development officers. Only a few had stated that they were identified through credit camps organized jointly by the District Rural Development Agency (DRDA) and Banks. This finding brings out a number of issues in the identification process of the IRDP beneficiaries in Andhra Pradesh. In spite of the various guidelines issued by the Ministry of Rural Reconstruction, the Government of India, to the effect that the selection of the households for the asset distribution under IRDP should be done in the gram sabha meetings, these directions had not been heeded in actual operation.

A related query we made, related to the role of village panchayats in organizing the meeting mentioned above. As already mentioned, for mally there is no involvement of the village panchayats in the anti-poverty programmes except the fact that the guidelines of the Ministry state that the village panchayat heads should be consulted by the local bureaucracy before finalizing the list of the beneficiaries. In this regard, it was observed in course of our field visit that village sarpanches were taken into confidence in their individual capacity while selecting the beneficiaries but not as representatives of the village panchayats as a whole. Given the power structure in the villages, the selection of the beneficiaries could not fulfil the criterion of justice. A substantial number of farmers with sound economic base who got infiltrated into the beneficiaries list.

CONCLUSION

It can be observed that a significant number of the beneficiaries in all the three blocks got an income of Rs. 5-10 each per day. This can be partly explained by the fact that for a majority of the beneficiaries, the low average investment per beneficiary was made under IRDP. This was more so in the case of the scheduled castes and the scheduled tribes and some artisan castes like carpenters, barbers, washermen etc. We observed in course of our field study that 'Dhobi units' got a paltry investment of Rs. 1,000. So was exactly the case with cycle units. Even in case of plough bullock on which the investment was only Rs. 1,500 for each unit, this was not found that entire income generating source, as the income ranged from Rs. 5/- to Rs. 11/- with the majority of the beneficiaries (nearly 80 per cent) who got this unit. Besides, our respondents stated that work was not available throughout the year.

In course of our field investigations we could perceive the lack of organisation among the rural poor to be a significant barrier in the way of their receiving substantive benefits or development under anti-poverty programmes. This further emphasised the dependence of the rural poor upon the local bureaucracy, since as we saw, they look to the Government officers for benefits under IRDP. In this connection, Goldsmith's following observation is revealing. It says that "large inequalities in assets have a tendency to reduce community solidarity and often make impossible the task of creating viable participatory organisations and projects.

References

Aziz, Abdul, 1989. Integrated Rural Development Programme in poverty alleviation in India, ed. V.M. Rao and Abdul Aziz, Ashish Publishing House, New Delhi, p. 102-38.

Bhattacharya, Mohit, "Global Governance", Mainstream, Vol.34, No.0, September 7,1996.

Eshwar Prasad, Y. 1987. An Evaluation Study of Integrated Rural Development Programme in Ananthapur district, Andhra Pradesh, Ph.D thesis (unpublished), university of agricultural sciences, Bangalore.

Hanumappa H G. and Ninan, K N, 1980. Rural poor and institutional credit where do we go from here in L K Naidu (eds), Bank of Finance for Rural Development, New Delhi: Ashish Publishing House.

Jain, C.M., "Rural Development: Some Aspects of Institutional and Administrative Change", Administrative Change, Jaipur, 1971.

Khatkar, R K, 1985. Rural Development, IRDP in Mahendragar district, New Delhi northern book center.

Kuria, N.T., "IRDP: How Relevant is it?", The Economic and Political Weekly, New Delhi, December 26, 1987.

Krishnan, Kutty, 1984. A case study of integrated rural development programme in a Kerala village. Indian Journal of Agricultural Economics 39(3): 433.

17

Economic Empowerment of Weaker Sections through Bank Credit – With Special Reference to Mysore District

Bhuvanendra, S.K.

INTRODUCTION

Our Nation's commitment to welfare of the poor and the weak is well evident from the fact that "justice- social, economic and political" has been kept as the first among the objectives in the preamble of the constitution of India. This was considered both necessary and essential for constituting India in to a sovereign, socialist, secular, democratic, republic. On account of various historical and social factors, women often referred to as "weaker sections", have limited access to assets and opportunities. This has affected their achieving equality of status and opportunity vis-à-vis others, as envisaged under the constitution. With a view to overcome the constraints and achieve the desired objectives, several specific provisions have been made in the constitution itself for empowerment of the women. Besides, special legislations have been enacted and the Governments, both at Central and State Level, have launched numbers of plans and programmes from time to time for welfare of the weaker sections.

The present study is on the "Bank credit and empowerment of weaker sections in Mysore district" in the fact that lending policy of commercial banks is one of the major instruments through which banks can bring about socio-economic changes, desirable for intensifying the pace of economic growth. Massive changes have been witnessed in the entire spectrum of Indian banking in general and in the area of their lending activities in particular. As such, the research work in this direction will throw more light on the developments, which have occurred so far, and also on how the lending techniques of banks have contributed towards achieving an egalitarian society and towards the fulfillment of broader economic objectives.

It is widely felt that there have been perceptible changes in the living conditions of the weaker sections mainly on economic side and relatively on social side. It is with this perceptional background that a detailed study has been undertaken to find out the economic impact of the commercial banking assistance on the empowerment of weaker sections.

Rural economy is the weaker sector of the national economy and even in the rural economy, a major segment is not only weak but in a miserable state. Banking institutions seem to be the only hope to inject strength and accelerate the growth of rural economy and ensure the development of the rural areas. Gandhiji observed that rural developemnt in India is recognsied as a sine qua non for faster economic development and welfare of common masses. Rural development is not merely development of rural areas but also the development of the rural people into self-reliant and self-sustaining modern little communities.

Objectives of the Study

The present study intends to

(1) analyse the role of bank credit in empowerment of weaker sections of the society in the study area, and

(2) offer suggestions to further effective improvement of bank credit in order to empower the weaker sections of the society.

Methodology

The study is based on primary data collected from field survey in Mysore district. We have interviewed the weaker sections to collect necessary information to evaluate the role played by banking institutions in order to empower the weaker sections of the society.

Results and Discusion

Creation of employment opportunities and generation of adequate income for the beneficiaries is the theme of all social banking programmes. The endeavour is to lift the weakest among the weaker sections of the society above the poverty line on a permanent basis. This part is devoted to the analysis of the impact of bank credit on the income level of the beneficiaries, and to gauge the extent to which financing under various social banking schemes, programmes were successful in fulfilling the objectives laid-down before the banking industry.

The increase in income level and there by improvement in the economic conditions of the beneficiaries, after the bank loans, was possible due to the favourable changes in the arrangements for procurement of inputs. The bank loans enabled them to become independent and to realize higher profit margin for their product.

It is evident from the table- 1 that average amount of post-loan income is substantially higher than pre-loan income for all the activities under study. In this sector, average pre-loan income is Rs.4096.15, which has risen to

Rs.6144.23 in the post-loan period. There are 21 respondents with pre-loan income range between Rs.3000 to Rs.5000 who were not able to improve their income. There is one beneficiary in the income Rs.5500 who is able to improve his income in post-loan period. The number of loaners in the income ranges Rs.6500 to Rs.9000 is 30 in the post-loan period. There is increase in the number of respondents in the higher income levels in the post-loan period. Median income of agricultural loaners indicates that 58 percent of the loaners of this sector are getting income above Rs.7000 in the post-loan period. The dispersion in income of the loaners is slightly higher in the post-loan period as compared to the pre-loan period.

Among the agricultural sector respondents, increase in income actually represents the saving of interest amount by availing bank credit and paying interest at a lower rate than they would have paid, had they borrowed the same amount from agricultural money lenders. The beneficiaries of tractor loans, on the other hand, were able to increase their income to a great extent.

A significantly positive correlation between pre-loan income and post-loan income establishes the point that those who had higher pre-loan income had higher income in the post-loan period as well. It can be inferred that those respondents who were using their own resources in the best possible manner and getting higher income were also in a position to earn a lot by using bank assistance.

Table - 1

Crop Loan Respondents pre-loan income

Sl.No	*Amount (Rs.)*	*Respondents*	*Percent*
01	3000	10	20.00
02	3500	3	6.00
03	4000	14	28.00
04	4500	12	24.00
05	5000	11	22.00
	Total	50	100.00

Crop Loan Respondents post- loan income

Sl.No	*Amount (Rs)*	*Respondents*	*Percent*
01	3000	7	14.00
02	3500	2	4.00
03	4000	4	8.00
04	4500	2	4.00
05	5000	5	10.00
06	5500	2	4.00
07	6500	2	4.00
08	7000	6	12.00
09	7500	4	8.00
10	8000	3	6.00
11	8500	7	14.00
12	9000	6	12.00
	Total	50	100.00

Impact of bank credit on respondents of tractor loaners

In this activity, above 70 percent of respondents pertain to tractor loans. Table - 2 indicates that, there are 15 respondents with pre-loan income range between Rs.5000 to Rs.7500 who are not able to improve their income after bank loans. The number of loaners in the income ranges between Rs.9000 to Rs.15000 is 34 in the post-loan period. This clearly shows that there is an increasing trend in the number of beneficiaries in the higher income levels in the post-loan period. Out of 50 beneficiaries selected under study 34 respondents have been improved their income. Median income of tractor loaners indicates that 70 percent of the loaners of this activity are getting income above Rs.10000 in the post-loan period.

Table - 2

Tractor Loaners: Pre-Loan period

Sl.No	*Amount (Rs)*	*Respondents*	*Percent*
01	5000	18	36.00
02	6500	15	30.00
03	7500	17	34.00

Tractor Loaners: Post-Loan period

Sl.No	Amount(Rs)	Respondents	Percent
01	5000	11	22.00
02	6500	03	6.00
03	7500	02	4.00
04	9000	06	12.00
05	10000	14	28.00
06	12000	06	12.00
07	15000	08	16.00

Impact on beneficiaries of dairy

It has been observed during the course of the study that in cases of direct financing by banks for the purchase of two buffaloes giving a gap of six months of the beneficiaries were able to get a continuous flow of income, resulting in repayment of loans and better income effect on the beneficiary. The dairy loans sponsored by animal husbandry department were found to have impressive effect on the income level of the beneficiaries. It is possible because of training imparted to the borrowers before sponsoring their cases to banks for providing loans. Some beneficiaries took up another allied to agriculture, namely piggery. By and large, the beneficiaries of this activity earned a good return because of low cost for running the activity.

Table- 3
Dairy Loaners: Pre-Loan period

Sl.No	Amount(Rs)	Respondents	Percent
01	10000	15	30.00
02	12000	19	38.00
03	15000	16	32.00

Dairy Loaners: Post-Loan period

Sl.No	Amount(Rs)	Respondents	Percent
01	10000	10	20.00
02	12000	6	12.00
03	15000	4	8.00
04	17500	11	22.00
05	20000	11	22.00
06	25000	8	16.00
	Total	50	100.00

In this activity, average pre-loan income is Rs.12256.80, which has risen to Rs.17500 in the post-loan period. Median income during pre-loan period of this sector was Rs.12000. hence it is clearly shows that Rs.5500 is the incremental income after obtaining the bank loan.

Impact on Bullock Carts beneficiaries

Table - 4 would enable us to appreciate the role played by regional rural banks in improving the income levels of the loaners of bullock Carts wells. It can be observed that a beneficiary, irrespective of age, family size, number of literate in the family, debts of the family, amount of loan and supplementary investment in the activity, can be successful in this activity. In this activity, average pre-loan income is Rs.12,255.81 which has risen to Rs.16,941.86 I the post-loan period. Median income of this activity loaners indicates that 65.2 percent of the loaners of this sector are getting income above Rs.17,500 in the post-loan period. Median income during pre-loan period of this sector was Rs.12,000. Hence it is clearly shows that Rs.5,500 rupees is the incremental income after obtaining the bank loan.

Table - 4

Bullock Carts activity loaners: Pre-loan period

Sl.No	Amount(Rs)	Respondents	Percent
01	10000	15	30.00
02	12000	17	34.00
03	15000	18	36.00
	Total	50	100.00

Bullock Carts activity loaners: Post-loan period

Sl.NoA	*mount(Rs)*	*Respondents*	*Percent*
01	10000	10	20.00
02	12000	5	10.00
03	15000	4	8.00
04	17500	12	24.00
05	20000	12	24.00
06	25000	7	14.00
	Total	50	100.00

Impact on Digging Wells activity

Out of 50 respondents, there were 24 loaners in the income range Rs.12,000 to Rs.17,500 in the pre-loan period and between in post-loan period also. On the other hand, there was a rise in the number of cases in the higher income levels i.e., from Rs.20,000 to Rs.27,500 in the post-loan provided as compared to pre-loan period. Average amount of income rose from Rs.15,127.27 to Rs.19,372.73 and median income jumped up from Rs.15,000 to Rs20,000 in the post loan period.

Table- 5

Digging Wells activity loaners: Pre-loan period

Sl.No	*Amount(Rs)*	*Respondents*	*Percent*
01	12000	21	42.00
02	15000	19	38.00
03	17500	10	20.00
	Total	50	100.00

Digging Wells activity loaners: Post-loan period

Sl.No	*Amount(Rs)*	*Respondents*	*Percent*
01	12000	14	28.00
02	15000	3	6.00
03	17500	7	14.00
04	20000	10	20.00
05	25000	11	22.00
06	27500	5	10.00
	Total	50	100.00

Source: Field Survey.

The above analysis indicates that, majority of the rural fold especially weaker sections of the society including small farmers are not able to meet their day-to-day requirements from their own sources of income not to speak of investigating in other productive enterprises for improving their economic conditions. Therefore, they have to depend on various financial agencies for getting funds for making investment. To bring about the overall development in the rural areas, financial assistance (especially regional rural banks assistance) to the rural poor needs emphasis.

Major Findings of the Study

Based on the analysis and discussion in the study of "Empowerment of Weaker Sections through Bank Credit", the following findings have been drawn:

1. The average amount of post-loan income is substantially higher than pre-loan income for all the activities under study. In this sector, average pre-loan income is Rs.4,096.15, which has risen to Rs.6,144.23 in the post-loan period. There are 21 respondents with pre-loan income range between Rs.3,000 to Rs.5,000 who were not able to improve their income. There is one beneficiary in the income Rs.5500 who is able to improve his income in post-loan period. The number of loaners in the income ranges Rs.6,500 to Rs.9,000 is 30 in the post-loan period. There is increase in the number of respondents in the higher income levels in the post-loan period.
2. It has been observed during the course of the study that in cases of direct financing by banks for the purchase of two buffaloes giving a gap of six months of the beneficiaries were able to get a continuous flow of income, resulting in repayment of loans and better income effect on the beneficiary.
3. The dairy loans sponsored by animal husbandry department were found to have impressive effect

on the income level of the beneficiaries. It is possible because of training imparted to the borrowers before sponsoring their cases to banks for providing loans. Some beneficiaries took up another allied to agriculture, namely piggery. By and large, the beneficiaries of this activity earned a good return because of low cost for running the activity.

4. When asked with farmers about the situation before availing of the KCC, majority of them have stated that their major area was under rain-fed conditions. As a result farmers were unable to earn good income from their agricultural activities. After availing KCC, initially most of the farmers in the study area spent their agricultural credit for enhancing area under irrigation. Of the total land of selected farmers, 45.83 percent comes under dry/ rainfed conditions. In this situation farmers should be appreciated for making use of credit in a productive manner to enhance area under irrigation facilities.

Policy Implications

On the basis of this study, the following suggestions are recorded to make lending advances under priority and non-priority sector by the Banks to be more effective and purposeful:

1. It is important to note that most of the beneficiaries are illiterate. Hence, the beneficiaries need to be educated about the formalities to be fulfilled in obtaining the necessary finance. The bank staff should help of the uneducated farmers in getting their credit sanctioned from the banks. If the beneficiaries are educated they can get loans easily from the banks.
2. To reduce the problem of overdues, banks should announce certain incentives in the form of cash discounts etc. The farmers who have cleared the

loan may be given rebate on interest and priority in giving loans by the bank. This would result in decreasing the number of defaulters in future.

3. The branches should provide credit assistance not only to their existing borrowers but also to other eligible persons within their command area provided they are not covered by any other financial agency. Immediate assistance would be needed for protecting and regenerating standing crops, repairs and protection of livestock sheds, for implements and for storage structure etc.

References

Batra,J.D.: Rural Banks for the Rural Poor. Kurukshetra, 26(2), 16 October 1977.

Bhatnagar, R.C. "Recovery of Agricultural Loans". State Banks of India Monthly Review, Vol.XXI, No.2, (Feb. 1982). PP. 43-48.

Bose, A., "Commercial Banks and Rural Finance" state bank of India monthly Review, Vol.XXI, No.6, (June, 1982) PP. 211-16.

Chatterji Biswajit and Amit Kundu (1999) " Rethinking Rural Financial Institution", paper presented in the 35th Annual Conference of the Indian Economic Society at Jaipur, march-1999.

Das, Tushar, K., "Agricultural Financing by Commercial Banks", Commerce, Pamphlet, No.99 (March. 1976).

Deshande D.V., Mudgal M.K., Gupta K.K (1996) Regional Rural Bank at Cross Roads, Bankers Institute of Rural Development, Lucknow.

Dhabatosh Dutta: Planning for Rural Banks. Economic and Political weekly, Vol.11,No.25, August 27th, 1977.

Ganesan P. (1996) A Study of Priority Sector Advances.vis-à-vis Profits and Profitability of Public Sector Banks in India: 1969-1993(an unpublished Ph.D. thesis) Bharathiar University, Coimbatore.TN.

Ganguti,A.K: Rural Banking, Margin, Vol.9.No.2, January, 1977.

Gian Kar (2001) "Nationalisation of Banks and Agricultural Credit in India", Deep and Deep Publications, New Delhi.

Jagdish Prasad and Sunil Kumar: Role of Regional Rural Banks. Kurukshetra , Vol.XXXIII, No.14, May,1985.

18

A Study on the Problem of Non-Performing Assets – With Reference to Canara Bank in Mandya

Gule Ariffa

INTRODUCTION

An attempt is made in this paper is to analyse the problem of non-performing assets in Canara Bank in Mandya district, in the course of analysis deposits, advances and priority sector advances as well as profitability position of Canara Bank has been covered. Analysis starts with brief organisational profile of the Canara Bank.

Banks have been viewed in the country's planning process as agents of social change. The performance of banks has been commendable during the last two decades in respect to fulfilling the objectives of nationalization, and they provided a powerful instrument in implementing the policies and programmes of the government directed towards achieving socio economic growth of the country. However, there has been steady erosion of profitability of Indian public sector banks in recent years. Declining profitability of banks has now become a subject of public debate. The ever-growing socio-developmental obligations cast on the shoulders. A more disquieting fact is that banks that have been considered sick are in the public sector.

Over the past two decades, banking policies and programmes have sought to achieve certain national objectives by reorienting the banking system towards a larger social purpose. As a result, the system has undergone a structural transformation in both quantitative and qualitative terms. The massive and speedy expansion of banking activities in the country has not been without constraints. Ever since nationalization in 1969, fulfilling of social obligation of the economy and rendering assistance to the people existing below the poverty line have been given the priority among the bank objectives, while earning profit has become almost secondary. Therefore, banks are facing two challenges -to improve their profitability on the one hand and to fulfil the social obligations by serving the society on the other. Concern in also being debated that if the present trend of declining bank profitability is continued; the financial viability of banks may be in the increasing quantum of non-performing assets. It may be observed that effective asset management is one of the important goals of banks and financial institutions as well.

Against this background, a modest attempt is made in this study to examine the causes for the declining of bank profitability, discuss the position of non-performing assets and suggest a few measures for making these assets more active to improve profitability.

Results and Discussion

Canara Bank was founded in 1906 by Shri.Ammembal Subba Rao Pai with an aim of serving the poor and needy. Over the years the bank has grown and has shown excellence in performance year after year. Ever since its inception, Canara Bank has attached high priority to customer satisfaction and has come out with innovative measures to enhance the same.

The bank as a network of over 2532 branches as on March 2006 with 100 percent computerization. The bank has an excellent record of making continuous profits year-after-year ever since its inception in 1906. During the financial year 2005-2006 the bank achieved a net profit of Rs.13443.22 crores, in the same period the capital risk weighted assets ratio 11.22 percent, vis a vis the bench mark of 9 percent. ROA 1.01 percent, NPA 1.12 percent and business per employee 4.42 crores. The total business of the bank stood at 196229 crores (both deposits and advances put together) registering a growth of 24.81 percent. Canara Bank has made available the benefits of technology to customers through facilities such as RTGS (CANSPEED), Western Money Union etc.

Achievements of Canara Bank

Achievements made by Canara Bank since its inception is in the following manner;

- Canara Bank was the 1st Bank in Asia to go in for ISO certification for its Sheshadripuram Branch way back in 1995. Also the CANCARD was the 1st credit card to be ISO 9002 certified.
- In the year 2005-06, nearly 29 branches and one administrative unit got ISO certification taking number of ISO certified branches to 805 and administrative units to 14.
- Canara Bank was the first bank in India to distinctly articulate and adopt the code of "Good Banking", our banks citizen charter for healthy practice in customer-banker relationship.
- The bank has a wide range of activities such as Corporate Cash Management Services, Rural Development and Self-employment Training Institutes etc. It has over 1000 quality circle active at various levels.

- The bank functions as a Financial Super Market with its seven subsidiaries offering a wide range of diverse service.
- Canara Bank has bagged awards for excellence in areas such as export financing activities, priority sector etc., "Shreyas" the banks house magazine won a host of awards/commendations. Canbank computer services ltd., a subsidy of the bank was awarded a certificate by American Society for quality.

Canara Bank through its strong work force and innovative measures aims at achieving higher standards of customer satisfaction. Though the corporate objective of the bank will continue to be EPOCH, the focus this year will be on 'Value Addition through Technology' a prime endeavor for any banking institution. The Vision of Canara Bank is to emerge as a world class bank with best practices in the realms of asset portfolio, customer orientation, product innovation, profitability and enhanced value for the stakeholders.

The Bank Today

Canara Bank's global business grew by 27 percent to reach Rs.2,22,504 crore up from Rs.1,75,092 crore as at December 2006. While deposits grew by 26 percent to reach Rs.131781 crore, credit growth continued to be buoyant at 29 percent, taking net advances of the bank to Rs.90723 crore. Productivity measured by business per employee shot up to Rs.5.04 crore.

Interest income on advances was up by a significant 36 % at Rs.349 crore as compared to Rs.3940 crore in the corresponding period of last year, resulting in 57 bps improvement in yield on advances to 8.82% as compared to March 2006. Performance excellence in the core activities is reflected in the bank's net interest income, which recorded a 14% growth. Total interest income earned, including interest on investments, amounted to Rs.8154 crore, signifying a 29% growth.

The bank registered a growth of 8 percent in its net profit for the nine months ended 31st December, 2006 compared to the corresponding period of the preceding financial. Its net profit of Rs.916 crore is after making a total provision of Rs.991 crore, including Rs.356 crore provided for NPAs. For the third quarter, the bank's net profit was Rs.363 crore as compared to Rs.356 crore in the corresponding period last year.

Capital risk weighted assets ratio as at December 2006 stood at 12.69% compared to 11.23% as at March, 2006. During the quarter, the bank went for its upper tier II offering under MTN programme raising USD 250 million from the international market. Oversubscribed by an impressive five times, the issue was well received by investors across Asia, Europe and offshore US accounts, vindicating investor confidence and the bank's impeccable track record.

With continued focus on Info Tech application, the number of branches under core banking solution has been further extended to 179 while ATM strength further increased to 918, spread over 379 centres. Under advanced payment system, the bank has enhanced its number of branches to 1101 under RTGS and NEFT. During the quarter, the bank joined the National Financial Switch ATM network of IDRBT and SBI ATM network under which the card holders of the bank would have access to more than 14500 ATMs across the country.

The bank won several awards and accolades for its varied endeavors and recent performance excellence. Notable among the awards were the Niryat Bandhu Gold Trophy for 2004-05 and Silver Trophy for 2003-04 for outstanding performance under export finance. It was also ranked as fourth largest among the 43 banks under total income, rated by Dun & Bradstreet, worldwide leaders in financial information. In recognition of its environmental friendly efforts, the bank also won the maiden award of

'Best Performing Bank' under solar water heater finance for the year 2005-06, instituted by the Ministry of New and Renewable Energy, Government of India.

The bank introduced several new products catering to specific niches. To step up the low cost resources, the bank launched HNI savings bank-gold campaign in Bangalore City branches, wherein HNIs were offered value-added facilities. On the children's day, 2006, the bank also launched Can Champ, a savings bank scheme for inculcating the habit of thrift among children and also making them eligible for education loans. This scheme has already attracted 1.39 lakh accounts just in a span of two months. The bank has added 1.2 million fresh deposit accounts to its clientele base during the current financial year, taking the overall clientele base to about 29 million.

Canara Bank advances to various sectors in Mandya

There are five branches of Canara Bank in Mandya in the following areas:

1. Mandipet Branch
2. Gandhinagar Branch
3. Bandhigowda Layout Branch
4. Factory Circle Branch
5. Shankara Nagar Branch

The performance of the Canara Bank under advances to various sectors in Mandya can be assessed with the help of the data furnished in table - 1. It is found that during the reference period total accounts and advances to various sectors showed an increasing trend. The amount of advances to SSI sector was to the tune of Rs.27.42 lakhs in 2001-02 which moved upward to Rs.40.25 lakhs in 2006-07. In agriculture sector also there is a positive trend since 2001-02 to 2006-07.

Table- 1
Composition of Advances

(Rs.in lakhs)

Year	*Agriculture*	*SSI*	*Retail Trade*	*Small Business*	*Professional & Self-employed*
2001-02	53.07	27.42	4.70	2.20	0.89
2002-03	55.01	29.05	5.01	2.89	1.02
2003-04	56.35	30.25	6.25	3.25	1.59
2004-05	59.89	32.55	7.01	4.25	2.00
2005-06	61.20	35.25	8.00	5.00	2.55
2006-07	65.25	40.25	9.25	6.50	3.00

Source: Canara Bank, Mandya. Personnel Collection.

Average advances of Canara Bank in Mandya district clearly show that since 2001-02 there has been an increasing trend. During 2001-02 there was 2320 lakhs of target and actual was 2307 lakh. It has been increased to 2500 target during 2006-07 and actuals was 2650 during the same period. The details are presented in the table - 2.

Table - 2
Average Advances of Canara Bank in Mandya

Year	*Target*	*Actuals*
2001-02	2320	2307
2002-03	2290	2416
2003-04	2340	2495
2004-05	2365	2509
2005-06	2400	2558
2006-07	2500	2650

Source: Canara Bank, Mandya. Personnel Collection.

Deposit mobilisation is essentially resource mobilisation. It implies tapping of potential savings and putting them in to the banking sector for productive uses. Canara Bank is now trying to attract more deposits by introducing attractive savings schemes. In Mandya district also Canara Bank has attracted more deposits. The details about target and actuals of average deposits are presented in table-3.

Table - 3
Average Deposits

Year	*Target*	*Actuals*
2001-02	3289	3692
2002-03	3555	3560
2003-04	3692	3648
2004-05	3560	3701
2005-06	3890	3905
2006-07	4050	4150

Source: Canara Bank, Mandya. Personnel Collection.

It is gratifying to note that, Canara Bank has accepted the new challenge and been making great efforts in finding out and exploting new sources of deposits and have made a commendable success in increasing their deposits in recent years. Especially, the performance of Canara Bank in the field of deposit mobilization in rural and semi-urban centres has been very commendable. Due to high attraction of deposits it could be possible to get high profit; the details of Canara Bank profitability income have been depicted in the table - 4.

Table - 4
Profitability Income

Year	*Expenditure*	*Income*	*Profit*
2001-02	49	63	14
2002-03	98	125	27
2003-04	129	192	63
2004-05	249	260	11
2005-06	252	275	23
2006-07	260	285	25

Source: Canara Bank, Mandya. Personnel Collection.

It is clear from the above tables that there has been a substantial growth of bank deposits advances since 2001-02. The index of growth of deposits and advances may be regarded as the index of the growth of Canara Bank business. Apart from the quantitative increase in deposits and advances, there has been an impressive qualitative shift. The number of small account holders with the bank is increasing day-by-day.

NPA in Priority SectorIn 1996-97, priority sector accounted for 47% of the total NPAs. Two points need to be underlined in this context. First, there is nothing inherent in the nature of business of priority sectors which makes them particularly vulnerable to loan defaults. In fact it may be added here that the recovery performance of a major nationalised bank in respect of priority sectors was reported to be very high in the early 1990s. Probably, the follow up of loans to these sectors leaves much to be desired.

It is suggested that instead of prescribing floor level for priority sector lending as a proportion of net bank credit, the norm should be such as to link priority sector lending with total bank deposit. If the share of priority sector lending is calculated as a percentage of total deposits, priority sector lending will be protected against fluctuations in the ratio of overall credit to total bank deposits. Due to effective functioning there has been increasing trend in profits of the Canara Bank, as a result of this even NPA ratio has also been declined when compared to other banks in Mandya district. The details of NPA in Canara Bank Mandya is depicted in table - 5.

It is clear from the above table is that NPA in Canara Bank has been gradually declined. During 2001-02, there was Rs.140 lakhs, during 2002-03 there was Rs.138, then in the year 2003-04 and 2004-05, Rs.120 and Rs.115 lakhs respectively and after 2005-06 and 2006-07 it has drastically declined to Rs.110 and Rs.75 lakhs of rupees respectively. This is due to personnel care taken by the bank authorities. Canara Bank is well-equipped and extremely efficient and highly profitable industry when compare to other nationalised banks in Mandya district. Customer relationship management and customer experience management would help the bank to go long way in laying the right foundation for better customer satisfaction.

Table - 5

NPA in Canara Bank in Mandya

Year	*NPA (in lakhs)*
2001-02	140
2002-03	138
2003-04	120
2004-05	115
2005-06	110
2006-07	75

Source: Canara Bank, Mandya Personnel Collection.

At the out set it can be summarized that the study provides massive scope towards customers and bankers in the different activities of the Canara Bank. Asset quality of banks registered significant improvements simultaneously with the rapid increase in the quantum of credit to the commercial sector. The robust industrial performance and wider options available to scheduled commercial banks for recovery of their dues showed up in a significant reduction in the level of NPAs. A significant improvement in recovery of NPAs combined with a sharp increase in gross loans and advances by scheduled commercial banks led to a sharp decline in gross NPAs to gross advances ratio. Customer relationship management and customer experience management would help the bank to go long way in laying the right foundation for better customer satisfaction in Canara Bank. This would give richest return by way of profitability by reducing the NPA.

Findings of the Study

Some of the major findings of this present study may be stated as under:

- The setting up of the Asset Reconstruction Company India Limited (ARCIL) provided a major boost to bank's efforts to recover dues.
- In the year 2005-06, nearly 29 branches and one administrative unit got ISO certification taking number of ISO certified branches to 805 and administrative units to 14.
- Canara Bank was the first bank in India to distinctly articulate and adopt the code of "Good Banking", our banks citizen charter for healthy practice in customer-banker relationship.
- The bank has a wide range of activities such as Corporate Cash Management Services, Rural Development and Self-employment Training Institutes etc. It has over 1000 quality circle active at various levels.
- The bank functions as a Financial Super Market with its seven subsidiaries offering a wide range of diverse service.
- The has registered a growth of 8% in its net profit for the nine months. Its net profit of Rs.916 crore is after making a total provision of Rs.991 crore, including Rs.356 crore provided for NPAs in Canara Bank in general, Canara Bank in Mandya district in particular.
- Canara Banks in Mandya are not provided loans and advances for non-economic viability activities. This could enable to get maximum profit. As result of this NPAs have been reduced.
- Canara Bank has taken good steps with concerned to repayment of the loans. This could enable to reduce the NPAs.
- Priority sector lending, is certainly a drag on the system in terms of affecting its income as well as in the creation of NPAs.
- Priority sector lending, which is not a Basle norm, gives a lower return and also has a very good chance of turning into a NPA. Therefore, this is

a double disadvantage for banks.

- Gross NPAs reflect the actual increase in deterioration in asset quality, while net NPAs can be a bit misleading as they are arrived at after making provisions and other adjustments.

Policy Implications

1. In order to quicken the turnaround process of the weak banks, carrying a large portion of non-performing advances, it is necessary to devise means to augment their income. It is perceived that the transfer of NPAs to a separate agency, Asset Reconstruction Company (ARC) would ensure a steady flow of income on such assets and that ARC would solely concentrate its efforts on recovery of dues and thus would be in a better position to recover the loans than the banks themselves.
2. The existing NPAs, which are dragging down the bank are due to certain historical factors and if these problem assets are removed to ARC, the bank should eventually return bank to profit earning.
3. In the light of the gravity of the NPA issues confronting the banks particularly the weak ones, the ARC mechanism can be given a trial expeditiously in a limited way and based on its success, can be extended on a large scale.
4. Infrastructure in Debt Recovery Tribunals (DRTs), to be augmented and DRTs should be given more powers to expedite recovery of bank's dues more particularly for disposal of mortgaged immovable properties.
5. There is a need to activate the economic and industrial activity, to check further degeneration of the loan portfolio in banks.
6. Growth in NPAs is a problem, especially so since the legal processes tend to favour the defaulter. Banks have to pay more attention to their credit

portfolio and implement stringent risk management practices to cherry pick customers.

Conclusion

To quote excerpts from the Narasimham Committee Report 1998: "NPAs constitute a real economic cause to the nation in that they reflect the application of scarce capital and credit funds to unproductive uses. The money locked up in NPAs are not available for productive use and to the extent that banks seek, to make provisions for NPAs or to writ them off, it is a charge on their profit. To be able to do so, banks have to charge their productive and diligent customers a higher rate of interest. It thus becomes a tax on efficiency. It is the customer who uses credit efficiency that subsidies the inefficiency represented by NPAs. This also raises the transaction costs in the system thus denying the diligent credit customers the benefits of lower rates, which would help them to be more efficient and competitive. NPAs, in short are not just a problem for the banks. They are bad for the economy". For example if we are able to contain NPAs to around four percent of the total advances, then the PLR of the bank could be brought down to say about, 10% which would provide the customer, the necessary competitive edge, over his counterparts overseas.

Nothing motivates a banker more today than effective NPA management. If NPA recovery rate were high, further disbursements would be automatically high. However, if NPAs rise beyond the manageable limits, the health of the banking system would be jeopardized and the recycling of funds which is the key element in development would be severely stifled. An effective monitoring and control, aided by proper legal reforms would change the contours of NPA in Indian banking on par with International standards and build resilience for a stronger and vibrant financial system to realise the objectives of the reform measures implemented so far. Canara Bank is well equipped to be an extremely efficient, highly profitable, financial sound, technically well equipped and highly customer responsive bank with good value system.

References

Chawla .A.S.,(1990) Nationalization and Growth of Indian Banking, deep and Deep Publications, New Delhi.

Dommen. M. A., (1990) "Banks in the Service of the Weaker Sections", Oxford and IBH Publishing Co., New Delhi.pp.13-34.

Das & Chakraborthy (2004) WTO: Opportunities and Challenges for Indian Banking, Himalaya Publishing House, and Bombay.

Rangarajan.C (2002) Indian Economy - Essays on Money and Finance, UBS Publishers & Distributors, New Delhi.

Tarapore.S.S(2000) Issues in Financial Sector Reforms, UBS Publishers & Distributors, New Delhi.

Angadi, V.B. "Banks" Advances to Priority Sectors- An Enquiry into the causes of concentration", Economic and Political Weekly, Vol. XXVIII, No. 13, (March 26,1983).

Bose, A., "Commercial Banks and Rural Finance" State Bank of India monthly Review, Vol.XXI, No.6, (June, 1982) PP. 211-16.

Bhatnagar, R.C. "Recovery of Agricultural Loans". State Banks of India Monthly Review, Vol.XXI, No.2, (Feb. 1982). PP. 43-48.

Chawla, O.P. and Patel, K.V, "Change and Development in the Village; Role of self - Help organisations". PRAJNAN, Vol. XVI, No.3, (July - Sept. 1987). PP. 283-298.

19

Empowering Women through Expansion of School Education in Karnataka

Krishnappa Madivala

INTRODUCTION

In this study an attempt has been made to examine (a) the poverty reduction efforts leading to enhanced school enrollment of children (male & female) during 1981-2001; (b) the efforts to improve the educational infrastructure and the quality of imparting school education has whether led to improvement in girl child school enrollment, attendance and retention positions; and (c) the problems of development of school education system in Karnataka.

Women's empowerment includes both a personal strengthening and enhancement of life chances, and collective participation in efforts to achieve, equality of opportunity and equity between different genders, ethnic groups, social classes, and age groups it enhances human potential at individual and social levels expressions. Empowerment is an essential starting point and a continuing process for realizing the ideals of human liberation and freedom for all.

Thus when we talk of women's development and women's status, it is important for us to recognize that interventions at all levels namely, social, cultural, political, economic are required and are possible (real changes) only if changes take place in the existing system and social structures, which are not at all, favorable to the women today.

Any intervention that does not contribute substantially towards women's active and critical participation in the over all development process of the society, needs to be re looked at as women's development in the real sense can take place only when the systems or structures of the society are changed in favour of women.

Recognizing the role of education as an effective instrument for bringing about changes in people in their socio-economic and socio-cultural conditions in an elaborate programme of pre-metric and post- metric scholarships, reservation of seats in the schools and colleges, establishment of hostels and ashram schools and many other beneficial schemes are in operation for the last five decades. It is of considerable interest to find out how these facilities have been actually beneficial for them (especially for females) and what is the level of their progress in the field of education. This study is aimed at knowing the truth in this regard in the state of Karnataka.

Karnataka is the eighth largest state in India both in area and population. It was formerly known as Mysore State. On November 1.1973 the name Mysore was changed into Karnataka under the Mysore State (Alteration of Name) Act 1973. Karnataka is predominantly rural and agrarian, about 76% of its people live in rural areas while about 7.11% of its working force is engaged in agriculture and allied activities, which generate 49% of the state income.

Karnataka is a south Indian State, which in many ways resembles the other Indian states too. In natural regions, languages, faiths and culture, it exhibits almost as much variety as the subcontinent itself. Its location is close to the nation's heartland and its boundary extent to the coastal periphery. In development attainments too, the state is at the median level in major sectors, reflecting generally where the country as a whole stands. Special attention has been paid to understanding regional developmental disparities, which are a major concern of the state today.

The All India Education Surveys conducted quinquennially on six occasions provide more reliable information on primary school enrollment. Even more significant is data regarding out of school enrollment. This is generally difficult to obtain the 1992-93 Survey of the International Institute of Population Sciences has some information on children between the age of six and fourteen attending school in both rural and urban areas. According to this source, 82% of children in urban areas go to school in India, but only63% of rural children also. In Karnataka, 65% of rural children attend primary school, which is higher than the national average of 63% (but far lower than the level of 95 in Kerala). In urban areas, the figure is 82% in Karnataka as is the country, here the figure for Kerala is 95% Karnataka appears to be also behind Assam, Gujarat, Haryana, Maharashtra, Orissa, Punjab and Tamilnadu as far as the attendance of rural children at primary school is concerned. An adequate and sustainable source of income is essential for a decent and comfortable life. Here too Karnataka is close to the national average. To per capita Net National Product of Karnataka at constant prices is marginally below the figure for the country (Rs.2551 against Rs.2608). Once again, the state ranks seventh among the fifteen major states Gujarat, Haryana Maharashtra, Punjab, Tamilnadu and West Bengal were ahead of Karnataka in per capita income in 1995-96. Between 1980-81 and 1995-96, however, only the states of Maharashtra, Gujarat and Tamilnadu achieved a higher growth rate than Karnataka.

A healthy life, access to education and an assured livelihood are necessary for improving the quality of human life. The Human Development Index evolved by the UNDP tries to capture the three facets of this concept. Comparisons among countries and provinces are possible when a common index of this kind is used. The tool will, therefore, be employed to find out Karnataka's developmental level with reference to the entire country in comparison with other states.

Growth of Literacy in Karnataka

The literacy rate in Karnataka State in 1961 was 25.4%, which increased to 31.5% in 1971, and 38.5% in 1981, on an average registering a growth rate of 0.6 during 1960's and 0.7 during 1970's. This growth is far lower than that of population, which was 2.2% during 1961-71 and 2.4% during the 1971-81. The combination of these two phenomena has resulted in the addition of illiterates in absolute terms. To begin with there were 14.11 lakh illiterates (aged 5 and above) in the state during 1961, which increased to 158.5 lakh and 182.3 lakh during 1971 and 1981 respectively. This illiteracy figure at the state level hides several disparities in terms of achievement of literacy across various segments of population. Even if one examines the literacy levels of school-going population of 5 -14age group as registered in the past three censuses, the literacy growth rate is more or less similar to the one observed for general population. This eventually suggests that the literacy growth that has been registered during the last two census decades between 1961-71 and 1971-81 can, in fact, be attributed to the performance of schooling, particularly at the compulsory primary education stage. One can also infer from this that there was no effective adult education programme in the state during the same periods: The above description using the literacy level of comparative age - groups between censuses reflects only a gross picture.

Karnataka, which now holds an esteemed position as one of the industrially advanced southern states in India enacted Compulsory primary Education Act during 1961 and vowed to achieve universal enrolment and retention among 6-10 years of children. Consequently the state has witnessed a tremendous expansion in primary education. The number of primary schools rose from 28,924 in 1961-62 to 35,549 in 1981-82. In fact according to Fifth All India Educational Survey (1986) conducted by NCERT, the state claims to have provided primary schools in 92.50% of habitations and for 57.24% of rural population within a walk able distance of 1 km. correspondingly, the expenditure in primary education has also increased from Rs.856.33 lakhs in 1961-62 to Rs.108.34 crores in 1981-82. Following this, the enrolment growth in primary schools also rose from 29.24 lakhs in 1961-62 to 52.63 lakhs in 1981-82. It should be noted that the reported enrolment also consists of over and under the target age-group children resulting in an inflated enrolment rate. However, the rate of enrolment growth has not been able to keep pace with population growth rate with the result universal enrolment has remained a distant dream. Further, all those enrolled do not complete their primary education resulting in failure of universal retention also. Literacy that forms one of the chief objectives of primary education has not been imparted adequately during the last three decades indicating rather a dismal performance of the existing formal education system.

Educational profile of the population matters in the context of globalization and ability to exploit new opportunities. The distribution of population by level of education for Karnataka, other south Indian States and all - India separately for males, females and persons for rural and urban sectors respectively. The distribution profile seems comparable with those for other south Indian States as well as all - India. Still Karnataka has some way to go before catching up with its southern neighbor Kerala with respect to higher levels of education as well as its gender dimension.

The Literacy Scenario

Literacy rate, given by the percentage of literate population aged 7 years and above, registered a substantial increase in Karnataka between 1991 and 2001. It increased from 56.04 to 67.04 percent. From a gender development perspective, it is important to note that the percentage point increase in female literacy rate (13.11 points from 44.34 percent in 1991 to 57.45 percent in 2001) was higher than that of male (9.03 points from 67.26 to 76.29 percent) Across districts, literacy rate was the highest in Bangalore (83.91 percent) followed by Dakshina Kannada and lowest in Raichur (49.54 percent) preceded by Gulbarga (50.65 percent). Literacy rate (for male & female combined) increased by more than ten percentage points in the districts of Bangalore Rural, Belgaum, Bidar, Bellary, Chamarajanagar, Chickmagalur, Chitradurga, Davanagere, Gadag, Gulbarga, Hassan, Haveri, Kolar and Tumkur. Among them, Belgaum, Davanagere, Gadag, Hassan, Haveri and Shimoga could register such an increase thanks to the creditable performance in promoting female literacy. because the percentage point increase in male literacy was less than ten in there districts. (Economic Survey - 2001-02 GOK Bangalore PP 321 - 322).

According to the 2001 census the literacy rate in Karnataka is 67.04 percent. In spite of the overall figures, analysis of the literacy data reveals certain problems. For instance, male literacy is 76.29 percent and female literacy is only 57.45 percent. Similarly, huge variations in literacy can be seen between regions, districts and between men and women.

Inter - district Disparity in Literacy in Karnataka

The level of literacy and educational attainment of both men and women is a vital indicator of the level of human development of a region / country. It may be noted that both male and female literacy and the general literacy have improved between 1991 and 2001. But the disturbing fact is that the inter-district variations in general literacy, male and female literacy continues to be a matter of serious concern in Karnataka. We may discern three types of trends in literacy at district levels in Karnataka between 1991 and 2001. They are namely; (a) the districts like Bangalore urban, Dakshina Kannada, Dharwad, Kodagu, Shimoga, Udupi and Dakshina Kannada has the highest literacy rate as per 1991 and 2001 census; these districts are also progressive districts in terms of other economic and social development indicators; so there is a close association between the high level of literacy and economic - social development in these districts. These are high literacy districts of the Karnataka State; (b) the second category of districts have good literacy and a increasing female literacy. Such districts are Bangalore (R), Belgaum, Davanagere, Gadag, Hassan, and Tumkur. These districts have a general literacy of 65 to 70% as per 2001 census. These districts are fairly prosperous with flourishing agriculture, horticulture and SSI's and are having in close proximity a few class I and class II urban centers (with population more than 3 or 4 lakhs; and (c) a large of economically backward districts are also socially backward, including lagging behind others even in literacy. The districts of Bidar, Gulbarga, Bellary, Raichur, Bijapur, Chitradurga, Chamarajanagar, Kolar, in this III category.

Dakshina Kannada and Bangalore have more than 80 percent of literacy. However, other like Gulbarga, Koppal, Raichur, Bellary, Bagalkot, Bijapur and Chamarajanagar had less than 60 percent literates in 2001. If we look at the division wise literacy data, Gulbarga (also known as Hyderabad Karnataka region) has only 55.04 percent of literacy. Except Bidar district, the other four districts, Bellary (58.04 percent), Gulbarga (50.65 percent), Koppal (55.02 percent) and Raichur (49.54 percent) have less than 60 percent literacy rate.

The Hyderabad-Karnataka (HK) region is one of the most neglected in the development of education not only in Karnataka but also in India. The divisions consist of five districts, Bellary, Bidar, Gulbarga, Koppal and Raichur. Though there are a few historical reasons for the backwardness of the HK region, efforts in the development of literacy are not a part of history.

Table - 1
Literacy Rate of Divisions in Karnataka and the Districts of HK Region

Divisons/Districts	1971	1981	1991	2001
Gulbarga	21.13	26.45	40.49	55.04
Belgaum	33.39	38.57	56.85	66.07
Bangalore	35.21	43.42	61.24	69.52
Mysore	32.44	40.44	58.49	69.88
Districts of HK region				
Bellary	25.12	30.64	45.89	58.04
Bidar	20.02	26.64	45.11	61.98
Gulbarga	18.74	24.94	38.54	50.65
Raichur	20.20	27.72	34.24	49.54
Koppal	-	-	38.23	55.02
Karnataka	31.52	38.46	56.04	67.04

Sources : Census of India 1981, 1991, 2001 - Directorate of Census Operations, Karnataka.

It is evident from the table that the highest number of illiterates is in the HK region. In all the four periods (1971-2000), the literacy rate in Gulbarga division is lower than the other divisions. And among its five districts, Raichur records the poorest performance, followed by Gulbarga. The literacy rate according to the 2001 census in Gulbarga and Raichur is 50.65 percent and 49.65 percent respectively.

It is important to note that there was a 10.39 percent gap in literacy between the HK region (21.13 percent) and the state average (31.52 percent) in 1971. However, the gap between the regions has widened since. It went up to 15.55 percent in 1991 and was 12 percent in 2001. However, the same is not the case for Mysore and Bangalore (69.52 percent) have a higher average literacy rate than the state average (67.04 percent), according to the 2001 census.

Literacy gap is the highest in all the districts of HK region. The literacy gap between Raichur district (49.54 percent) and the state average (67.04 percent) is 17.50 percent and that between Gulbarga and the state is 16.39 percent. In 2001, there were 12 districts where the literacy rate was above the state average. But of these, nine belong to south Karnataka. No district from the KH region has literacy above the state average. Elaborate, extensive literacy improvement measures are necessary to lift the districts of HK region. Otherwise, these districts will continue to lag behind others in all spheres of socio-economic development.

The problem of literacy is more clear when we look at the numbers. According to the 2001 census, the total population of Karnataka is 5,27,33,958. Of these, males constitute 2,68,56,343 (50.92 percent) and the female population is 2,58,77,615 (49.08 percent). For the purpose of calculating literacy, Census 2001 excluded the 0-6 age group. Therefore, literacy rate is the percentage of literates to the population aged seven years and above, which constitutes 4.59,07,990, including a male population of 2,33,54,844 (50.87 percent) and female population of 2,25,52,946 (49.13 percent) (Table- 2).

Table - 2
Division wise Total Number of Literates and Illiterates (2001)

Divisons	Total No of Literates	Division's Share in State's Total	Total No. of illiterates	Division's Share in State's Total
Bangalore	11866557	38.56	4409631	29.14
Mysore	7238905	23.53	3206382	21.18
Belgaum	73277480	23.80	3876631	25.62
Gulbarga	4342046	14.10	3640138	24.06
South Karnataka	19105462	62.08	7616013	50.32
North Karnataka	11669526	37.92	7516789	49.68
Karnataka	30774988 (69.03)	100.00	15132802 (32.97)	100.00

Sources: Census of India 2001, Karnataka Provision Population Tables, p. 48.

There are 3,07,74,988 literates (67.03 percent) and 1,51,32,802 literates (32.97 percent) in Karnataka in 2001 out of the total population. Of the total literates, 62.08 percent are in south Karnataka and the rest in north Karnataka. Karnataka still has 1.5 crores illiterate people. Unless the state makes sincere efforts to eradicate illiteracy, these sections of the population will not be included in the socio-economic sphere of human activity. Further, it is significant to note that nearly 40 percent of the literates are in Bangalore division. However, a mere 14.10 percent is in Gulbarga division.

Education of women has a major impact on the overall development of a society. Jawaharlal Nehru said, "If our nation is to rise, how can it do so if the half of the nation, of our women kind, lag behind and remain ignorant and uneducated?" In Karnataka, the development and growth of literacy among women is far from satisfactory. In fact, the state's performance in this area is poorer than other southern states. However, the problem of literacy among women in Karnataka is not uniform. Some districts like Bangalore, Dakshina Kannada and Udupi have a favourable literacy rate compared with the districts of north Karnataka. For instance, in all the divisions total male literates (1,78,17,682) outnumbered male illiterates (55,37,162) in 2001 (Table - 3).

Table - 3
Division wise Number of Literate and Illiterates Men, 2001**

Divisions	Total No of Literates	Division's Share in State's Total	Total No. of Illiterates	Division's Share in State's Total
Bangalore	6755144	37.90	1630273	29.45
Mysore	4009365	22.50	1196493	21.60
Belgaum	4359699	24.50	1354337	24.46
Gulbarga	2693474	15.10	1356059	24.49
Sourth Karnataka	10764509	60.42	2826766	51.05
North Karnataka	7053173	39.58	2710396	48.95
Karnataka	17817682 (76.29)**	100.00	5537162 (23.71)**	100.00

However, this is not so in the case of women literates. In north Karnataka, both the divisions, have more number of women illiterates than literates. This problem is further deepened in the case of Gulbarga division has a total of 39,32,671 females of which 22,84,099 are illiterate and only 16,48,572 are literate (Table - 4). Disparities and discrimination against women's education is a universal phenomenon. But in Karnataka it is more pronounced in the north.

Table - 4
Division wise Number of Literates and Illiterates Women, 2001**

Divisions	Total No of Literates	Division's Share in State's Total	Total No. of illiterates	Division's Share in State's Total
Bangalore	5111413	39.15	2449358	28.96
Mysore	3229540	24.92	20009889	20.95
Belgaum	2967781	22.70	2522294	26.28
Gulbarga	1648572	12.73	2288884099	23.80
Sourth Karnataka	8340953	64.37	4789247	49.92
North Karnataka	4616353	35.63	4806393	50.08
Karnataka	12957306 (57.45)**	100.00	9595640 (42.55)**	100.00

Notes: ++ = Excluding 0-6age group population; ** Divided by state's total male population, that is 2,25,52,946 (Excluding 0-6 age group population).

Variations in literacy rates among women are more visible when we examine their share in the total population and their share in literacy and illiteracy. Their share in the population (except in Mysore division) is less then that of their male counterparts. But their share in the total illiteracy rate is higher than the males' average in all divisions (Table - 5).

Table - 5
Women's Share in Population, Literacy and Illiteracy, 2001**

Divisons	Women's Share in Population	Women's Share in Literacy	Women's Share in illiteracy
Bangalore	48.48	43.07	63.02
Mysore	50.16	44.61	62.68
Belgaum	49.00	40.50	65.06
Gulbarga	49.26	37.96	62.74
Sourth Karnataka	49.13	43.65	62.88
North Karnataka	49.11	39.55	63.74
Karnataka	49.12	42.10	63.40

Notes: ++ = Excluding 0-6 age group population ;
Source : Census of India 2001, Karnataka

Gender gap in literacy indicates the status accorded to women in a society. If there is higher rate of disparity between men and women in literacy, it shows that women in that region are severely neglected. Most women in Karnataka remain illiterate even after several literacy campaigns. These variations in literacy are further aggravated when we analyze female literacy by district and division. In the case of male literacy Dakshina Kannada has the distinction of having the highest percentage of literates of 89.74 percent. In fact, in most districts male literacy is above 70 percent. However, the same is not true in the case of women. In most districts, female literacy is less than 60 percent. The literacy deprivation is severe in the HK region. For instance, in 1971 out of 100 women only 10 women were in a position to read and write; this figure increased to 42 in 2001. Table - 6 shows a wide literacy gap in all the divisions of the state. In all the four periods (1971-1991), literacy rates of both male and female in Gulbarga are lower than the other three divisions of the state.

Table - 6
Division Wise Male and Female Literacy, Gender Gap in Literacy

	Gulbarga	Belgaum	Bangalore	Mysore	Karnataka
1971					
Female literacy	10.11	20.76	25.00	23.74	20.95
Male literacy	31.13	45.45	44.73	40.93	41.62
Gap between male and female	-21.02	-24.69	-1973	-17.19	-20.65
1981					
Female literacy	14.89	26.11	33.11	31.13	27.71
Male literacy	37.77	50.54	53.10	48.81	48.81
Gap between male and female	-22.88	-24.43	-20.00	17.68	-21.10
1991					
Female literacy	26.52	43.10	50.82	49.15	44.34
Male literacy	54.01	69.99	71.48	67.79	67.26
Gap between male and female	-27.49	26.89	-20.66	-18.64	-22.92
2001					
Female literacy	42.43	54.81	62.27	60.62	57.45
Male literacy	67.31	76.91	77.54	78.03	76.29
Gap between male and female	-24.88	-22.1	-15.27	-17.41	-18.84

Sources: Census of India.

The gap in literacy rates between men and women increased during 1971-1991. However, in 1991-2001 it decreased. It is important to note that the gap in literacy was highest in Belgaum, rather than in Gulbarga division, in 1971 and 1981. But in 1991 and 2001, Gulbarga division showed the largest literacy gap. This shows that in Belgaum division, efforts have been made to improve literacy among women. But HK region, instead of improving, has lagged behind considerably.

Gender gap in literacy worsens further when we look at the five districts of the HK region. Table - 7 makes it clear that all the districts of this region are far from the state's average gap in literacy (18.84 percent) in 2001. For instance, the gap is 28.39 percent and 25.18 percent in Koppal and Raichur districts respectively. However, it is only 9.38 percent, 12.35 percent and 11.27 percent in Bangalore, Dakshina Kannada and Kodagu respectively.

Table - 7
Literacy Gaps in HK Region and Other Districts

Region / Divisions	Female Literacy	Male Literacy	Gap
Raichur	36.84	62.02	25.18
Bidar	50.01	73.29	23.28
Koppal	40.76	69.15	28.39
Gulbarga	38.40	62.52	24.12
Bangalore ®	46.16	69.54	23.43
Bangalore	78.98	88.36	9.38
D. Kannada	77.39	89.74	12.35
Kodagu	72.53	83.80	11.27
Karnataka	57.45	76.29	18.84

Source: Census of India 2001.

A comprehensive programme is required to improve the poor level of literacy among the women of Karnataka in general and women of the HK region in particular. HK region consists of a large number of agricultural labourers. As a result, these sections of the population have had to miss out on the available literacy facility. In order to improve their literacy level more educational facilities should be made available to the women of the HK region. But mere provision of literacy is not enough, it should reach them and they must become literate.

Planners must plan programmes of action to improve educational conditions in North Karnataka in general and Gulbarga division in particular. A participatory development approach should be developing the HK region. Balanced regional development approach should be given utmost importance. Priority should be shifted from investment and income criteria to education and health in the developmental strategy. Women's education should be encouraged particularly in north Karnataka. Girl students should get special incentives to improve their educational status.

Policy Initiatives/Programmers for Expansion and Development of School Education in Karnataka

The government has taken several initiatives to improve economic opportunities for and reduce poverty of the SC/ ST and back ward class communities and minorities viz:,

- A new programmed called kaushalya with a provision of Rs.5 crore to train 5,000 SC and ST 5,000 Back ward class unemployed women in different occupations;
- Construction of 15,000 houses for homeless ST families;
- Setting up 75 new hostels for SC, ST and Backwardclass students in the districts of Bijapur, Bagalkot, Bidar, Raichur, Gulbaraga, Koppal and Bellary; and
- 30 percent of these institutions will be reserved for girl students.

Midday Meals Programme

The Government's programme "Akshara Dasoha", a midday meal scheme for children studying received well in the rural areas. The district panchayat bodies and "Sthree Shakti" groups implement the scheme. The scheme provides for serving hot meals and vitamin A and iron tablets to children. The Government has made a budgetary provision of Rs.200crore for this programme during the year 2003-04. The scheme is implemented in 27 districts benefiting about 46 lakh children.

The indirect benefits of the programme are quite note worthy children from different start of society eat together overriding all caste factors; the scheme has provided employment to more than 80,000 women who are employed as cooks. To ensure sustainability of the programme, the Government has decided to meet its cost from the proceeds of on-line lottery. Further, the Government has also decided to dedicate all future receipts from lotteries for the development of primary education in the state. (Economic Survey of Karnataka 2003-04 PP: 330)

The state has an extensive network of schooling facilities with over 51 thousand primary schools and 9500 high schools. Over 86 lakh students are studying in standard I-VII and about 19.5 lakh students are in VIII-X standards. About 3.22 lakh teachers are working in primary and secondary schools. During the past 4 years about 8 lakh children have been brought back to the formal schooling system. The state has launched a special enrollment drive under programmers such as "Chinnara Angala", 'Ba Marali Shalege', 'Coolyinda Shalege', 'Ba Bale Shalege', etc., all habitations with a population of over 200 have been provided primary schools.

To encourage girl's education, free education is given to all girl students studying in standards I-XII in government institutions. Free textbooks and uniforms are given to girl students studying in standards VIII-X in government institutions. Free textbooks and uniforms are also given to all students studying in I-VII standards in government institutions covering about 70.4lakhs students. A Massive midday meal programme initially started in the 7 northeastern districts in 2000-01, has been extended to all the remaining districts during the current year. This has resulted in an increase in school attendance by about 2.75 percent as per the preliminary indications. During the past 4 years. In service training was imparted to over 5 lakh teachers under programmes of DSERT, DIET etc., school development and monitoring committees have been constituted with a view to encourage community participation in school development. The dropout rate that was about 14 percent in classed I-V in 1999-2000 has come down to about 8 percent in 2003-04.

The following programs are being implemented in order to bring the out-of-school Children (6-14 years age) into schools.

1. **Children Census:** the number of out of schools

children is determined by taking up children various programs are organized to bring back to main scaffold.

2. **Enrolment Drive:** During every academic year this programme encourages children who do not return to school even after one month of enrolment for several reasons. The parents of the children who do not join the schools are convinced about the importance of children.
3. **Chinnara Angala:** Chinnara Angala is an innovative summer Bridge course programme for main steaming 6-14 age group out of school children to formal schools. The duration of the course is 2 months.
4. **Cooliyinda Shalege (from labour to school):** This is a programme to convince the owners of establishments where children are working as laborers and the working children between the age group of 6-14 about the need of education and bring these children to the main stream of education.
5. **Beediyinda Shalege (from street to school):** This is a special programme for mainstreaming all 6-14 age group out of school children who are orphans, rag pickers and children living in streets through voluntary organizations to mainstream.
6. **Baa Baale Shalege:** This programme is specially meant for mainstreaming all 6-14 age group out of schoolgirls to formal schools. The objective of this programme is to provide minimum 8 years of school education and there by reduce the gender disparity.
7. **Baa Marali Shalege (come back to school):** A campaign has been organized during the Kannada Rajyothsava month in November every Year. It aimed to bring back the out of school children and Un enrolled children to the school fold. In this programme every; Monday before the school start

teachers, students SDMC members and the community leaders visit the houses of dropouts to convince the parents and children to bring the kids back to the schools.

8. **Flexi schools (Sadaa Shale):** This programme is to help the children preferably working in different establishments between the age group of 6-14. The schools run at the timings convenient to these children to create interest in learning and thereby bring them back to mainstream of education.
9. **The National programme for Education of Girls Elementary level:** This is a Special programme meant for girl's education formulated and implemented by the Sarva Shiksha Abhiyana- a centrally sponsored scheme. This programme aims to provide 8 years of elementary education, increase female literacy rate and to reduce gender disparity.

Conclusion

Education has a vital role to play in increasing the capacity of the family and community for a better quality of life through the competencies they develop. Not only are they empowered through such competency based career development but, it turn, they can extend it through their work to the community and vulnerable groups, thus leading to social development, and particularly to the development, and particularly to the development of women through self-awareness and acquiring skills. It is worthwhile to create the awakening among women so that they can come up by taking care of themselves.

References

Ashagrie, Kebebew. 1997. Statistics on Working Children and Hazardous Child Labour in Brief. Geneva: International Labor Office.

Athreya, V.B., and Chunkath, S.R (1996), Literacy and Empowerment (New Delhi : Sage).

Bashir, Sajitha (2000), and Government Expenditure on Elementary Education in the Nineties (New Delhi: The European Commission).

Bashir, Sajitha and Ayyar, R.V. Vidyanatha (2001), 'District Primary Education Programme, Mimeo, National Council of Educational Research and Training, New Delhi: In Encyclopedia of India Education (New Delhi: NCERT).

Basu K., P.Pattanaik, and Suzumura K. (edit.,) (2000) 'Choice, Welfare, and Development; A Festchrift in Honor of Amartya Sen. (New Delhi; Oxford University Press).

Behrman, J.R., and Wolfe, B.L. (1984), 'More Evidence on Nutrition Demand: Income Seems Overrated and Women's Schooling Underemphasized', Journal of Development Economics, 14: 108-28.

Bhargaya, Pramila H (2003); The Elimination of Child Labour Whose Responsibility?, (New Delhi: Sage Publications)

20

Visveswaraya Grameena Bank and Rural Development - A Study in Mandya District

Narayana, N.

INTRODUCTION

Institutional credit system has been playing a vital role in the economic development of rural India particularly at this important juncture when we are entering 21st century. Rural sector plays a significant role in Indian economy. It affects directly or indirectly almost all the economic activities in the country. It employs the maximum number of people. It is also the most important source of national income in India. It also supplies food for the survival of the entire population of India. It also supplies materials necessary for the major industries of India. A large part of the revenue of the government is also obtained from rural sector. In short, rural sector can be rightly considered as the backbone of our economy. In spite of the significant role of the rural sector, it continues to be neglected. The magnitude of poverty, illiteracy, and ill health is of higher order in the rural areas as compared to the urban areas.

India is a land of villages and they constitute the backbone of the country. Since time immemorial India has been cherishing the village life. Villages continue to dominate the Indian way of life as they have done before. An over whelming majority of India's population lives in more than 6.38 lakh villages. According to 1991 census, the village population in India was about 74.28% of the total population and it slightly decreased to 72% in 2001. The urban population of India was 10.8% in 1901; it increased to 25.72% in 1991 and then to 28% in 2001. As these figures indicate the dominance of villages still continues.

Though India is known as the classical land of the villages her villages are not free from problems. Ever since the Muslim rule the Indian villages have been receiving one or the other setbacks. The village could no longer preserve their self-sufficiency and autonomy. The village gradually becomes the centers of problems. The economic problems are the main problem of the villages.

Indian farmers are born in debts and finally die in debts. Village economy gives little scope for saving. The poor position of the Indian farmers compels him to borrow money from the local moneylenders who charge exorbitant interests and squeeze their clients to the maximum. Absence of good banking facility and the procedural delay involved in the sanctioning of loan also make many to go to moneylenders for immediate financial help. According to All India Rural Credit Survey Report of the year 1951 moneylenders at hat time accounted fro 70% of all rural credit. However, in 1991 they accounted for only 17.6% of the rural credit.

Majority of the rural fold is not able to meet their day-to-day requirements from their own sources of income not to speak of investigating in other productive enterprises for improving their economic conditions. Therefore, they have to depend on various financial agencies for getting funds for making investment. To bring about the overall development in the rural areas, financial assistance to the rural poor, particularly institutional assistance for the development of agriculture needs no emphasis. Finance is an essential requirement for almost every activity. If required finance is not available out of ones own income then one needs credit. In rural areas of India, credit requirements are more pressing. Rural credit in India is a part and parcel of its economic development. Rural population is composed of agricultural producers, tenant cultivators, village artisans and landless labour. All these categories are in need of credit. To provide the credit requirements to these categories regional rural banks play very significant role.

Objectives of the Study

The specific objectives of the present study are;

1. To examine the performance of Visweswaraya Grameena Bank in Mandya district in terms of branch expansion, deposit mobilization, loans and advances to agricultural development and recovery of loans.
2. To study the effective functioning and over all performance of Visweswaraya Grameena Bank in Mandya district.
3. To make suggestions for further improvement of schemes adopted by the Visweswaraya Grameena Bank for the development of agriculture sector in Mandya district.

Results and Discussion

The Visveshvaraya Grameena Bank has 20 branches in rural centers out of 25 branches. At present, the bank has a strong and wide network of branches covering the entire part of the district and no License is pending. The backward for Opening of the branch. Region and taluks were given topmost priority in Opening the branches. The branch expansion of Visveshvaraya Grameena Bank is shown in the Table 4.14. The bank has totally 25 branches spread over all the seven taluks of the district, out of Which 1 in urban, 4 in Semi urban and 20 in rural centers, This Was to facilitate the increase of deposits and provide advances of the Bank of priority sector in rural development.

Deposit position of VGB during the year 2006-07 was Rs. 2896.31 lakhs. The deposit mix of the bank with comparative position over the last year is depicted in table - 1.

Table - 1
Deposits of Visveshvaraya Grameena Bank.

(Rs. in iakhs)

	Deposits	*2004-05*	*2005-06*	*2006-07*
1.	Deposits	2002.03	2358.66	2896.31
	Growth %	34%	18%	23%
2.	Average Deposits	1456.54	1917.35	2486.50
	Growth %	35%	32%	30%

Source: Annual Reports of Visvesvaraya Grameena Bank, Head Office, Mandya.

It is clear from the table, the bank has achieved the target under aggregate and average deposits. The average deposit of the bank stood at Rs.2486.50 lakhs during 2006-07 as compared to Rs.1917.35 lakhs during the previous year, thereby recording a growth rate of 30% over previous year per branch deposit of the bank which stood at Rs.94 lakhs at the end of March 1998 has been increased to Rs.116 lakhs as at the end of March 2007 Similarly, per employee deposit has been increased from Rs.22.68 lakh is to Rs.28. 12 lakhs is during 1he current year. Out of 25 branches, 10 branches have achieved the aggregate deposit target and 5 branches have achieved the average deposit target.

Priority Sector lending

Visveshvaraya Grameen Bank, since its inception, has been playing a very significant role by way of lending credit to the priority sector in the rural areas of Mandya district covering crop loan. Small scale Industry (including Artisan, village industry and Tiny industry), Retail trade, small business, professional and self-employed, SC/ST, Minority and Weaker Section. Table - 2 shows the priority sector advances of Visveshvaraya Grameena Bank during the year 2006-07. It is clear from the table that, the advances made by the bank to the priority sector is remarkable. The highest amount disbursed to the weaker sections of Rs.810 lakhs, for retail trade Rs.9.15 lakhs, small business Rs.6.47 lakhs SC/ST beneficiaries Rs. 16.61, Minority Rs. 15.60 lakhs and for crop loans Rs. 810 lakhs.

Table - 2
Priority Sector Advances of Bank (up to 2006-07)

Sl.No.	*Activity*	***Amount Disbursed (in lakhs)***
1.	Crop Loan	437.30
2.	Retail T rode	9.15
3.	Small business	6.47
4.	Professional and Self-employed	6.74
5.	Scheduled Categories / Scheduled Tribes	16.61
6.	Small Scale Industries	21.76
7.	Minority	15.60
8.	Weaker Section	810.00
9.	Term Loan for agriculture purpose	
	a . Tractor / Power Tiller	43.53
	b. Others	100.83
	Total priority	**1467.99**

Source: Annual Reports of VGB, Head Office, Mandya.

The Role of Bank in Government Sponsored Schemes

The bank has involved in successful implementation of government sponsored schemes like IRDP, SCP and other government special schemes in the district. The performance of the bank in this sector is furnished in Table – 3. Efforts have been made by the bank to upgrade the quality of the rural poor under the government sponsored schemes.

Table - 3
Details of the outstanding advances under the government sponsored schemes

Name of the Programme	*Target for*		*Disbursements made out standing position*			
	2005-06		*2005-06*		*2006-07*	
	A/C	*Amount*	*A/C*	*Amount*	*A/C*	*Amount*
IRDP	-	58	536	53.29	3283	208.88
SC/ST (SCP)	41	-	92	5.38	363	16.61
Other Govt. Sponsored Schemes	133	-	90	5.45	288	21.05
Total	**174**	**58**	**718**	**64.32**	**3932**	**246.05**

Source: Visvesvaraya Grameena Bank, Head Office, Mandya

Table - 4
Performance of the VGB at a Glance

Sl. No.	*Key performance indicators*	*2004-05*	*2005-06*	*2006-07*
1.	No. of Districts covered	1	1	1
2.	Total Staff	105	104	103
3.	Deposits	2002.03	2358.60	2896.31
	Growth %	34%	18%	23%
4.	Borrowings outstanding	379.84	536.12	601.15
		25%	41%	12%
5.	Gross loans & advances	1231.24	1711.37	2019.50
	Outstanding Growth %	18%	39%	18%

Sl. No.	Key performance indicators	2004-05	2005-06	2006-07
	i) Loan to prioritysector	892.93	1120.08	1283.41
		468.59	686.14	873.41
	ii) Loans to NTH	49.25	68.48	80.78
	iii)Loans to SC/ST	424.34	433.94	810.00
	iv) Loans to SF/MF/AL	11.08	13.691	5.60
	v) Loans to minorities	-	-	-
6.	Investment outstanding	1409.09	932.51	1470.79
	Growth %	39%	11%	58%

Source: Annual Reports of VGB, Head Office, Mandya.

Self Help Groups (SHGs)

Formation of Self Help Groups was encouraged throughout the district by the bank. A training programme was arranged exclusively for Branch Managers at Halagur Branch to encourage them for formation of Self Help Groups in the district. The programme was conducted jointly by BYRADA Mysore, Vikas Rural Development Society (VRDS) Malavalli and NABARD Mandya. The programme was quite successful. At present, there are 81 self Help Groups in the district formulated by the Visvesvaraya Grameena Bank.

Category-wise disbursement of Advances

The bank has extended the financial assistance to the priority and non-priority sectors during the year 2005-06 and 2006-07. From the Table -5. it is clear that in the year 2005-06 the amount of advances given by the bank was Rs.2237.16 lakhs, but in 2006-07 it was raised to Rs.2523.36 lakhs. The disbursement of credit has been made fairly with greater attention on to weaker sections rather than target group. There has been considerable increase in the amount of advances made available to the non-target group. Scheduled caste and scheduled tribes received very significant proportion of total advances of the bank.

Table - 5
Category-wise Disbursement of Advances by the Bank During the year 2006-07

(Rs. In lakhs)

Sl. No.	*Particulars*	*2005-06*	*2006-07*
1.	Target Group	749.88	799.27
2.	Non-target Group	689.44	873.41
3.	SC/ST	44.16	48.28
4.	Minority	3.80	3.13
5.	Weaker Section	749.88	799.27
	TOTAL	2237.16	2523.36

Source: Annual Reports of Visveshvaraya Grameena Bank, Head Office, Mandya.

The study of the Visveshvaraya Grameena Bank reveals that, it has largely achieved the objective for which it was setup. It has made significant progress in all the directions. Visveshvaraya Grameena Bank covers all the villages of the district through the strong network of 25 branches. Inspite of many odds the bank has successfully reached every nook and corner of the district and has stood in prime place in the implementation of government sponsored agricultural development programmes and poverty alleviation programmes.

Major Findings of the Study

1. Though the 'progress of the Visvesvaraya Grameena Bank in terms of deposits, advances and in other aspects i.e. priority sector advances is commendable, still it appears that here are certain gaps in the effective functioning of Visvesvaraya Grameena Bank.
2. The study of the Visveshvaraya Grameena Bank reveals that, it has largely achieved the objective

for which it was setup. It has made significant progress in all the directions. Visveshvaraya Grameena Bank covers all the villages of the district through the strong network of 25 branches. Inspite of many odds the bank has successfully reached every nook and corner of the district and has stood in prime place in the implementation of government sponsored agricultural development programmes and poverty alleviation programmes.

3. The disbursement of credit has been made fairly with greater attention on to the weaker sections rather than target group. There has been considerable increase in the amount of advances made available to the non-target group. Scheduled caste and scheduled tribes received very significant proportion of total advances of the Visweswaraya Grameena Bank.
4. There is 100% recovery against advances made to self help groups. The bank has planned to link at least 50 groups in the next year. This is the extensive work done by the bank in the district with the main objective to raise the saving activities by the people and to raise the standard of living of the rural people. This has also established Vikas Volunteer Vahini Club (VVV Club), its activities which included Meet & Match programme on Organic Farming and Vegetable cultivation, seminar on cultivation of 'Gerkins' vegetables. The club frequently arranged field visit trips for the benefit of the members.

Suggestions

In the light of our findings and observations some suggestions are made about Visvesvaraya Grameena Bank in rural development. The suggestions are listed as follows:

1. Proper premises should be provided to

Visvesvaraya Grameena Bank branches as money lack proper premises.

2. Staff should be given proper and appropriate training.
3. To reduce the problem of over dues, Visvesvaraya Grameena Bank should announce certain incentives in the form of cash discounts, etc.
4. The VGB branches should provide credit assistance not only to their existing borrowers but also to other eligible persons within their command area.
5. It is very important to note that, most of the beneficiaries are illiterate. Hence, the borrowers of Visvesvaraya Grameena Bank need to be educated about the formalities to be fulfilled in obtaining the necessary finance.
6. While identifying the borrowers under self employment schemes, it would be better to avoid political influence.
7. There is urgent need to streamline the procedures at branch-level and bank-level for the quick disposal of the loan applications.
8. Priority sector lending and rural banking do not adversely affect the bank profitability to a significant extent and hence should not be blamed for the declining trends in bank profitability. Advancing to priority sector and opening of rural branches may be extended in the larger interests of the society.

References

Badruzzama Siddiqui (2002) Priority Sector Lending: Some Major Issues, Kurukshetra, Vol.50 No.10 New Delhi.

Rakesh Malhotra (2002) Regional Rural Banks: The Forgotten case in Financial Sector Reforms, Kurukshetra, Vol.50 No.10 New Delhi.

Patel .A.R (2005) Rural Credit System: Need for Revamping, Kurukshetra, Vol.50 No.10 New Delhi.

Alak Ghosh ; Role of Regional Rural Banks. The Economic Studies, Vol.17, No.1, July, 1976.

Agarwal, R.K.: Evaluation of the Working of Regional Rural Banks. Mittal Publications, New Delhi, 1991.

Agarwal, R.N.: Rural Banking in India, Oxford and I.B.H Publishers, New Delhi.

Angadi.V.B (1983) Banks advances to Priority Sectors: An Enquiry into Causes of Concentration, Economic and Political Weekly, New Delhi, Vol.XVIII, No.13.

Batra,J.D.: Rural Banks for the Rural Poor. Kurukshetra, 26(2), 16 October, 1977.

Balamohandas.V., Regional Rural Banks and Rural Credit, Discovery Publishing House, New Delshi, 1991.

21

Role of Information Technology in Economic Growth of India

Nagesha

INTRODUCTION

The main objective of this paper is to evaluating the role of IT sector as an essential factor of the development of our economy and suggests suitable measures to further improvement of the IT sector in order to develop the economy. Until 1991, India has barely participated in the export of few technical and engineering goods. It has, however, established itself as a leading exporter of Software and Information Technology Enabled Services (ITES) to OECD markets. Software has been a leading sector growing more rapidly over the past decade and presuming that it can continue for some time even in future. Yet, major debatable questions and controversies are emerged like how far the benefits of the software and IT sectors growth are reaching the Indian masses as opposed to a small, educated elite population. Hence, to explore the hidden truth related to the contribution of IT sector to broad based economic development the present study is under taken.

The dualistic nature of Indian economy influencing by both the traditional and modern mode of techniques, where each one influence is differ significantly. IT sector as a part of modern mode of technique started to influence of our economy slowly in 1991 and it become more influential factor after 1996. For the past couple of years, our economy significantly increased her share in the international market through exporting software products and ensures that the Indian IT sector is dominant player in the global market and emerging as one of the leading countries of the millennium in software export. However, it makes sense to have questions like how much of hope we can keep on IT industry? What its correlation with India's overall economic development? Is it helping our economy in reducing the poverty and income inequality? Can it improving the benefits to only the educated elite population with access to jobs and power? Or is it improving the over all welfare of the economy?

The predominant growth rate of the one sector of our economy is influencing the overall growth of the economy, through which most of the objectives of the economy can be achievable. However, the growth of this sector is limited to certain area which possessed with all modern means of infrastructure. Both the World Bank and the Indian government are keen to play up the success of the information technology industry and its role as a path to a new era of prosperity. But information technology only contributes 3.5 percent of total GDP and employs 1.5 million people. More than 230 million people are employed in the agricultural sector. India's poor primarily live in rural areas, farming small plots of land or working as agricultural laborers. Moreover they are unlikely to benefit directly from the technology boom because the social and economic mechanisms for redistributing the gains of the information technology industry have been eroded by the introduction of taxes and cuts in social welfare programs. Job creation in the urban information technology sector does little to create economic gains for India's rural poor.

Hence, it is worth to discuss about the impact of IT sector on economic and social inequality.

To accelerate the pace of the growth of the economy, the sector which has more spill over effects, back ward and forward linkages is needed. The sector imbibing with all these attributes not only succeed in the growth of the economy but also reduces the inequality and helps in development. Thus, the concept of welfare is reflected through the condition of less disparity. However, the biggest task of IT sector in India is undoubtedly increasing growth, but its role in reducing disparity is still questionable. Thus, the present study is taken as a task of research to lighten the hidden reality of the Indian economic scenario. The major interest of the present study is covering this issue of the IT sector and inequality. However, the major studies came to light at the national level whereas the issues are not taken into care at regional level. Hence, the present study is focusing this issue both at national level and regional level of our state.

Results and Discussion

The software technology parks in India are spread over the wide geographical area in which the head centre is in New Delhi. Software Technology Parks of India is a society set up by the Ministry of Communication and Information Technology, Government of India in 1991, with the objective in promoting the software exports from India.

STPI scheme is a 100% Export Oriented Unit for the development and software data communication links or by physical media. STPI take care of all the statutory needs like project approval, software export certification etc. The efficiency in the performance can be judged on the basis of the export of these units over a period of time. This analysis helps in drawing norms towards the new policy issues for the smooth spread and improving the capabilities of these units.

Table - 1
Software Exports (Registered Units of STPI From 1999-00 to 2000-03)

(Rs. In crores)

STATES	*1999-00*	*2000-01*	*2001-02*	*2002-03*
Andhra Pradesh	1059	2017	2805	3638
Karnataka	4321	7475	9904	12350
Tamil Nadu	1874	2956	5014	6305
Kerala	67	141	159	165
Maharashtra	1534	2570	4603	5508
West Bengal	150	250	604	1200
Uttar Pradesh	1220	1660	2000	2514
Delhi	795	1100	1750	2065
Haryana	405	1450	2140	2734
Orissa	89	200	213	260
Others	93	232	331	410

Source: Compiled from NASSCOM website, concerned state IT website.

PRESENT SCENARIO: STATEWISE

According to the STPI, its member units have exported software of over Rs.1,00,809 crores estimated by the end of fiscal year 2005-2006. The total exports by STPI units in the previous year were Rs. 74019 crore. The growth in exports for the fiscal year 2005-2006 as compared to fiscal year 2004-05 is an impressive 36% to touch $22 billion mark.

The table - 2 reveals that the % growth in software exports in Andhra Pradesh, Punjab, Uttar Pradesh, Delhi and Haryana is impressive over the previous year. However, in the proportion of share to total export of software, the Karnataka IT industry stand first (36.70%), followed by Maharastra (15.38%), Tamilnadu (13.85%) and Andhra Pradesh (12.40%). The share of the South Indian share to total software exports of the nation accounts more than 78.6%!

Table - 2
Estimated Statewise Exports By STPI Registered Units

(Rs. In Crores)

Name of the State	Export in FY 2004-0	Exports in FY 2005-06	% Growth
Karnataka	27600	37000	34
Maharastra	11542	15500	34
Tamilnadu	10790	13960	29
Andhra Pradesh	8270	12500	51
Haryana	5953	8358	40
Uttar Pradesh	3825	5476	43
Delhi	2453	3520	43
West Bengal	2000	2500	25
Orissa	400	465	16
Kerala	270	296	10
Chandigrah	225	294	31
Rajasthan	200	271	36
Gujarat	187	247	32
Madhya Pradesh	140	189	35
Punjab	125	182	46
Pondicherry	30	40	33
Others	8.8	11	25
Total	74018.8	100809	36

Source: STPI WEBSITE.

The study of present scenario of the STPI units in statewise depicts the disparity in the revenue generation through export. This even continues in India in terms of city wise.

Table - 3
Estimated Citywise Exports of Selected Centres (2000-01)

STPI Centres	Exports (Rs. Crores)
Bangalore	7475
Bhuvaneshwar	200

STPI Centres	*Exports (Rs. Crores)*
Chennai	2956
Gandhinagar	102
Hyderabad	1990
Jaipur	30
Kolkata	250
Mohali	40
Navi Mumbai	1610
Noida	4350
Pune	960
Trivandrum	88

Source: STPI WEBSITE.

INDIAN DOMESTIC MARKET

Indian IT vendors are increasingly turning attention to domestic market. The Indian user industries are outsourcing parts or entire IT infrastructure to specialized vendors. Recognizing the growing importance of the domestic market, NASSCOM had has put the domestic software and services segment at US $ 3.9 billion during 2003-04, up from US $ 3.0 billion in 2002-03.

Table - 4

Composition of the Domestic IT Market

Category	*2002-03*	*2003-04*	*2004-05*
IT services & products	2.8	3.6	4.3
ITES-BPO	0.2	0.3	0.6
Hardware	3.3	4.3	5.3
Total domestic IT Market	6.3	8.2	10.2

Source: NASSCOM REPORT

ANUUAL SIMPLE GROWTH RATE (in percentage)

Category	*2002-03 to 2003-04*	*2003-04 to 04-05*
IT services & products	22.22	19.44
ITES-BPO	33.33	100.00
Hardware	23.26	23.26
Total domestic IT Market	23.17	24.39

The annual growth rate of domestic IT market showing optimistic nature IT vendors. However, despite this encouraging trend, the domestic software market size continues to grow at a marginally lower rate, as compared with software services exports, due to a higher level piracy, pressure on software prices and lower level of sophistication in IT spending for most Indian companies.

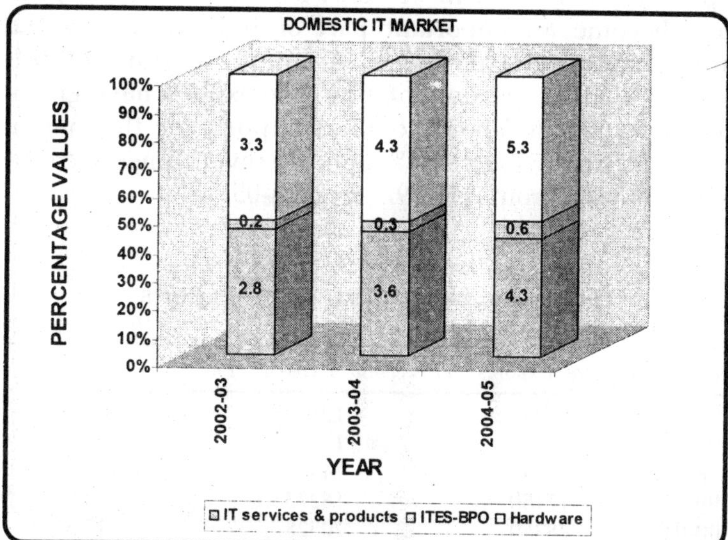

In domestic It markets Banking and financial services, manufacturing, telecom, healthcare, retail, government are the key verticals having different share in consumption. In the year 2003-04, the banking and financial segment accounts for largest share of the domestic market (24%), followed by others (23%), telecom (17%), small office and home (14%), government (13%), manufacturing (10%).

IT AND ECONOMIC GROWTH

From the Tables it can be visualized as IT industries are playing significant role in export earning of the nation and generating good receipts which perpetually motivating them expand the size of the industries. However, other contributions of the IT industries are also accounts as a part of nation wealth and economic progress. Hence, it is worth to point outing the different scenario of the It industries in the path of progress of the economy.

Share of IT software exports to total exports

IT industries have made significant progress in software export. From 1996-97 to 2004-05, the software exports have become an important part of India's exports and India's international image. A unique feature of this industry is the export orientation. The exports have grown sharply and the share to total exports of the nation increased from 3% to 21.2% almost seven times increase in percentage from 1996-97 to 2004-05.

Table - 5
Software Exports to Total Exports

(In Rs. Crore)

Year	*Software Exports (1)**	*Total Exports (2)*	*(1) as % of (2)*
1996-97	3700	121193	3.05
1997-98	6500	132703	4.90
1998-99	10940	144436	7.57
1999-00	17150	162753	10.54
2000-01	28350	205287	13.81
2001-02	36500	213345	17.11
2002-03	46100	260079	17.73
2003-04	58240	303915	19.16
2004-05	78230	368427	21.23

Source: Compiled from Economic Survey 2002-03 and 2005-06

Note: * it includes both IT and ITES.

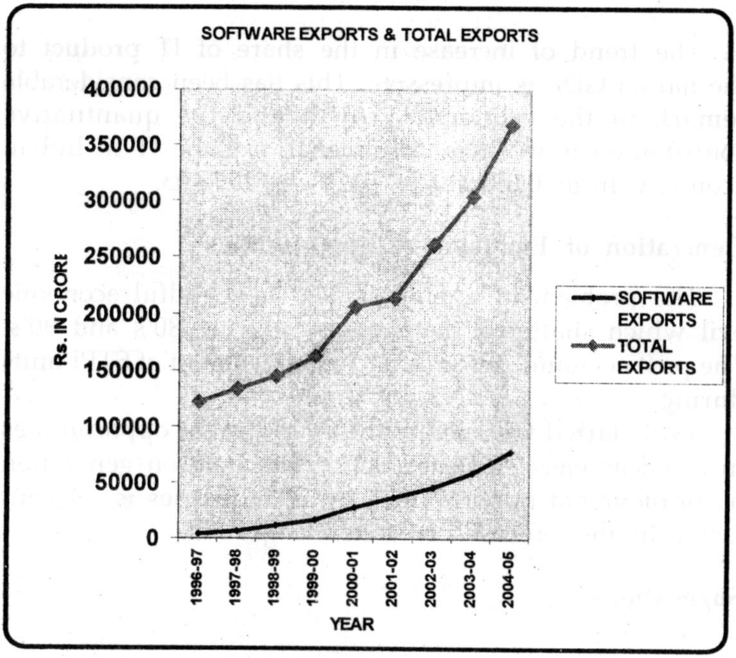

Share of IT sector in India's GDP

The statistics on the overall size of GDP and on the size of the IT industry in billions of current rupees provides vivid picture on the important role of IT industries.

Table - 6
IT Product And GDP

Year	*IT Product (1)*	*GDP at current prices (2)*	*(1) As percentage of (2)*
1994-95	6345	917026	0.692
1997-98	18641	1390148	1.341
1998-99	25307	1598127	1.584
1999-00	36179	1761932	2.053
2000-01	56592	1930184	2.932
2001-02	65768	2097446	3.136
2002-03	79337	2255574	3.517

Source: Compiled From Asian Development Bank Website

The trend of increase in the share of IT product to the nation GDP is impressive. This has been considerable remark in the economic growth and the quantitative contribution is worth noting scenario of the IT in Indian economy from 0.692% to 3.517% in 2002-03.

Generation of Employment opportunities

The problem of unemployment is dreadful economic evil which shattered the economy during 80's and 90's. The post economic reforms and establishment of STPI units during

1991 started to generate the employment opportunities in rapid accelerated pace. Hence, the note on generation of employment opportunities by IT industries is relevant factor in the process of economic growth.

Suggestions

- Enhancing the physical infrastructure to the major part of the economy so that diffusion of benefits of ICTs will take place and over all economic welfare of the economy will improve.
- The flexibility in the economic policy needed to enhance the STPI units provisions in under developed regions. This gradually make the under developed regions better off in the future days.
- The moderate balanced growth strategy needed by the government to take care in reducing the disparity.
- The greater influencing strength of ICTs should be enhanced directly or indirectly, if possible, to peripheral area of the centre petal region of the IT industries.

Conclusion

The total direct employment in the India IT-ITES sector is estimated to have grown by over a million, from 284,000 in fiscal year 1999-2000 to a projected 1,287,000 in the current fiscal year (2005-06). In addition to this, Indian IT-ITES is estimated to have helped in creating an additional 3 million job opportunities through indirect and induced employment. The overall analysis of IT industries of India in this study revealed that the performance of the IT industries in domestic sale of IT software and products as well as in international market accelerating the growth rate of the economy. The objective of India vision 2020 requires the GDP growth rate of 8.1% per annum which intensively need the coordination of different sector of the economy. In this regard the IT sector contributing more through export orientation approach in earning foreign exchange and by generating income , employment to the people of the nation. Hence, the role of IT in export, share to GDP, employment, income etc is miracle and splendid in short span of time. Thus, India to shine in 2020 let this sector perpetually contribute even more than this.

References

Anand, Jaideep and Bruce Kogut, 1997. "Technological capabilities of countries, firm

rivalry and foreign direct investment," *Journal of International Business Studies,* Third

Quarter: 445-65.

Asiedu, E. (2002), 'On the Determinants of Foreign Direct Investment to Developing Countries:

Is Africa Different?' *World Development,* 30(1), pp. 107-119

Balasubramanyan, V.N., Salisu, M. and D. Sapsford. 1996. "Foreign Direct Investment

and Growth in EP Countries and IP Countries," The Economic Journal, 106: 92-105.

Ball, N. 1983. Defense and development: A critique of the Benoit study. Economic Development and Cultural Change 31 (3): 507-24.

Barro, Robert J. 1990, "Government Spending in a Simple Model of Endogenous

Growth", Journal of Political Economy, XCVIII, 103-25

Barro, Robert J. 1991. "Economic Growth in a Cross Section of Countries." *Quarterly*

Journal of Economics 106, vol. 2 (May): 407-433.

Barro, Robert J. 1995, Determinants of Economic Growth, The MIT Press, London

Barro, R.J. 1997. Macroeconomics, MIT Press, London.

Barro, R. and Sala-i-Martin, X. 1997. "Technological Diffusion, Convergence and

Growth," Journal of Economic Growth, 2, June: 1-26.

Barro, R. and Sala-i-Martin, X. 1998. "Economic Growth. The MIT Press, Cambridge, MA.

22

Growth in Livestock Population and Its Role in the Development of Karnataka Economy

M.Chandra Naik

INTRODCUTION

The main objective of this paper is to evaluate the growth in livestock population and its role in the development of Karnataka economy. The livestock population includes cattle, buffaloes, sheep goats, pigs and poultry. Under five year plans of the state the livestock development has been given priority in Karnataka with a view to supply animals as a source of energy for agricultural operations, as means of meat supply (food supply) and also as the source of milk supply. In 1983 the total size of live stock population in Karnataka was 36.51 million, of which, 11.30 million cattle and 3.65 million were buffaloes. By 1990, the total size of livestock population of Karnataka State was 38.34 million, of which, the size of cattle population was 10.18 million and the size of buffaloes was 4.37 million. Between 1983-1990, there was a modest decline in the total size of cattle population whereas a modest increase in the total size of buffaloes. The most important feature of the cattle and buffaloes population of Karnataka State has been that nearly 90 per cent of it has been the native breed livestock. Therefore, the milk yield from the native breed cattle and buffaloes population is low. This situation has to be changed by increasing the total size of cross breed cows and buffaloes to increase the supply of milk and make dairying a productive employment and economically viable rural enterprise.

Growth of Veterinary Services

The modern veterinary services are provided by the state government through a network of veterinary hospitals and dispensaries as well as mobile veterinary service units. The veterinary services in traditional sense are also supplied by the village community. Table-1 reveals that the total number of different types of veterinary institutions in the state sector has increased from 1356 to 2817 between 1995-96 and 2007-08. The total number of veterinary hospitals have increased from 152 to 210; veterinary dispensaries from 250 to 581 and primary veterinary centres from 580 to 1263 during 1995-96 to 2007-08. The veterinary hospitals and dispensaries are located at the large and small towns whereas the primary veterinary centres are located in large villages. The state government has shown interest in setting up of artificial insemination centres. The total number of artificial insemination centres have increased from 300 to 590 during 1995-96 to 2007-08 . In Karnataka State a good network of veterinary institutions exists comprising the state veterinary institutions and the mobile veterinary service units operated by district milk unions.

Animal husbandry sector in modern time to produce improved bullocks for agriculture, to increase per capita available good poultry, to provide better veterinary aid and to increase the nutritional level of livestock forms an integral part of agriculture. The integration of farming with animal husbandry facilities, better utilization of farm by - product, maintenance of soil fertility and better utilization of man and animal power increases the rural incomes.

Table - 1
Livestock Population in the State

Sl. No.	*Livestock*	*1995-96*	*2007-08*	*Percentage Increase (+) / Decrease (-)*
1.	Cattle	11.30 (30.95)	10.18 (26.55)	(-) 10
2.	Buffaloes	3.65 (10.00)	4.37 (11.40)	(+) 20
3.	Sheep	4.79 (13.12)	4.73 (12.34)	(-) 1
4.	Goats	4.35 (11.91)	3.69 (9.62)	(-) 15
5.	Pigs	0.32 (0.88)	0.30 (0.78)	(-) 6
6.	Poultry	12.10 (33.14)	15.07 (39.31)	(+) 25
	Total	36.51 (100.00)	38.34 (100.00)	(+) 5

*Source:*Draft VIII Five year plan, P. VII - E.1, Based on census of Livestock in Karnataka.

Karnataka State is endowed with significant assets of livestock wealth, which in its number and variety could be compared to any other state in the country. The multitude of livestock depended on scientific leves would not only provide protein of high quality which is so urgently need at present but also promote socio-economic progress of weaker sections of the society.

The state has some famous breeds of cattle and sheep. The 'Hallikar' and 'Amritmahal' cows are famous in the country for their drought quality and the 'Khilari' breed in Dharwad and Bijapur districts is also known for draught purposes. Another important breed 'Cenoi' is found in parts of Bidar and Gulbarga districts known for milk and brought purposes. Buffaloes form an important component in milk production and also agriculture operations, Buffaloes in Dharwad and Bijapur districts are superior milk producers. The state has four breeds of sheep namely Bellary, Dharwad, Hassan & Bannur.

Table - 2
Trends in the Growth of Veterinary Institutions in Karnataka State(Numbers)

Sl. No	*Institutions*	*1995-96*	*2001-02*	*2007-08*
1.	Hospitals	152	187	210
2.	Dispensaries	250	452	581
3.	Primary Veterinary Centres	580	942	1263
4.	Mobile Dispensaries	74	164	173
5.	Artificial Insemination Centres	300	610	590
	Total Institutions	1356	2355	2817

Source: GOK, Karnataka at a glance, Directorate of Economics and Statistics, Bangalore.

Dairy Development Programme is one of the important programmes and it has kept pace with the cattle development programme. The government dairies and the rural dairy centers in the state offer the milk produced in the rural areas assured marketing facilities for the milk produced throughout the year balanced cattle feed, helping the ryots to grow the required green fodder in their fields etc. In a nutshell these centers are doing all the spadework at the field level to build up the dairy industry for the welfare of the farmers engaged in dairy development activities.

Milk Procurement in Karnataka State

In India, Karnataka is one of the leading states as far as milk production is concerned. The details of milk production in the state of Karnataka are presented in the table - 3. The milk production in the state of Karnataka includes 1977-78 to 2007-08.

Table - 3
Milk Production in Karnataka State

(In lakh Kgs)

Year	*Milk Production*	*Amount(in lakhs)*
1977-78	422	442
1978-79	508	812
1979-80	579	1091
1980-81	783	1500
1981-82	580	1573
1982-83	821	1821
1983-84	1031	2374
1984-85	1338	3372
1985-86	1817	5256
1999-00	2473	7681
2000-01	3021	9577
2001-02	3091	10380
2002-03	3438	12431
2003-04	3341	12544
2004-05	3038	14381
2005-06	4000	22236
2006-07	4305	24495
2007-08	4143	23793

Source : National Dairy Development Board, Bangalore.

It could be seen that the milk production is steadily increasing and increase being very rapid since 1981-82. This increase is not only attributed to buffer breeding ghee and management practiced but increased facilities for milk procurement by Dairy Development Department.

Milk Procurement in Karnataka State in Organized Sector

In the table - 4 milk procurement by organized sectors in the state of Karnataka details are depicted. This details includes from 1977-78 to 2007-08. The data in the table clearly indicates that milk procurement in the state has been gradually increased.

Table - 4
Milk Procurement by organized Sectors in Karnataka

Year	*Average Milk Procurement / day (lakh KPD)*
1977-78	0.94
1978-79	1.39
1979-80	1.82
1980-81	2.14
1981-82	2.04
1982-83	2.25
1983-84	2.82
1984-85	3.67
1985-86	4.98
1999-00	2.82
2000-01	3.67
2001-02	4.98
2002-03	6.77
2003-04	8.25
2004-05	8.74
2005-06	9.42
2006-07	9.15
2007-08	11.35

Source : National Dairy Development Board, Bangalore

In the above table it is interesting to note that milk procurement per day in the state increased as shown in the above table. In 1977-78 milk procurement per day 0.94 lakh LPD. Milk production is steadily increasing and increases being very low production in the 2.04 lakh KPD 1981-82. The milk procurement is expected to surge forward with coming years increased being very rapid since 1989-90. The Annual average milk procurement has nearly decade doubled during last two years 9.15 and 9.04 in 2006-07. And 2007-08 the average milk procurement in Karnataka region was the years increase being very rapid since milk procurement.

Performance Highlights of Karnataka Dairy Development: Karnataka State entirely covered by dairy development.

2. Elected board in position in 9 unions and Federation
3. Processing units controlled by respective milk producer's unions.
4. 90% of functioning milk producer's co-operative societies earning profit.
5. In the last 10years for milk procured Rs.1,980 crores has been paid to dairy farmers.
6. At present an average of Rs.1.09 lakhs is paid per day to milk producers.
7. High capacity utilization of cattle feed plants
8. Bulk supplies of SMP WMP to Army.
9. Low price spread between procurement and sale prices.
10. Successful implementation of silvipasture and decentralized nursery scheme.
11. Wide-spread dispersal of cross bred cattle.
12. Coverage of 2,51,392 numbers of women members (17%) and about 2,40,804 numbers of landless labourers (17%) under the project.
13. Milk supply to Calcutta Mother Dairy through Railway tankers from Mother Dairy Bangalore.
14. Successful implementation of State Government aided Dairy Development Programmes through SC/ST Development.

Dairy cooperative society is a basic organisation unit functioning at the village level. democracy is practiced at the grassroots level in these societies which are organized on cooperative principles. These societies collect the milk from the primary milk producers, process it through milk unions at the district level, and finally market it through the unions as well as their milk marketing federation at the state level called as Karnataka Milk Federation (KMF). The KMF is representing dairy farmers organisation and the responsibility of the milk procurement, marketing, formation of societies and extension support for milk producers to promote dairy development in the state.

Conclusion

The dairy sector in Karnataka plays an important role in the state's agro economy due to the rapid pace of its growth and the shifting food demand patterns in favour of dairy products as a result of to changing incomes and urbanization. This sector ensures an alternative source of income to the farm families and leads to all round socio-economic development at the village level. there is need to sustain through planned and comprehensive strategies for future development of dairy sector in Karnataka under global competitiveness. The dairy sector has vast potential for further growth thereby augmenting rural employment opportunity besides improving the economic condition of people. In addition, the nutritional levels of people could be improved. Thus, by developing dairy sector the rural economy would benefit in more than one way. There is a strong need to provide this sector with necessary funds and create better environment and facilities for its unstinted growth.

References

Alderman, Harold (1987) Cooperative Dairy Development in Karnataka, India, International Food Policy Research Institute, Washington.

Puttaswamaiah,K (1980) "Economic Development of Karnataka, Oxford and IBH Publishing Co, New Delhi,pp.397-437.

Setty, Rajappa (1980) "Karnataka Dairy Development Project: Profile of Performance", Southern Economist, November 1, 1980, pp.57-59.

Pasha, Syed Ajmal and G.V.Ramakrishna (1999) "White Revolution of Karnataka Issues and Prospects", in Economic Development of Karnataka - Leading Issues, D.T.Nanjegowda and M.V.Srinivasa Gowda (Edts), pp.149-157.

Karnataka Milk Federation (2007) Harbinger of Rural Prosperity" KMF, Bangalore.

Government of Karnataka (2007-08) Report on Integrated Sample Survey for Estimation of Production of Milk, Egg, Wool and Meat, Directorate of Animal Husbandry and Veterinary Services, Bangalore.

Index

I

K

L

M